WATER STORIES

of

NATIVE AMERICAN AND ASIAN INDIANS

LEGENDS OF RAIN, RIVERS AND LAKES

Water Stories

of

Native American and Asian Indians

LEGENDS OF RAIN, RIVERS AND LAKES
Stories Retold

TERESA PIJOAN, PhD

AND

ARUN CHINTAMAN PRABHUNE, PhD

SUNSTONE
PRESS

SANTA FE

Chapter illustrations by Claire M. Connally and Tejas S. Prabhune.
Cover artwork by Nicole D. Garling

Sunstone books may be purchased for educational, business, or sales promotional use.
For information please write: Special Markets Department, Sunstone Press,
P.O. Box 2321, Santa Fe, New Mexico 87504-2321.

Book and cover design › R. Ahl
Printed on acid-free paper

∞

Library of Congress Cataloging-in-Publication Data

Names: Pijoan, Teresa, 1951- author. | Prabhune, Arun Chintaman, 1949- author.
Title: Water stories of Native American and Asian Indians: legends of
  rain, rivers and lakes / Teresa Pijoan, PhD and Arun Chintaman Prabhune, PhD.
Description: Santa Fe, New Mexico: Sunstone Press, [2020] | Includes
  bibliographical references. | Summary: "Water themed stories from Native
  American Indians and Asian Indians based on traditional rituals, faiths,
  and beliefs from these two cultures. These stories give insight into the
  resemblances of these two native peoples"-- Provided by publisher.
Identifiers: LCCN 2019044270 | ISBN 9781632932976 (paperback) | ISBN
  9781611395877 (epub)
Subjects: LCSH: Indians of North America--Folklore. | East
  Indians--India--Folklore. | Water--Folklore.
Classification: LCC E98.F6 P84 2019 | DDC 398.2089/97--dc23
LC record available at https://lccn.loc.gov/2019044270

WWW.SUNSTONEPRESS.COM
SUNSTONE PRESS / POST OFFICE BOX 2321 / SANTA FE, NM 87504-2321 /USA
(505) 988-4418 / FAX (505) 988-1025

TERESA PIJOAN wishes to dedicate this book to: Russell Canfield, Healer

With Appreciation to: Rhonda Brown Jackson
Arun and Usha Prabhune
Thomas E. Van Etten
Uday Prabhune
Nicole and Joseph Garling
Claire M. and Lillian M. Connally
Tejas Prabhune
Kimberly and Joseph Jimenez
Manuel Garcia S.V. Librarian
Carolyn L. Doyle and Cole Doyle
Patricia and Louie Tapia
Anthony Ornelas Marquez
Andrew Miller
Enrique Chavez and his mules Chico and Nacho
Mary Portillo
Robert Wallach, Matthew Patton, Jose Reyna, Krishna Tripuraneni, Douglas Allen, Shaunequa Harvey, Olivia Guiterrez and Cheyan Ingrao, and all the Story Holders in the World.

ARUN PRABHUNE wishes to dedicate this book to: Prof. Kenneth Fields, Stanford University

With Appreciation to: Tejas S. Prabhune
Nicole D. Garling and Claire M. Connally
Teresa Pijoan, PhD
Sudhir Rasal, PhD
Balasaheb Labade, PhD
Savitri Jagdale
Dr. Umakant Walvekar
Dr. Madhuri Walvekar
Hrishikesh Wakadkar
Nitin Anwekar
Bhimanna Durgo Patil
Harish Dasare
Nilesh Jamadar
Pritam Birla
Prashant Talnikar
Deepak Chiddarwar, PhD
Greg Graves
Manisha Joshi
Usha Prabhune, Uday and Pradnya, Reva, and Ravi Prabhune, Satyavrat and Shruti, Ojas Prabhune, and all well wishers.

Contents

Introductions
Teresa Pijoan, PhD ~ 11
Arun Prabhune, PhD ~ 13

1
Rain Control Ceremonies

Rain Stopped for *Prasad* Bhojan / Asian Indian ~ 16
Stopping the Rain, Guiana / Native American ~ 27

2
Sacred Spirits Save Lives

The River Goddess Appears / Asian Indian ~ 34
Deganawida, the Peace Maker / Native American ~ 44

3
Magical Water Appears

Eternal Holy Nanak Zara / Asian Indian ~ 62
Water Flows, Chiricahua and Lipan Apache / Native American ~ 68

4
Reincarnation by Water

The Savior Sea God / Asian Indian ~ 86
Stone Boy Saves Uncles, Brule Sioux / Native American ~ 99

5
Evil Threatening Mediums

Well and the New Bride / Asian Indian ~ 118
Stolen Wife, Cochiti / Native American ~ 130

6
Medicinal Healing

Dangya Lake and Whooping Cough / Asian Indian ~ 150
The Lake of the Beginning, Tsimshian / Native American ~ 158

7
Spiritual Wisdom Saves Lives

An Angry River Calmed Down / Asian Indian ~ 170
The Story of the Rain Na'wai, Tsia / Native American ~ 184

8
Appeasing Solitary Ghosts

The Legend of the Ghost in Kirtan Wadi Lake / Asian Indian ~ 199
Spirit Woman Ghost, Paiute / Native American ~ 208

9
The Weeping of Earth Mother

The Story of the New Mother Well, Red Water Well / Asian Indian ~ 225
Chief's Burial, Chickasaw / Native American ~ 245

10
Fertile Blessings

Blessings of Bhivai Devi / Asian Indian ~ 264
Water Blessings, Yurok / Native American ~ 277

Map for Asian Indian Stories ~ 298
Maps for Native American Stories ~ 300
Asian Indian Bibliography ~ 302
Native American Bibliography ~ 303

Introductions

TERESA PIJOAN

Our objective is to compare and contrast Native American and Asian Indian mythology in regard to rain, lakes and rivers generally readable for students and travelers who desire knowledge, understanding and authentic information. The concept of "Indian" reflects the cultures from two continents, one being the Americas and the other being East Asia. The cultures have intertwining beliefs even though the religions, languages and mores are vastly different.

Native Americans and East Asians have many physical similarities noted by anthropologists. And all of these people come with an awareness of a 'Great Spirit.' This celestial entity includes a wide spectrum of magic, spirituality, hope and fear. There are beings who are neither feared nor worshiped, but are simply wonderful or terrifying with great spiritual strength.

Different Native American groups, clans or tribes have a term for the one original supernatural entity. Great Spirit can refer to the one Creator or the Boss, who is the universal image and under him are the many gods or spirits. Southwestern native people have kat'sina or 'spirit beings' who enter humans after a cleansing or purging to perform in respectful dances or healings. Nomadic groups have natural elements such as wind, rain, clouds, rivers, and animals who can enter into a meditative human's spirit to enlighten after a cleansing or a dream quest.

Mythology holds a waking spiritual consciousness molded within cultural awareness. This consciousness traditionally shapes the moral order within an individual, which in turn develops traditional religious beliefs. It is important to note that "Culture" is not a 'thing,' but a 'Process' or an 'Emergence.' Native American and East Asian Indian peoples represented within this book reflect their religious socio-similarities. Today, the rise and fall of cultures has been infringed upon by outsiders and yet, personal honor remains strong within these groups. This book strives to reflect the original unblemished cultural belief systems relevant to the two continents. Cultures shift and change over time and what was once believed has been watered down or mixed with newer concepts. The stories within were gathered by people who in order to survive have been assimilated into modern cultures. Their voices are deserving, collected and recorded with respect.

Traditional family life and cultural survival are related to being 'honorable' for it is a person's honor that allows the spirits to bless them. This form of traditional honor allows others to learn from their words of wisdom and authority. Grandfathers teach the importance of movement and rest. The spiritual gods move about making the trees, the animals, the clouds and then they stop. When there is a 'stop' this is the time to meditate on life, on what is around you, on what you have accomplished. Where the spiritual gods have rested become places of worship to that god, which brings learning of oneself. Nature is appealed to, not controlled, for the ways of life are learned through 'personal' spirituality.

Prayer is powerful. Many prayers are given while dancing and chanting to the spirit world. Pounding feet allow Native American dancers to humble themselves to the Earth Mother. Drums rhythmically beat, echoing the heartbeat of life to Sky Father. Throbbing sounds pulse outward as a show of respect. Prayers are given with hands open-upward illustrating vulnerability and trust with the willingness to accept wisdom. Meditation and dreams are also ways of finding one's spirit-path or awareness. Remembering, teaching and telling in lessons learned and past wisdom. It is our hope that the reader will retain the wisdom within this book and pass the gained insight to others as they travel through life honorably.

This research was done with Arun Prabhune, PhD, a professor of Marathi Literature. Marathi is the language of the state of Maharashtra in India. His interest is in the study of comparative folk literature as is mine. Since 2008, Dr. Prabhune has been an advisor to the prestigious Marathi literary periodical *Akshar Wangmay* and was on the editorial board of the Marathi literary periodical *Pratishthan* for twenty-five years. This periodical is published by the Marathawada Sahitya Parishad or Marathawada regional literary organization. Dr. Prabhune has published critical articles on comparative folk literature and drama literature. The Prabhune family collectively has helped with this work as has my family.

We have maintained our families being involved in the tradition of story keeping. Both Dr. Prabhune and myself have traveled extensively, spoken to many tellers and have worked diligently to perfect this work.

ARUN PRABHUNE

During my study of the Native American bear folk tales in the year 2000, I studied the Native American culture and rituals, mythologies and myths, and compared the same with those of Asian Indians. I noticed many similarities in these cultures. Some mythological stories and folk tales are also based on some similar themes. The Americas and India are thousands of miles apart, and yet there are similarities. So, I continued my reading in this regard.

Researchers such as Emily Hoskins Vokes, Chaman Lal, Charles James Ryan, Gordon F. Ekholm, Gene Matlock, and many others have studied and pointed out the India-America cultural relationship as well as similarities and discussed this in their publications and books.

In the year 2008, when I was a visiting scholar at Stanford University, professor Kenneth Fields suggested an interesting topic for my research project: "Rain in Native Americans and Asian Indians." Rain is a water source. So, I decided to focus on an expanded "rain" project, that is "Water stories of Native American and Asian Indians."

My research friend Teresa Pijoan and I were both interested to work on similarity-based water stories. So, we started to work jointly on the water stories project since Asian Indians and Native Americans are culturally rich and they have dramatic traditional stories. We hadn't come across a book which is based on similarity-based stories from Asian Indians and Native Americans. So, if we could collect the stories from both cultures, we believed that it would make a different type of book.

We decided to collect the stories of sea, rain, rivers, streams, ponds, lakes, and wells. We were eager and enthusiastic to find out particulars of stories. We were interested in several questions: How had these water sources appeared in these different cultures? How did the people of these two cultures think about water sources? How is it that the human mind and human emotions are the same or similar even when these exist a great distance apart? What are the rituals related to water sources in these cultures? What are the rain-making and rain-stopping rituals? Is there a possessor of supernatural powers such as an avtar or an embodiment who is able to control the water element in both the cultures? Are there different aspects of water elements reflected in the stories—for water can be kind but it can be furious, it is useful but can be destructive, it is transparent but can be mysterious. So, we believed that it would be interesting to collect the stories, put together the pairs, compare those, and find out the similarities within the stories.

We have selected different types of stories. There are ancient tales of spiritual personalities and cultural heroes who performed miracles with their supernatural powers; these give us an experience of unwavering faith. There are legends related to historical architecture and environment demonstrating great moral values. There are modern stories told by those who are still alive and have survived their thrilling experiences. Each story highlights man's life-threatening struggle with nature and, in particular, the water element.

We have selected the stories from nomadic and settled groups of the different Native American regions, but most of the Asian Indian stories are from rural India. The folk may be nomadic or indigenous, rural or urban, still the human mind faced with a very helpless situation tends to think in the same way. When folk-mind creates literature, the regional values, concepts, beliefs, faiths, fears, and rituals are reflected in their creation. Thus, we were able to find similarities even though these regions are located so far away from each other.

There are ten pairs of stories. Each pair has a story from India and a Native American story. Notes and a glossary can be found at the end of each story. Readers can also enjoy the similarities and cultural references because they will get to know the different types of characters, personalities, traditional dresses, traditional foods, emotions, wishes, views, moral values, rituals, faiths, and beliefs from these two cultures.

The comparative study of two cultures and of the similarities between two different cultural folk tales is a field of research. However, we believe that the similarity-based stories from two different cultures would also be very interesting to general readers. This book is for general readers to give an insight into the resemblances of these two native peoples.

Our family friend and researcher Teresa Pijoan, PhD, has been a valuable contributor in my prior books and publications over the last two decades. She has been of immense help in all aspects of this book, providing valuable suggestions to add appropriate clarifications for non-

Indian readers in case of the Asian Indian stories. Her family as well as mine have also been of much assistance, support and encouragement in this extensive project.

Prashant Talnikar, who is a writer in Marathi and a professional translator, provided English translations for the stories in a very short time. The translations were helpful in preliminary discussions and in selecting the stories. The actual stories included in the book are in my own words.

I remain indebted to my teacher and former research guide, professor Sudhir Rasal, PhD, from India for his continual support even to this day. His keen interest in the project, suggestions, and moral support helped in my commitment to complete this book.

1

RAIN CONTROL CEREMONIES

Rain Stopped for *Prasad Bhojan*
ASIAN INDIAN

This is the miracle story of the nineteenth century. There lived a virtuous man named Ganesh Bhatt Tembe and his wife Ramabai who were a religious family. They were Brahman by caste. Haribatt and his wife were blessed with a son and lived happily in the small village of Mangaon. It is in the Konkan region of the Maharashtra State. This region is famous for heavy monsoon rains. Generally, the rain-free months are after December. In the rainy months if someone wants to host and celebrate an event in a space outside, there is the chance of heavy rains and the event may get washed away. Therefore, no one dares to plan on hosting an open event during this rainy period.

The Tembe family were great worship followers of Lord Dattatreya. Ganesh Bhatt and his father Haribhatt spent hours together in worship. Ganesh Bhatt married, but he felt the need to complete his religious deep meditation away from family responsibilities and worry. After twelve years of extensive education with his father, Ganesh Bhatt moved to live in a village called Ganagapura in the state of Karnataka, India. There he was completely engrossed in the worship and meditation of Lord Dattatreya. One fine night, he had a dream where there appeared a yellow golden light with a cool breeze and sweet-smelling air. After a moment, the light became brighter and brighter and, in the light, there appeared Lord Dattatreya. In the dream, Ganesh Bhatt made an obeisance to Lord Dattatreya who blessed him. Lord Dattatreya ordered Ganesh Bhatt to return to Mangaon and see to his wife who would give birth to a son that would be the embodiment of Lord Dattatreya. Then He disappeared. Ganesh Bhatt opened his eyes. He was very happy to see Lord Dattatreya in his dream.

As per order, Ganesh Bhatt left Ganagapura and went to Mangaon for he was anxious to share the account of his dream with his wife. Ramabai welcomed her husband for she was pleased to have him home. Ganesh Bhatt took a bath and then worshipped his home gods. After his devotions, he was in a good mood and with joy he narrated his dream to his wife.

He said, "We are blessed for soon you will be pregnant with a son who will be Datt avatar. Our son will be the embodiment of Lord Dattatreya. He will be part of our family."

Hearing of her husband's dream, Ramabai felt truly sanctified. After a year, on August 13, 1854, she gave birth to a little boy. Both Ramabai and Ganesh Bhatt were extremely pleased for they thought, "Our family is a spiritual family for we have received the holy blessings of Lord Dattatreya. This boy is the avatar with the embodiment of Lord Dattatreya here on earth."

On the twelfth day, after the birth, was the ritual of the naming ceremony. Flowers decorated the home in celebration. Ganesh Bhatt and Ramabai bathed and then carefully washed their infant son. The paternal and maternal grandparents, relatives and close friends were invited. Wrapped in new clothes, the baby was put in a beautiful cradle. In this ceremony, the paternal aunt had the importance of naming the baby. As per tradition, she whispered the name in the newborn's ear. Turning to the gathered family and friends, she announced, "This little one's name is Vasudev." Everyone was pleased with the name. Indian sweet pedhas were shared with the guests.

Vasudev grew as children do, day by day. He was not fair in color but his eyes were bright and intelligent. He learned quickly and retained information at a higher level than most children. His eloquence was impressive. When Vasudev was eight years old, his grandfather Shri Haribhatt performed his Thread Ceremony or Upanayana samskara. This is the rite of passage a young boy takes for he is no longer considered a child, but now is known as a serious student solely focused on formal learning. It is the start of a new life for a boy, given to him in this ceremony called *yagnopaveetham*, the receiving of sacred thread.

After the Thread Ceremony, Vasudev concentrated his mind fully on his studies. His sincerity, intelligence, a remarkable memory, and his hard work helped him to complete his studies earlier than was normally expected. His powerful ability to understand knowledge and his memory retention were incomparable to other students. Soon, he mastered the art of speaking and writing in the Sanskrit language, as well as a command of the Vedas; the Vedas are the most ancient of the sacred Hindu literatures compromising more than one hundred extant books holding thousands of relating legends, rituals, and religious-philosophical speculations. While studying, he also worked on his expertise in priestly duties. At a very young age Vasudev was well respected in his society.

Vasudev was focused on his daily religious duties and did not participate in the family's day-to-day activities. He meditated at Mangaon where there was a hill covered by a dense forest of huge trees of Banyan, Pimpal, Kadulimb and Palash. The forest was home to tigers, lions, wolves, foxes and many other animals. People were fearful of this area because of the wild predatory animals, but Vasudev enjoyed the silence for the hill was an ideal place for meditation and yoga. Many times, he would go to a small cave on this hill for deep meditation, sitting there for weeks without any food. Due to his extreme fasting, he became slender but his mental strength increased. He acquired supernatural powers through the Vedic *mantras* and also by practicing his Yoga. For years, he would go to this cave near Mangaon to perform his yoga.

When he came down from the hill, people in Mangaon would come to meet him and pay their respects to him. They were well aware of his knowledge and spiritual powers. They knew the Tembe family had a deep faith and a timeless tradition of worshipping Lord Dattatreya as did Vasudev since childhood. At the age of thirty, Vasudev built a temple to Lord Dattatreya at Mangaon and dedicated his complete life to Lord Dattatreya.

Observing Vasudev's simple living, deep knowledge, scholarly writing, virtuous and religious character, devotional worship, and dedication towards Dattatreya, people held such high respect for him. People's admiration for Vasudev increased and soon the young Vasudev became known as the most honorable Tembe Swami Maharaj.

In the self-built small temple to Lord Dattatreya, Tembe Swami placed a beautiful brass idol of Lord Dattatreya where he would sit for hours to reflect on his love for Him. There, Tembe Swami would meditate and converse with Lord Dattatreya while concentrating his mind in deep meditation. Tembe Swami worshipped and served Him, being devoted to the observances related to the temple. Also, he was occupied with the proper celebrating of the festivals. One of these celebrations was regarding *Guru Dwadashi*. Tembe Swami planned this carefully for this festivity was in appreciation of his guru Shripad ShriVallabha or Sripada Srivallabha. Every year on this day, the number of followers participating in this celebration increased by the hundreds to gather at Mangaon.

The celebration of *Guru Dwadashi* comes in the month of October or November. These months are not rain free months in the Konkan area and the fear of heavy rainfall worried many, yet usually rain never disturbed this celebration. As usual, hundreds of followers arrived at Mangaon to celebrate *Guru Dwadashi* with Tembe Swami. There was excitement and eagerness in the preparations in order to beautify the village. Front yards were swept clean and washed with water to keep the dust settled. In front of the homes, women drew rangoli designs filled with colors. All of the decorated front yards were attractive. Bunting decorated the village with red, green, yellow, and blue colored flags flapping in the breeze. People were dressed in bright colored clothes as the women wore red, yellow, orange, dark green and soft green, mixed with white and black *sarees*. Their appearance was captivating with their jewellery of small post earrings in each ear with a larger dangling nose ring to enhance their beauty. *Kunku*, a red spot was placed on the women's foreheads. Everyone appreciated one another's ceremonial outfits.

Men wore a white *dhotar* as well as colorful shirts. Red, blue, and orange colored *phetas* were wrapped around their heads. Most of the younger boys were wearing shorts with colorful shirts. Girls wore colorful frocks. The children played games for this was going to be a fine day of worship to *Guru Dwadashi*.

The temple had been decorated by Tembe Swami's followers with garlands of marigold flowers. Tembe Swami bathed as usual, early in the dawn hours and then he entered the temple of Lord Dattatreya where he worshipped the idol and performed his holy rituals. Then he worshipped his guru Shripad ShriVallabha Swami by praising him and chanting mantras. Many of the followers gathered around him to watch for everyone was enthusiastic about the celebrations.

Outside of the temple of Lord Dattatreya, a gazebo had been erected with wooden poles, wrapped cotton sheets for sides, and *sarees* and *dhotar*s were used to cover the top and the three sides. The entire village and many other followers from all the nearby villages were expected for this *prasad bhojan*, so a lot of food needed to be prepared. Fire pits had been dug into the ground for the cooking and preparation. Men gathered wood for the fires from the dead and down tree branches nearby. Large cooking pots and huge round trays were available, along with all the necessary foods such as white raw rice, potatoes, tomatoes, pigeon peas, semolina, ghee, peanut oil, mustard seeds, cumin, turmeric, and hot chili powder.

The fires were lit in the fire pits and the cooking was started early in the morning. After some time, the aroma of heated turmeric, cumin and curries floated in the air. The hot oils cooked mustard seeds, browned the curry leaves and red chili powder as the women stirred and mixed delicacies for this event. The sweet dish *shira* is an Indian sweet dish with semolina, ghee and brown sugar, was made in quantity.

Outside of the large gazebo, men and boys were busy stitching fat leaves together, preparing *patravali* and *dron* or leaf-plates and leaf-bowls respectively, for *prasad bhojan*. They are made from broad *palash* leaves sewn together with small twigs. After completing their work, the *patravali* and *dron* were placed on the ground next to one another in long lines with space left for people to sit in front of them and eat. These leaf plates and leaf bowls known as *patravali* and dron were placed on the ground outside of the temple premises in the open courtyard.

The *puja* was over in the Temple where the atmosphere was religious. All of the followers were pleased to see the *puja* performed with such devotion. First Tembe Swami offered the fresh food to Lord Dattatreya and thereafter everyone gathered to sing *aarti* to Lord Dattatreya and His guru Shripada ShriVallabha. Tembe Swami then paid his obeisance to Lord Dattatreya by lying prone before the idol. The teeming devotees shouted praises.

After this it was time for the *prasad bhojan*. The followers were hungry and eager to taste the delicious *prasad* food. The delicious odour's coming from the cooking area stimulated their appetites. People lined up ready to eat their meal of *prasad*. Suddenly, dark rain clouds appeared in the sky accompanied by strong winds.

Within a few minutes the atmosphere changed for now the shining sun and blue sky were covered with thick black clouds. Thunder started rumbling loudly with flashes of lightning. Trees began swaying as the sheer force of the wind flung the leaf plates and leaf bowls up into the air. The temporary gazebo started to pull apart as the *sarees* and *dhotars* were battered by forceful gales. People were running to the fire pits, hurrying to care for the fires and trying to cover the already cooked food ready to be served. The women, who so painstakingly prepared the tasty meals, were afraid all would go to waste with the rain coming at any moment. Frantically, they covered as much food as possible. Everyone was disheartened with this sudden change of climate and a possible fiasco for the meal.

Many of the followers felt they may have been to blame for the bad weather in that they had done something to incur the wrath of Lord Dattatreya. Perhaps they weren't fated to eat the ceremonial meal *prasad*. It was a tense time for all. Some followers asked, "Why did the climate change all of a sudden? *Guru Dwadashi* is a holy day. It is a happy day. Pious Tembe Swami worshiped his guru with dedication. He should be blessed. Isn't He happy by this worship? Hasn't He accepted this worship? We are here to pray to Him with full devotion. Doesn't He know our honest feelings? Doesn't He want to give us the feast after the ceremony or *prasad bhojan*? Let us go to Tembe Swami and request him to remove this rain."

The followers were anxious and afraid for if the rain came everything would be ruined. The people felt helpless and hopeless. The situation was dramatic and stressful for the people had worked hard to sew the clothes, decorate the area, gather and cook the food. Minute by minute the situation became more and more serious and more critical.

Tembe Swami stepped out of the temple to take a look at the dark clouds, hear the thunder and see the lightning. Studying the sky, the clouds started rumbling loudly. Tembe Swami smiled. As he stood there calmly, the people ran to him calling out. "Swamiji, Swamiji, please have mercy on us. Please do something about the rain. We won't be able to take the holy *prasad bhojan*."

Hearing their pleas for help, Tembe Swami stared at the sky. Again, at the same time thunder rumbled loudly and again Swamiji smiled. He lifted his right hand skyward to the rumbling clouds. Closing his eyes, Tembe Swami called out to Lord Dattatreya evoking his supernatural powers as he quietly chanted some *mantras*. Suddenly, he opened his eyes to stare at the clouded sky and spoke loudly, "O, Rain God, I understand your message. You sent it by rumbling. I know, you are also eager to eat guru's *prasad*! I can understand your wish. But if you hurry to come here for eating *prasad* food, it will be spoiled. No one would be able to eat the *prasad* except you. No, it is not good. Don't be selfish! Think about these worshippers and followers. Stop! Stop there for a few minutes! Don't you understand, your arrival is not welcome? Your arrival creates a serious problem. Stop! I will place some of the *prasad-patravali* aside for you. Eat it and be satisfied. Don't worry, before our followers start their meal, we will offer you the *prasad*."

Tembe Swami stopped speaking and suddenly there was a loud rumbling from the clouds! Swamiji smiled. He understood the meaning of this for the Rain God had sent a message. Tembe Swami said, "He is happy to eat *prasad*. He will not disturb our feast of the *prasad bhojan*."

Turning to the people, Tembe Swami spoke loudly, "Don't worry. Be quiet. The Rain God is no longer coming to spoil our meal. In fact, he is as eager to accept the Lord's feast or *prasad* as you are, but he wants it before you. So, please serve a plate first for him."

The followers of Tembe Swami knew of his greatness and his supernatural power and they had deep faith in him. When the followers heard his order, one of them ran into the shelter to gather a *patravali*.

Women put the delicious *prasad* food on it and poured water in a glass. Followers asked Tembe Swami, "This is the *prasad* for the Rain God and a glass of water to drink. Where should we put this?"

Swamiji went with the followers a distance away from the large group. One of the followers asked Swamiji, "Why we are putting this *patravali* of *prasad* so far away from our temple?"

Swamiji nodded to the clouded sky and said, "The Rain God is eager to come here for the *prasad* and if we keep the *prasad* near the temple, do you know what will happen? The Rain God will come and all our arrangements will be washed away! Our food will be soaked in rain water. Now, if we put the food here, far away from our gathering, the Rain God will not disturb us or our cooking and meal arrangements and our temple and the surrounding area will be dry. Place the *prasad* way over here, so the rain will fall. We will be safe and the Rain God will be pleased with his food."

Smiling, Tembe Swami added, "The Rain God will notice the guru followers and he, too, will be pleased to see how everyone is enjoying the *prasad bhojan*! Now, hurry and put down the food. Then we shall go and do all the necessary arrangements for the *bhojan*. People are hungry!"

Saying such words, Tembe Swami spoke to the cloudy sky, saying loudly, "Are you looking at us? We have come here for you with guru *prasad*. Now, you can come and enjoy the *prasad*, but take care of the worshippers and followers. Remember, there should not be any disturbance in guru *prasad bhojan* and the related arrangements. After the *bhojan*, you, may come into this area and you will be most welcome!"

At the exact moment when Tembe Swami stopped his speech there was a loud rumbling. It meant the Rain God responded to his request.

The followers who stayed with Tembe Swami placed the *patravali* of *prasad bhojan* and the glass of drinking water carefully on the ground and they paid obeisance to the Rain God. As Tembe Swami and his followers hurried back to the temple, they heard a loud rumbling and rain fell, but only where they had placed *patravali* of *prasad*, for the Rain God was pleased.

Sheets of rain circumvented the festivities, however, not a drop fell on the temple, or the cooking shed, or where the meal arrangements were arranged. There were clouds darkening the sky all around, but no rain fell on the celebration! It was as if there was a specified area filled with sunlight, but all around were dark clouds and hard falling rain. The temple area was completely dry, but the surrounding land was saturated! Worshippers and followers were astounded. Work was forgotten as they watched mystified at this miracle. Tears of joy came to the eyes of these followers for they believed they were the luckiest people in the world to witness such a great miracle! They paid their obeisance to Tembe Swami for stopping the Rain for *prasad bhojan*.

Tembe Swami called to them, "Followers, hurry up and serve everyone. Enjoy the *prasad* by the grace of Lord Dattatreya."

Rain Stopped for Prasad Bhojan

Then everyone remembered their hunger and rushed for the delicious food preparations. The women busily put food on the *patravali* as the men gathered the children to eat. All was well. All were happy. All enjoyed the guru *prasad bhojan* with joy and mindful devotion. Group after group of people lined up for the food of *prasad bhojan* without any disruption. The rain did not disturb *bhojan* or their prayers. The land was dry where the people were, yet surrounding them, a hard rain fell, pounding the ground. The followers watched this miracle with incredulous eyes! They couldn't believe what they were seeing and experiencing. It was unheard of, it was unimaginable! They considered themselves very fortunate to have witnessed this amazing happening and felt their lives were fulfilled for they had experienced the supernatural powers of the embodiment person they knew as Tembe Swami. They praised Tembe Swami and his greatness for his capability of controlling and stopping the rain.

Notes:

This story describes the miraculous abilities of Shri Tembe Swami. In this Eastern Indian story Shri Vasudevanand Saraswati Tembe Swami, regarded as an avtar (avatar) or the embodiment of Lord Dattatreya, holds-off rain storms for a sacred ceremony.

The devotees believe that people who are avtars (avatars) possess sacred spiritual powers, which enable miracles to happen. Keeping rain storms from falling on sacred celebrations while rain fell hard all around, brings these events of Shri Tembe Swami to be widely accepted as truths.

Glossary:

Aarti – A last part of puja ritual or worship. At the final stage of puja worshiper puts a burning lamp of ghee in his hand and sings of praise of the deity.

Avtar – Embodiment of a deity. A superhuman being or a deity in another form.

Bhajan – Prayers and religious songs sung by followers and worshippers in the evening in front of deity and also at some special religious celebrations.

Bhojan – Meal. Lunch and supper.

Dhotar or Dhoti – A rectangular piece of unstitched fifteen feet long white cloth. It is a traditional garment of men. Men wrap it around the waist and the legs, and then tie a knot at the waist.

Guru Dwadashi – In this context, Guru is referring to Shripad Shrivallabh Swami (b. 1320 - d. 1350). He is the first avtar or embodiment of Lord Dattatreya, So, he is the guru of the Datta sect. Dwadashi means twelfth day. On the twelfth day of the Indian month *Kartik* (October-November), guru Shripad Shrivallabh Swami 'closed' his avtar. This is his 'avatar closing or disappearance day'. So, it is considered as a holy day.

Kadulimb or Neem – A type of evergreen tree (Azadirachta indica) native to India.

Kunku or Kumkuma – It is a red powder made from turmeric or any other local materials. Women put red colored kunku on their forehead. It looks like a red spot. It has a cultural significant importance. It represents prosperity. It is also widely used for worshiping the Hindu gods and goddesses. It is a sign of respect in social life.

Lord Dattatreya or Dattatreya or Datt – A Hindu deity is considered to be an avatar or embodiment of the gods Brahma, Vishnu, and Shiva. Brahma is creative power, Vishnu is the preserver and protector while Shiva is the destroyer of evil and the transformer. So, he has three heads and six hands but two legs.

Mantras – Sacred Sanskrit utterance with spiritual powers.

Palash – Butea monosperma. It is a species of Butea native to tropical and sub-tropical parts of the Indian Subcontinent and Southeast Asia.

Pheta – The traditional turban worn in Maharashtra, India.

Pimpal or Peepal or Bodhi tree – Ficus religiosa or sacred fig. It is a species of fig native to the Indian subcontinent.

Pooja or Puja – A prayer ritual performed by Hindus of devotional worship to one or more deities. It is a Sanskrit word. It means reverence, honor, homage, adoration, and worship.

Prasad bhojan – Meal of *prasad*a. *Prasad*a means food offering to a deity after worship. 'Bhojan' means a meal. Worshippers take meals from the food offered to the deity.

Prasad patravali – A *patravali* with *prasad*-bhojan. Patraval (plural is *patravali*) is a traditional Indian eating plate made in a circular shape by stitching six to eight leaves (usually sal or banyan tree leaves) with tiny wooden sticks.

Rangoli – An art form of sand powder painting. The purpose of rangoli is decoration.

Thread Ceremony or Upanayana samskara – It is a Hindu rite-of-passage ritual. Traditionally, this ceremony was performed to mark the point at which male children began their formal education. In ancient times, people used to perform this ceremony before sending a child to Guru (teacher) for studying Vedas.

Stopping the Rain, Guiana
NATIVE AMERICAN

Deep in the mountains of Venezuela, following the Interior Range of *Cerro Negro*, Cerro El Papelon, and Cerro El Pequito, is a sacred mountain with one particular cavern called Guacharo. This cavernous mountain range is made of rough country with steep canyons, sky high cliffs with sheer cut inclines dropping clear sparkling waterfalls. Fast flowing water cuts through the narrow valleys to feed the various types of rich green fauna and illustrious flora. Tall ferns of lime green with darkened edges and rare wild orchids of shocking colors grow in the shade of wild fruit trees and teak, giving the air a sweet smell. The forest is thick with intertwining vines, letting only a slight bit of sunlight to peek through to the ground covered in moss.

Tapirs waddle under trees while other peccaries forge for roots. Red deer and whitetail deer trot wild through the undergrowth while chocolate brown paca scurry about under the red howler and capuchin monkeys. The foxes, red and brown coati awake from their day's sleep to hunt at night. Lounging in trees overhead are large pumas and spotted ocelots, waiting for the right animal to attack for their noses are attuned to the rich odors of the dense forest.

Guacharo birds, otherwise known as oil birds, fly in the night sky with vibrant green-black plumed curassow birds. Noisy Chachalaca birds race about in packs of three, squabbling over wild melon seeds and fallen fruit on the forest floor. Night time thrives well under the majestic shimmering colored leaves glistening in the moonlight as birds from the Guacharo cavern swiftly dart through shadows barely missing branches. Porcupines and raccoons noisily rummage in the dark while various species of snakes stealthily slither surviving in the dense under brush, in the night, around and in the Guacharo cavern.

The daredevil racing birds rest in this particular cavern during the day. These fast flying, fruit eating birds are one of a kind in the world. Guacharo birds feast on Oil Palms and tropical Laurel bushes. This strict diet produces within them a natural oil, which is a delicacy used in cooking for feasts and ceremonial practices. Flying at night, using their sonar vision, they make a clicking noise, which allows hunters to locate them. During the day, they perch asleep in the cavern between the stalagmite and stalactite formations. No living human dares to enter this cavern either in the night or the day.

Guacharo cavern is known as the dwelling Place of the Dead. Deep inside this cavern are labyrinths of tunnels and chambers formed by underground aquafers of fast flowing water. Mists mix with the deafening sound of pounding water as caves hemorrhage cold, clear liquid from the upper cavern into the interior lower caves, allowing the dead to travel to the Other Side. During the rainy season, a twenty-foot wall of pulsing water rips at the land, surging long distances to birth magical waterfalls, glistening in an array of colors only to quietly wind through the calm forest as a peaceful river, the giver of life.

The lifeless bodies, items and gifts of the deceased must pass testings within the deepest portion of the Guacharo cavern in order to find peace in the next other world. Souls of the dead must have been good in life, without reproach, in order to pass easily through this cavern. The deceased who did not live an honorable life, did not share in human kindness and were not understanding must wait for a longer period of time to reach salvation. One's character among the living relied on their afterlife's blessings.

In the night, Guacharo Cavern emits bloodcurdling human sounds mixed with souls groaning in agony or moaning in despair, also, sorrowful crying can be heard. Such is the horror of the dead souls who became trapped, punished and tested in order to slide to the Other Side. T h o s e living family members who wish to help the deceased transfer easily to the Other Side, without pain and agony within the cavern, preform a feasting ceremony to appease the spirits of Guacharo Cavern.

The forest heat allows the men to go naked as they cut the low lying branches with their machetes, forging a path through the thick forest. The adult men have facial piercings of long, white-bamboo toothpicks projecting from their lips, nasal bone, cheeks and eyebrow areas. Brave hunters who have gone through extreme events will have tattoos of solid red or solid black pigment in wild designs covering their whole face, down the neck and onto their hands. Married men retain tattoo spots or designs going from one shoulder down to the center abdomen. If someone in their immediate family has died, they will get a tattoo representing the loss and eternal life of that loved one somewhere on their body. The young adult males have various tattoos, but not as many as the older well experienced males. All of the males wear leather sacks to hold their private parts up and away from their body. These leather sacks are strung around their waists with leather thongs. Scars from tribal wars show dark on the bodies of these mature men. The young boys run about bare, waiting for their times of testings.

The younger men who are strong, follow carrying the ceremonial heavy cooking pots of burnt clay and others bring the newly killed meat. White-lipped wild pig and fat tapir bodies hang from skewer poles carried by hunters who killed these animals using sharp spears. This feast has monkey meat, brought down using blowguns. Large birds with feathers now plucked swing from ropes tied over shoulders. Older grandfathers carefully bring the celebratory natural alcoholic drink made from cassava, known as *parakari* or *kari*, in black clay pots wrapped in leather strapping, corked with thinly cut tree bark. Food bundles of plantain bananas, maize, sweet potatoes, cassava tuberous roots, and wild fruit are tightly tied in colorful cotton cloths balanced on the heads of the women or tied in woven basket bundles over their shoulders. Brown clay jars filled with fresh golden honey are carried by the girls.

Bamboo tubes pierce and decorate the women's faces. Many of the women have their faces painted with red, yellow and black natural pigments and wear necklaces of shells strung on leather thongs crisscrossing over their sternum to fall over their bare breasts. After menstruation begins, females wear a leather thong between their legs. Some women are tattooed with random spots decorating their bodies. Hair is shaved close to the scalp to inhibit the infestation of bugs or skin diseases due to the hot humid climate. Children dance in the procession, carrying flutes and drums for the musical part of the celebration known as the Feast for the Dead. Little girls have shells strung on leather, woven into dyed cotton yarn crisscrossing their small chests. The women have two stripes drawn from each shoulder down over each breast to the middle abdomen. While the younger women have three narrow stripes tattooed around the upper thigh. This permanent tattoo color comes from a madder family of flowering plants an unripe fruit known as Rubiaceae and includes pigment from plants such as the coffee or bedstraw fruit. These terrestrial trees are found within the South American forests.

Fire pits are dug by the men. Women gather dried wood. Flames are fanned as the hot cooking pots are brought to a boil filled with maize or tiny ears of multi-colored corn and small wild squash. Tubers and sweet potatoes are wrapped in wet shredded bark to be buried in the dirt under the fire pits. The husks of the cassava roots are removed and shredded. For the husk to be cooked or eaten raw converts to a cyanide poison. Remains of the cassava are ground down into a gritty flour to make flat bread or when mixed with honey a sweet cake. Some cassava is ground into a powder and fried in animal oil to become a crunchy brittle cookie known as farofa. Some cassava powder is put aside to be toasted or used as a condiment, giving the food a nutty flavor.

The hot humid dense air becomes saturated with rich odors of roasted nuts, hot peppers and various spices. Large, wide leaves gathered from wild grapevines and flowering vines are gathered by the men to use in the wrapping of the cooked celebratory food. Children race, chasing various small animals away. While around the perimeter of this area youths bang on drums to scare snakes away. The gift of good food to the Guacharo Cavern Gods helps the families' deceased move more quickly to the Other Side.

Below the elevated cavern, the echoing Shaman voices intermingle as they sing songs while paddling their canoes on the canyon river with steep sides. The shaman wears a stiff grass halo dyed yellow, black and red around his head and has his chest and face painted red from animal's blood. A packed plug of tobacco is stuck in his lower lip, which allows the gods to bring messages to him for the people. Each shaman must go through times of isolation, purging and hallucinogenic out-of-body experiences in order to lead a ritual for the dead. Tribes guard their shaman carefully for they have magical healing abilities and are able to foretell events of hardship or wealth. Both men and woman can become shaman.

Below the sacred cavern runs a river filled with life. Today, the family men and women are holding long spears as they balance in low sided canoes on the river, hunting fish. Down the river, children throw rocks in the water to bring fish to the surface, allowing the fishers to spear with a clean throw. At the bend in the river, near the cooking area, men pull in strong woven nets filled with flapping fish. This feast shall have plenty for all the gods and all the families who have come together in this solemn time of prayer, song and joy in sharing family stories and to beg for the release of the dead.

Young fishermen brag, begging to compete with others as to who will spear the most fish. Others flaunt their new tattoos. Men challenge one another as to who is the strongest in pulling in a net filled heavy with fish. The women chatter while standing over cooking pots, sharing family stories and traditional cooking recipes. The elders sit on the river's cool bank, soaking their feet. Infants and toddlers are carefully watched by family who are sitting in the shade, fanning with large leafs. Young boys climb trees, laughing as they take frightening chances. Unmarried young women giggle and gossip as they watch the single men.

The area is deliciously cool, for the heat from the overhead sun is lessened with the help of the heavy forest's trees and the soft canyon breezes. All of this human activity is a celebration of life, which rises up to Guacharo Cavern to help those tortured souls move to a place of peace.

Suddenly, there is the loud call. A fisherman who is pointing to the sky visible through a clearing in the forest, shouts out excitedly, "Rain! Rain is coming! Look above, see the dark clouds moving toward us!"

As if on cue, wind rips at the tops of the giant trees, slamming one into the other. Huge branches crack as screaming howler monkeys set off a raucous of noise. Thick blankets of loose leaves spin in wide chaotic whirlwinds, pelting down with swirling dirt on everyone in the area. Hurriedly, the mothers pass off their infants to those hiding under the tall bush only to hurry back to cover the cooking pots. The small children scream while racing to their nearest relative. The elderly struggle to stand, wanting to move further away from the fast rising river. Young women race to help those in need while the canoes and small boats bounce on the river's surface. Flash floods in a canyon are deadly, fast and impatient.

Those on the river quickly paddle eagerly wanting to be on dry land. Chaos and hysteria fill the people's calm day for the heavy monsoon rains bring death by drowning. Everyone was busy, no one took notice of the one canoe still afloat in the middle of the fast flowing river.

An elderly shaman stood in his bouncing canoe in the middle of the fast flowing river. His scraggly gray hair flew around his head and with his gnarly fingers he shook his hands at the sky. Slapping around his thighs was his loin cloth and his spindly legs kept him balanced. Waving his hands erratically in the air, it was a miracle he didn't flip into the water, he screamed at the rain clouds. Flinging his arms in large circles, he yelled incantations that scared the birds in the trees and the clouds in the sky. Regaining his

Clay of Cloud

Guiana Stopping the Rain Story number 1

balance, he continued to shake his hands at the dark clouds as if pushing them away. Children pointed, adults turned to stare at this crazy shaman.

Again and again, the elderly shaman's voice roared loud over the gushing river, "Sun be strong! Wind blow the rain clouds away! Rain clouds we must celebrate! Sun, shine strong! Wind blow the rain clouds! Rain clouds, we must celebrate!"

Slowly, the dark clouds coasted away from view. Tree tops became still. The flowing river calmed to a quiet gurgle. The shaman stopped yelling to abruptly sit in his wet canoe, his stern face still pointed skyward, threatening.

A young boy burst out laughing as he pointed to the sky, "Look! The clouds are afraid of our shaman grandfather! They are moving away!"

Mothers walked out from under bushes, releasing their young who they had protected. The elders clapped their hands together for certainly this was a miracle. Fishermen and women pushed their canoes back into the river, paddling out to the shaman. When he saw them approaching, the elderly shaman stood to dance a jig in his canoe, shouting, "It worked! It worked! We shall have a feast! The rain is afraid of this old man!"

It did not rain that day nor the next. Rain did come the following day as the people walked back through the forest to their thatched homes and villages. The Feast for the Dead was a success, thanks to the dancing shaman. The gods of the Guacharo cavern were given respect and good food. This was a ceremony to remember. People still speak of this event today and keep a shaman with them when they return to this forest ceremony.

Notes:

Magical Guacharo birds guard the Cavern of the Dead where no living person dare to adventure. The dead cannot travel to the place of peace without the help of the living who have a celebratory feast to appease the spirits of death. Those who have not lead a life of goodness, kindness and generosity can find their spirit stuck in a place of limbo, a horrible terrifying location. On this occasion, it is only thanks to the magical threats of the shaman who pushed back the rain and these lost souls achieved peace by the ceremonial feast. This story was told to me by a fellow who was married to a woman who once lived in Tesuque Pueblo in New Mexico some years ago.

Glossary:

Canoe – A boat made from a hollowed out tree trunk.

Cassaava Root – Poisonous tubor must be shucked and cooked, used for flour.

Cerro Negro – Refers to an active new volcano in the Cordillera de Los Maribios mountain range in Nicaragua, South America. English translation: Black Road.

Guiana – Area or region in north South America.

Guasharo – Refers to nocturnal fruit eating bird in South America.

Shaman – Person who has access to spirits, does rituals, divinations and healing.

Tapir – Large pig-like mammal, related to horses and rhinos.

2

SACRED SPIRITS SAVE LIVES

The River Goddess Appears
ASIAN INDIAN

The adventure here was narrated by Late Sagunabai Prabhune, mother of Arun Prabhune, approximately fifty years ago. Arun Prabhune has written it down to the best of his memory. Arun Prabhune tells of his trip, when he was a teenager, to the Narmada River. After graduation, being the age of seventeen years, this was an honorable trip. His goal was to visit *Garudeshwar* on the banks of the Narmada River, in Gujarat state of India. The planned trip included flat bread with dried onion curry wrapped in cloth, and he travelled about four hundred miles using various means of transportation. At that time, his home was in Vaijapur in the state of Maharashtra. Nearest railroad station for Vaijapur was Rotagaon which was nearby. His father rented a horse carriage that was covered and had four seats. The fifth person was the driver up front. The road to the train station was bumpy. By the time they arrived at the station everyone's back was sore.

At the train station, tickets were bought. Arun Prabhune's father Chintamanrao, who was a medical doctor, as well as his wife Sagunabai, were honoured to accompany their son on this adventure to a Holy place. The train was crowded with different classes of people. The red train had first, second and third class compartments. This was a new view of the simple life on trains for Arun Prabhune. They did have their own seats, which was a blessing. Many of the poor people shared seats or stood in the aisles. The train trip to Mumbai took seven hours and then they continued on by express train to Ahmedabad to stop at Ankelashwar. It was now four a.m. as they dismounted the train car, out in the middle of nowhere.

Waiting for six hours with two or three other people, the red narrow-gauge railway arrived with four cars. It was the Rajpipla State Railway, and the train was Ankelashwar to Rajpipla. Everyone boarded, but the four cars were mostly empty even at this hour at 10:00 A.M. in the morning. This small train chugged along for two hours until it arrived at Rajpipla where they waited two hours to board a bus that took them in the late afternoon to *Garudeshwar*, a tiny village. Here a Hindu priest rented rooms to the worshippers. Each room was eight by six feet in size with pallets on the floor. The teenaged Prabhune and his parents shared a room. Different classes of people shared for there was no discrimination at a Holy Place.

When it was time to worship, there was the ringing of the bell at the temple. Once the bell stopped, birds were heard chirping loudly in the tall trees. Many of the villagers walked into the water naked, slapping clothes to wash against the rocks. Other followers wore their saffron loin cloths or long wrapped pants to the temple. People stood in awe of the temple, the river and the splendid beauty of the Narmada River. Visitors chose to be discreet and not watch the naked villagers.

It is about one hundred and fifty steps from the temple to the sweet water of the Narmada River. Many of the people who were there to worship believed the Holy water would cure their illness. Arun Prabhune's father further explained:

"Goddess Narmada rides a huge crocodile that lives in the depths of the river. This crocodile has long sharp teeth in his terrifying black mouth. His long tail is deadly as are his claws for he will protect her at all cost. Some have seen her ride the crocodile, but that was long ago.

"Garudeshwar is a blessed place. It is on the banks of the Holy *Narmada Mata* (Narmada mother, Goddess) and is the resting place of Tembe Swami. There are times when *Narmada Mata* gives *darshan* (appearance) to her followers. This allows them to appreciate her and to believe in her for she is there for them."

Studying the clouds overhead, his father said, "It is vital when coming here to not point at anyone. Do not pass judgement on anyone. Be calm, quiet and peaceful for to wave your arms about or shout will bring trouble in your life. The gentle, supplicating nature is needed here for this will bring you a blessed existence."

Young Arun asked his father, "Has the River Goddess been seen by anyone? Where does she live? How does she look? What does she do?"

Father said, "Narmada River is long and winds her way through India along mountain ranges and small villages. This river at times is graceful and then as she pulses through canyons, she falls from tall waterfalls to become treacherous and deadly. Many of these villages have temples and places of worship at her banks. At one of these small villages called Omkareshwar, there is a great temple of Lord Shiva. Your mother knows the story in detail. She will tell you the story of the Narmada River Goddess."

Mother Sagunabai said, "Sure, let me tell you the story." Then she continued, "The story took place at Omkareshwar, where the Goddess Narmada appeared and was seen by many people. This was when Shri Gajanan Maharaj of Shegaon was crossing the Narmada River by boat along with his followers. Arun, the story goes like this:

"Early in the late 19th century, at the time of this occurrence the Shri Gajanan Maharaj was living in Shagaon. Just like today, at that time also, there were many followers of Shri Gajanan Maharaj. Shri Gajanan Maharaj is believed to be the reincarnation of Lord Ganesha and Lord Dattatreya. Lord Ganesha promises success, prosperity, and peace. It is his responsibility to decide if a follower will be successful or will fail. Praying to him allows removal of obstacles and makes possible the fulfillment of one's wishes. Lord Dattatreya is a powerful god for he has the three heads representing the Lord Brahma, Lord Vishnu and Lord Shiva. Brahma is creative power, Vishnu is the preserver and protector while Shiva is the destroyer of evil and the transformer. Lord Dattatreya has six hands each holding different items. In one hand, he holds a drum (*damaru*) in the other a discus-like-weapon (*chakra*). His third hand holds a conch shell (*sankh*), the fourth hand keeps the rosary (*japa mala*), the fifth hand carefully balances the water vessel (*kamandalu*) and the last hand proudly grasps the trident (*trisula*).

"Shri Gajanan Maharaj was a holy person. Thousands of his followers came to Shegaon to receive his *darshan* and blessings. How he was able to transform wicked people from their evil sins into kind honest believers is unknown. Shri Gajanan Maharaj was tall and had great strength from practicing yoga. He was an *ajanbahu*. It means his arms were extended to his knees. He wore only a humble loin cloth. His skin was tanned from the sun as was his head, which was bald. He chose to walk barefoot as was his pious manner. When a person came to him, immediately they felt his electric charisma and magnetic charm. People were drawn to him for his wisdom, teachings and deep meditation. At the time while he was living in Shegaon, he chanted, '*Gan Gan Ganat Bote ... Gan Gan Ganat Bote....*' No one, not even today, really knows the exact meaning of these words, though many people have given their own interpretations of these words.

"An interesting and dramatic incident happened on a *Somvati Amavasya* or a day when No Moon Day happens to occur on a Monday. It is believed that *Somwar*, which is a Monday, is the day of Shiva. So, if Amavasya, which is a No Moon Day and considered a time of great power, occurs on a Monday then it is a very sacred time. It is believed that a person is able to cleanse their sins by bathing in the river Narmada on that specific day. Keeping this belief in mind, some followers of Gajanan Maharaj came, praying for him to go with them to Omkareshwar. This temple of Lord Shiva is placed on the island called Mandhata or Shivpur on the Narmada River. This island itself is shaped similar to the Hindu symbol that represents the meditative sound of '*OM*.'

"Shri Gajanan Maharaj warned his followers, 'If you go by yourselves you should be fine, but I cannot go with you for if I do, there will be perilous trouble.' The followers pleaded, begged and prayed for him to go with them. Finally, he agreed. They started their journey by train to the railroad station at Khedi. They hired a bullock cart, which is a two-wheeled vehicle pulled by oxen, from Khedi to Omkareshwar by a narrow Narmada bridge.

"Once there, they were absorbed into the magnitude thousands of devotees who had also arrived to worship through prayer and to cleanse their sins in the river. Because this was the day of *Somvati Amavasya* – New Moon Day, the area was overflowing with people, making it difficult to walk. Women were cooking in their large pots in a cleared area. Men were singing *bhajans* or prayers. Children were running and playing. Some were swimming with their families, enjoying the clear, cool Narmada water. Some worshippers were wading into the river to wash, while others were washing their clothes on the rocks at the side of the river.

"The Narmada River is shallow in places only to drop into deep chasms of fast swirling current. As one wades further into the center of the river, it can drop several feet, becoming unsafe. Some worshippers were making human chains as they waded into the flowing cold water. Others were cautious and only waded up to their ankles. Children were held fast by their parents as they were dunked into the cleansing river water. The Narmada River is filled with healing minerals brought down from the mountains. Gajanan Maharaj was sitting on the bank of the Narmada River. He was in a trance and chanting, '*Gan Gan Ganat Bote ... Gan Gan Ganat Bote....*'"

"On the far side of the Narmada River was the Khedi railroad station. The people with Shri Gajanan Maharaj were on the opposite side from the train station. Resting and watching others lineup to take boat rides to the far side, they agreed it would be best to go early in the afternoon.

"After worshipping to Lord Shiva, the followers thought of returning to Shegaon, not by bridge road but by boat because of heavy traffic. They requested Shri Gajanan Maharaj to go into the Narmada River by boat to Khedi where there was the railroad station.

"Shri Gajanan Maharaj listened to their request. Then he said, 'I would not want to go by boat."

"His followers once again persuaded him to get into the boat, telling him, 'Now we can return home to Shegaon by train. This will take less time and be easier for all of us."

"Shri Gajanan Maharaj shook his head, 'It would not be wise for you to go into the river by boat with me.' His eyes sparkled, trying to convey to them how important it was for them to listen. The followers insisted he go with them in the boat. Finally, he agreed, once again, to do as they wished.

"Boats lined the river's shoreline, waiting for people to load. The carriers in the water were everything from large rafts, canoes, boats, large and small. These were poled or rowed to the other bank of Narmada River. Fast churning river water shoved and pushed at the sides of each craft. Some were actually running into one another along the Narmada River. This was certainly a busy and dangerous place. There was confusion as families tried to get everyone on a boat one that would not hold so many. People were not calm or peaceful, but pushy and anxious.

"As the followers of Shri Gajanan Maharaj moved to the boat loading area, other worshippers moved out of his way for they recognized him as a holy person. The two boatmen boarded Shri Gajanan Maharaj and his followers on a small boat. The boatmen were struggling to pole clear of the large boulders in the center of the Narmada River. The current pulled the boat one way, the boatmen another and they lost control. The boat slammed into one of the pointed river boulders, ramming a large hole into the bottom of the boat. The boatmen jumped into the river for the safety of their lives. People standing on the shores began yelling at them, 'Your boat is sinking! Your boat is sinking! Get out! Get out!'

"Other boats were trying to reach them, but for some strange reason they were pulled away. The followers on this boat with Shri Gajanan Maharaj were crying, screaming for help. While chaos grew around him, Shri Gajanan Maharaj remained calm. Shaking his head, he reminded the terrified people around him, 'You were told not to come here. You were told not to get into the boat with me. Yet here we are and this is not good.' He laughed and started chanting, '*Gan Gan Ganat Bote ... Gan Gan Ganat Bote....*"

"The followers fell on their knees in the wet boat to say, 'You were correct! It was our mistake not to listen to your wise words. We surrender to you! We will listen to you in the future, please save our lives!"

"Now Shri Gajanan Maharaj was not saying anything, he was in a trance and singing his beloved words, 'Gan Gan Ganat Bote ... *Gan Gan Ganat Bote ... Gan Gan Ganat Bote....*"

"Then he said, 'Don't worry, Mother Narmada will come, she will not let us sink or die in her river.' Saying so, Shri Gajanan Maharaj started reciting the praise of Narmada, he began to pray, 'Come, Mother Narmada, Come! Please forgive the people. Let them live.'"

"The river flowed around them in the sinking boat. His followers were kneeling, praying to Narmada.

"Suddenly, water in the boat began to disappear. Feeling weightless, they realized the boat was being lifted up and out of the flowing river. They were being carried to the far shore. As the boat was gently set on the sandy river bank, a young beautiful woman with piercing blue-green eyes just like the color of Narmada water appeared out from under it. Her long dark hair was wavy as it floated in the river water behind her. Her youthful face glowed as water dripped down her chin. On her forehead was a bright vermilion *bindi*, a red dot on the center of her forehead. The *bindi* retains spiritual energy and strengthens intellect.

"Goddess Narmada's cherry-red lips framed her pearl-white teeth. She demurely smiled at Shri Gajanan Maharaj. Tilting her long slender neck, she smoothed down her light moss-green *saree*. It was similar to those worn by the fisherwomen who lived at the river's edge. Shocked by her appearance, people stared, questioning her, 'Who are you? Where are you from? It's dangerous in the fast current of the river, you should come ashore! Your clothes are soaking wet!'

"Warmly smiling at the people, she answered, 'I am the daughter of fisherman Omkar and my name is Narmada. I live in this river. I came here for Shri Gajanan Maharaj. Wishing to see him. Honor him.' Stepping onto the sandy beach of the river, she walked to Shri Gajanan Maharaj to kneel reverently at his feet. No sooner had she touched his feet, did she disappear.

"Gasping at her magic, the people asked Shri Gajanan Maharaj, 'Who is that woman? Who is the fisherman Omkar? Is that woman magical for she vanished?"

"Putting his hands up to stop the questions, he answered, 'Omkar is the fisherman who is none other than Lord Shiva of Omkareshwar. The woman who appeared in human form is his daughter, the Goddess of this Narmada River. She herself is Holy Narmada River. She protects those who come here to worship. It was she who lifted our boat and brought us to the shoreline. It was her protection and divine power that saved us.

"The followers were pleased. They realized the greatness of

The River Goddess Appears

Shri Gajanan Maharaj. All of them and all the other people nearby knelt reverently at Shri Maharaj's feet. Shri Maharaj didn't notice for he was in a trance, chanting his beloved words, '*Gan Gan Ganat Bote ... Gan Gan Ganat Bote....*' While going back to Shegaon the followers were very pleased because they could worship Lord Shiva on the day of *Somvati Amavasya* and also could see the great holy River, the Goddess Narmada in human form."

Arun Prabhune smiled, "The River Narmada is a most spiritual place. I have gone every year for the last forty years to give my respects. Now, people come from all over the world to appreciate her beauty."

Notes:

Believers regard Shri Gajanan Maharaj as the embodiment of Lord Dattatreya. He was first seen in the town of Shegaon, in the state of Maharashtra, India. The date he took *Samadhi* (renounced life) was the eighth of September, 1910. Many accounts of his miracles and how he performed them are prevalent among millions of his followers throughout India and even abroad. There are various narratives regarding Shri Gajanan Maharaj and how he alleviated the troubles and woes of hundreds and thousands of his devotees. People also share their own experiences as they relate to Shri Gajanan Maharaja's divine intervention into their lives. There are many such extraordinary incidents and anecdotes, and these are narrated in the spiritual book 'Gajanan Vijay' by his devotee Shri Dasganu. The East Indian culture worships the rivers as goddesses. Devotees believe if a person is pure and has a pious soul, this person will receive the divine gift of seeing a river goddess in person. This recount is about such a miraculous encounter.

The wide and long flowing Narmada River is one of the most important rivers in India and considered holy. This story is considered a history, repeated and listened to by many, over and over again. Naturally, there are various versions of this, which are more prevalent. The legend is retold in my own words.

Glossary:

Ajanbahu – A person whose arms are extended to his knees is called ajanbahu. This is a Sanskrit word with a cultural significance in Indian culture. Persons with such physical characteristics are Gods, saints, kings or great warriors.

Bhajan – Prayers and religious songs sung by followers and *worshippers* in front of a deity and also during some special religious celebrations.

Garudeshwar – Garudeshwar is a small village situated on the banks of Narmada river. Lord Shiva once took the form of Garuda (Great Eagle) and saved the people of the village from a catastrophe. The villagers then built a temple of the god and named it Garudeshwar. Over time the village got the name of the temple itself. This lord Shiva's temple is about 2000 years old.

Darshan – An opportunity or occasion of seeing a holy person or the image of a deity.

Shegaon – A town in Buldana district in the state of Maharashtra, India.

Somwati Amavasya – A New Moon Day that falls on a Monday. This day is considered a very holy day. On this day, one should take bath in any holy river like Narmada, Ganga, Yamuna, etc.

Deganawida, the Peace Maker
NATIVE AMERICAN

Above our Earth Mother is a place known as Sky Land. Many guardian spirits live there to watch and protect the people below on land. Once, there was a Spirit Mother who walked along a cloud path calling, "Blue Sun? Where are you? Daughter!" There was no reply.

Tall Cloud chanced to meet her, "Spirit Mother, your daughter is no longer in Sky Land. Come, let us speak with *Ha-Wen-Neyu* our Boss."

Spirit Mother stared at Tall Cloud. He towered over her with his white hair dancing around his pale face as his chalk blue eyes peered down at her. She had one brown eye and one light blue eye. Tall Cloud puckered his thin white lips as he waited for her answer. She was hesitant to believe him for he was known to tell tall-tales. One of his many long arms opened, gesturing for her to move in front of him, "Please, it is important. There is trouble on Earth Mother and *Ha-Wen-Neyu* knows what has happened with your daughter. Come."

Spirit Mother nodded to him, letting her long white hair bounce around her being. As his thin fingers wrapped around her upper arm, she stared at his three toed feet and followed him to *Ha-Wen-Neyu*.

Ha-Wen-Neyu or boss is larger than a thundercloud. Spirit Mother asked Him, "Do you know where my daughter could be?"

A long arm grew from the side of the thundercloud as *Ha-Wen-Neyu* nodded, "People are fighting and killing one another. This is not good. This is not good at all."

Spirit Mother agreed, "We have worked long and hard to make the Earth People. It is not right for them to kill one another or to hurt one another." She wiped a rain drop from her puffy cheek, "Please, tell me where my daughter Blue Sun is, please."

Ha-Wen-Neyu studied Spirit Woman's constantly changing shape, "Your daughter Blue Sun is down with the Earth People. She has been given an important purpose. Perhaps she will not understand it at first, but it will come to her. She was raised here in Sky Land with us, but her memory of this place was removed when she was placed on earth. Now

Blue Sun is one of the Earth People. These beings are complicated, easily confused. If you wish, you may watch her and her life through the evening clouds. Blue Sun has an important purpose, be patient and be proud of her. Your pain in losing her to an Earth Purpose is appreciated."

Spirit Woman drifted away to think. If her daughter was to be remembered by the Earth People, this would be a great gift. Billowing near the opening of some thick gray-blue clouds, Spirit Woman peered down to earth. There was her beautiful daughter gifted with two firm legs and two strong arms. Dark hair flowed around Blue Sun's round face with large brown eyes and a thin nose above pursed pink lips. A flowing white buckskin dress covered her strong body. Blue Sun's feet were covered in short bleached moccasins decorated with intricate bead work of red, green, white and yellow. Blue Sun was now in solid form, standing strong near the glistening waters of a large lake surrounded by tall trees of spruce, fir, poplar, birch, maple, elm, oak and pine. Each leaf was a different shade of green, some were brown mixed with red. Spirit Woman sighed, blowing smaller clouds from her as she envied her daughter's form and purpose.

Blue Sun was placed beside Lake Simcoe near the shores of the Great Lakes near the Huron or *Wyandot* people. Rubbing her eyes, she tried to think of what she must do to survive for she had no conscious memory of being or experiencing life in this place. Slowly, through trial experimentation, Blue Sun built a large rounded wooden frame tied together with shredded and wrapped birch bark strips. Taking platter sized birch bark panels, she wrapped and tied these together for a roof with four poles on each side and two going from front to back. The thatched roof of thick branches woven with grasses and vines protected her from the hot sun.

Quickly, she practiced weaving baskets to make nets and traps. Fire was gathered from lightning strikes and kept burning in a pit. Cooking food became an art for her as different herbs, rodents, fish and plants were found to be edible. Seasonal chilly winds brought about the creativity of skinning squirrels to make fur blankets, woven together with vines from the dark forest.

Meat was dried to make venison jerky. While fresh water was used for washing, cleaning food and storing. Soon, the cold gales of winter blew across the lake, bringing fat clouds dropping deep levels of snow. Ice formed on the lake and surrounding streams, making the fire pit all the more important for she needed heat. The cold of winter with dangerous layers of snow were a challenge, but she met these with clever concepts and survival knowledge. Spring brought ferocious flashfloods that rampaged through the forest, dissolving her hut and drowning her fire pit. Thankfully, the changing weather brought not only torrential rains with loud thunder, but plenty of lightning strikes for fire.

Blue Sun discovered how to make a lid for her fire pit, formed from wet wood covered in clay with one large hole in the center. Finally, the heat and humidity of summer brought a feeling of solitude and peaceful isolation. Blue Sun had no knowledge that there were others such as herself.

One fall night, as she slept on fur skins in her hut, she dreamt of giving birth to a small child. A voice spoke to her saying this daughter would become the mother of a strong man who would be involved with the Earth People and their deadly wars. When she awoke, Blue Sun ached for someone with whom to share her life. Slowly, Blue Sun's body became plumper and her legs ached. Her hunger increased, but hunting and gathering wood became difficult. As months passed and the spring fog had lifted from the lake, she grimaced in pain as a strong wave of contractions radiated through her body. An early morning frost kissed the ground around her as she squatted over a bed of wet leaves. She was in severe agony. Her hands pressed firmly against the trunk of a spruce tree as her fingers tore at the layers of loose bark. Pain riddled her body as she pushed down with tears flowing from her eyes. Finally, with one hard push and a gritting of teeth, a small infant fell onto the pile of leaves between her feet. Blue Sun collapsed when her body emptied the afterbirth. Lying on the soft leaves, she lifted her infant daughter to her breast. This little one's warm smile and sparkling eyes filled her with love and devotion.

Blue Sun named this baby girl White Frost. Mother and daughter grew together learning of the earth and further adventures of survival. Spirit Mother in the Sky Land watched over these two earthlings. How she ached to share with them and have them safe with her, but *Ha-Wen-Neyu* had a magical purpose for them and this needed to be respected. Blue Sun and White Frost played together by the lake, washed in the water, and carried dried wood to stack outside the hut now thicker with tree bark and more moss on the roof.

Blue Sun taught her daughter how to weave, sew nets, set traps and carry a spear with a sharpened point for a better direct hit for larger game. They worked at skinning, bleaching buckskin in the sun and weaving grass clothing. Life was good and White Frost grew strong and tall with her mother's guidance. The further they explored, the more foods they found such as different berries, roots, wild squash, sunflowers and multitude of different healing herbs and grasses.

As White Frost grew into a young woman, she was able to go alone out in the morning to gather wood from the forest. She was always within calling distance of her mother. One morning, White Frost bent over to pry a dried log from the forest's floor. A strong gust of wind blew up her grass dress, up between her legs, giving her a feverish chill. White Frost hurriedly brought the firewood back to the hut only to sit down quickly, "Mother, all of a sudden I feel tired, worn out and my stomach hurts. Do you think we have enough firewood for today?"

Blue Sun hurried to her daughter to feel her forehead. "You are not feverish. You have never been sick before, do you want to lie down or go to cool yourself in the lake?"

Shaking her head, White Frost said, "Perhaps to rest for all of my energy has gone from my body. I shall sleep and tomorrow we can finish gathering wood."

As the days passed, Blue Sun noticed her daughter growing plump, her legs became swollen and it was difficult for her daughter to bend at the waist. Blue Sun asked her daughter White Frost, "Have you been with another? Have you seen anyone else while you were out gathering wood or bringing in water?"

White Frost smiled respectfully, "No, Mother, you are the only person I have seen since I was born. There has been no one around here to help us or share news with us. I am tired. Even if we did meet others, would we be able to understand them?"

Blue Sun had no answer. She was not certain about communicating with others. Would they be friendly or would they try to hunt them? Blue Sun had no awareness of language or how her daughter understood what she said. Was it learned from being alone or was her voice a gift? Worried for her daughter's safety, Blue Sun watched her daughter grow larger day by day. As the weeks passed, White Frost waddled more and more when she walked beside her mother. Now, Blue Sun did most of the chores alone. This weighed on her mind for Blue Sun knew her ability was limited in caring for her daughter, but there was no way she would be able to care for a grandchild as well!

The summer nights became hot and humid. When the two women were asleep on their palettes outside of their hut, Blue Sun had a reoccurring dream of her daughter giving birth to a son. He would be given the name Deganawida, which meant "Two River Currents Flowing Together." Blue Sun knew if this boy was to become a Peace Keeper, he would need to know the people around them. In the morning, she explained to White

Frost her dream. White Frost sat outside the birchbark hut, watching her mother gather all of their household items. They were going to find others to help them survive.

After several days of slow travel, they came near to a village. The loud noise of children and the smells of good food cooking brought them near a Huron village longhouse. White Frost peered down on the place of people. The one long building covered in birchbark panels was filled with families. Smoke rose from the roof holes. The tall, arched building had two doors, one at each end. She watched as men sharpened arrows. Other men had long poles walking shoulder-to-shoulder with dead animals from the forest, carrying them to place by the pit fires, burning outside of the Long House. Using sharp bone and stone knives, the women stripped the fur and skin from the animals to cut thick slices of meat.

The men had their heads shaved on each side with a long mane of hair falling from their forehead to the nape of their necks. Their bare chested muscles glistened in the sun. Breechcloths were wrapped around the men's waists, leggings protected their legs and birchbark type sandals were tied to protect their ankles and feet. Some of the men had beaver furs tied around their wrists.

White Frost called to her mother, "Look, look at the women. They are wearing what we wear! They must belong to us!"

Blue Sun stared at the women wearing wrap skirts of long grasses. Some women had on leather dresses tied over their shoulders falling to their knees. The women's long hair was either wrapped in two leather thongs, one over each shoulder or pulled up and back, tied with a leather strip. The children ran around clothed in leather and woven grasses.

Blue Sun and White Frost spent days, stripping bark from tree branches to make poles, burying them deeply for the framework of their wigwam. Branches were laid over the ceiling frame as smaller branches were woven through to form a roof. Mud was plastered into the walls' crevices to assure privacy and keep out the wind. Each day that passed, White Frost became larger with child and found it more difficult to move. Blue Sun helped her daughter bathe in the river and made a dress for her that would cover her body. At night, Blue Sun sang to the night sky. Her voice carried down into the valley where the Long House people lived.

During the day, children would creep through the forest to peek at the two women. At times, young women would come to stand and stare. Blue Sun and White Frost were not sure if it would be wise to speak with them. The *Huron* people were cautious as well for these lone women were strangers and could be spies from warring neighbor tribes.

Every morning, Blue Sun brushed White Frost's hair with a small brush made of spruce branch needles. They sat outside of their solidly made hut, showing the *Huron* people how they were clean and neat. As time passed, the *Huron* people walked around them, squinting. Finally, a small boy asked Blue Sun a question. She was amazed to find they spoke the same language. The Huron women were skeptical of these two who just showed up without any warning. The men were friendly, some even stacked firewood around their hut. One little girl brought them some food.

Elders conversed about these strange women who were not in union with a man nor did they have family. It was obvious the second younger woman was expecting a child. If the women had no men to help them, they could not be accepted within the tribe, and could be used to find out about the other tribes and their warring plans. The Elders, however, didn't have the courage to ask Blue Sun or White Frost their purpose for these strange women were polite, helpful and knew of healing herbs.

The summer passed into fall and these women stayed, appearing to be friendly and in need. An older man, who had lost his woman in childbirth, took Blue Sun to be his new woman for she was older and wise in the ways of raising children as he had four small ones who needed a mother. This man was strong and a respected member of the *Huron* people. It was in late morning, when he walked to the bark hut to reach down lifting Blue Sun's water basket. Nodding to her, he asked her to be his woman. When she nodded to him, the man smiled.

Behind him was a younger man, who was known as a brave hunter. His courage carried him directly to White Frost where he lifted the basket she was weaving. Solemnly, he asked her to be his woman, "You are a strong woman with child and will have many more. These children will need a father to teach them the ways of making canoes, stretching bows, hunting and fighting. Let us have these children as one family." White Frost's eyes sparkled as he helped her to stand. Now, life was settled for these two women.

On the night before Deganawida's birth, Blue Sun had another dream. This was a vision of Deganawida being responsible for the destruction of the Huron tribe. This dream came with images of death, bloody killings and gatherings of strangers. Quietly in the morning, she shared this dream with her daughter. It was decided that the moment the infant was born, they would go down to where the river fed into Lake Simcoe and drown him without anyone else knowing. They would tell the people that White Frost's baby had been born dead. This would save the *Huron* people and keep them safe from death.

White Frost made excuses to her man of needing to stay with her mother once her contractions started. Going far into the forest, the two made a soft bed in the broken leaves to receive the infant into the world. This small infant's birth was quiet and peaceful for the baby boy did not scream or cause a fuss. Quickly, the two women wrapped the small infant in soft deerskin, taking the cooing baby to the mouth of the Lake. Carefully, as they waded into the deep waters, they took turns keeping his small body underwater. They held him all night until the sun rose in the east. Tearfully, White Frost lifted the quiet bundle out of the water and handed it to her mother. Blue Sun's tears fell onto the tight deerskin wrapped around the infant. Spirit Mother watched from above, letting her tears fall to earth as morning dew. More than anything in her being, she wanted to reach down and hold the three of them. What they were accomplishing was a testing for this infant, but the earth women did not know of this. There was nothing Sky Mother could do to help them!

Blue Sun gasped as the baby kicked and tugged at the tightness around his tiny body. Quickly, she unwrapped the cloth to find the little boy alive, sucking on his thumb, hungry. His large caramel brown eyes peered up at his grandmother. Wiping the tears from her eyes, Blue Sun held him to her daughter, "He's been under water since sunset to sunrise! How is he still alive?"

White Frost eagerly held the baby to her breast to nurse. "Mother, are you sure we are doing right by trying to kill my beautiful baby?"

"Daughter, visions tell us how to live our lives and how to follow testings. This is what we must do! Please be strong!" They rested under a tall tree as White Frost nursed the baby.

Blue Sun watched the birds fly and dip over the tranquil lake. Pain riddled her body as she spoke, "We cannot let this one live for he will bring death to the people we know and love. There must be another way to bring about his death." As the day warmed, the women fell asleep with the baby in White-Frost's arms. Blue-Sun awoke with a start.

Pushing her daughter's long brown hair from her face, she said, "I have had another vision. We are to take the baby to the River of Stadacona. There we will tie a stone around him, drop him into the river at sunrise and wait until sunset to lift his body from the water."

Carefully avoiding other people, the women walked through the thick forest to the river then known as the River of the Stadacona or known today as the Saint Lawrence River. Again, White Frost cried silently as her mother took a strip of deerskin to tie around a heavy stone with the leather's other end wrapped, tied about the baby's thick neck. Shaking in emotional pain, she waded into the fast flowing river. There she dropped the stone tied to the infant into the water. The baby boy disappeared under the fast flowing water, cold and deep. The two women sat on the riverbank with their backs against a tall tree. They stared at the water as they waited for sunset.

Fearful of her infant son's death, White Frost put her head down on her arms as she sat with her knees up to her chest. She couldn't watch her mother bravely swim into the fast river to retrieve her son's dead body. Shivering, with tears falling onto her lap, White Frost prayed with all her might for her son to still be alive. The stone had held him down under the freezing cold water all the day, but maybe the Spirits would allow him to live. Please, Spirits allow him to live, please. She was crying so hard, she barely heard her mother's voice calling to her.

"White Frost, look! Look! Your son is still alive! He is hungry and how he is crying!" Blue Sun's news tugged at her daughter's heart. Calling out to her more loudly, Blue Sun yelled, "Daughter, daughter, this one will not go! He is with us yet! He is hungry and is squirming for your arms. Come and get him from me for this water is pulling me under!"

White Frost fought the water's current as she charged to her baby and her mother. Happy tears fell quickly as she called out with open arms, "Oh, Mother, this is truly magical! The Spirits must want him to live! We must stop this. Please, Mother!"

Blue Sun leaned to her daughter's eager arms, "Here, here, he lives! He wants his mother to feed him and love him! Please, take him for my joy has made me weak!" Mother handed the baby to White Frost as the two of them locked arms, forging their way through the fast water to the shoreline. Together they collapsed under the same tree that had held their prayers. White Frost nursed her infant while her mother slept. Again, Blue Sun had a dream. The river they were near fed into Lake Ontario. In her dream, the river they needed was the Huron River that fed into Lake Erie.

Sun woke the women and the infant. Cautiously, Blue Sun told her daughter of their need to go to Huron River. White Frost stared at her mother, "No! We cannot go through this again! This is my baby and we have tried twice to kill him and he has refused to die. We cannot do this again! We cannot!" White Frost pulled away from her mother's hold on the infant.

"We have no choice, this is what the Spirits have told us to do. We have to do this! Please, this is more important than what we need or want, please!" Again, the two women walked for three days to the Huron River. Neither of them spoke to the other. White Frost held her infant close to her chest, nursing him as her tears bathed him. Anger filled her body toward her mother and her mother's dreams of death. Blue Sun moved with a hypnotic trance closer and closer to their destination. This was not her doing, but the request of the Spirits.

They arrived early in the morning. Blue Sun gingerly took the infant from her daughter's hesitant arms. Blue Sun tightly wrapped the deerskin once again around the baby boy. The baby squirmed, wrestled to be free and screamed to be back with his mother. Wading into the fast river, red with mud from falling rain, Blue Sun held her grandson, once again, underwater. She rocked him gently under the water until he was still. Singing to the Spirits in the sky, she asked them for a sign. Spirit Mother brought clouds to shade her daughter. Sun warmed Blue Sun's body, giving her strength to believe. White Frost screamed and cried as she frantically watched from the shore.

As the orange sun began to set, Mother lifted the baby boy from under the mud red water. Once again, the baby boy was squirming, sucking on the deerskin over his mouth and very much alive. Raising the infant over her head, Blue Sun thanked the Spirits. This one was to live. This one was to do great things that did not have to do with killing. Laughing as she waded to her daughter, she smiled, "He is to live. His name is to be Deganawida for he has joined two rivers together to be the one who saves lives. The clouds gave me this sign. He is a peacekeeper who shall have a sacred tree named for him for we have sat under many trees to watch him live."

Both the women agreed to return to the village. Their men were pleased to see them for everyone was worried they had gone to another tribe. White Frost's man was pleased to have a son to teach. Learning how to plant pumpkins, wild squash seeds and gather berries, White Frost lived as the other women. Blue Sun continued to weave her baskets and her fishing nets. She became well known for her tight weaving and her man was very proud of her as he traded her weaving works to other tribes. Life was good for these two women as they learned the ways of the *Huron* people.

Deganawida grew fast and learned quickly. Soon he had six brothers to learn with regarding canoe making, bow stretching and arrow balancing, swimming races and hunting. He learned the languages of the different people who came to trade with his adopted father who taught him and his brothers how to hunt with the Huron. Deganawida became strong as he learned to fell fat tree trunks with sharpened axes. Bending soaked hickory planks for canoe braces was easy for him. His big canoes carried four or five men with heavy furs for trade. He chose not to take a wife, but to move among the different tribes around the Huron village, learning their customs and their ways was most important to him.

As he met and absorbed the traditions from others, a woman named *Jigonhsasee* became known to him as a peacekeeper. This woman traveled to and from battlegrounds, helping wounded warriors find their way home. There were stories of her going to tribal chiefs, asking them to come to her village longhouse to discuss options for peace. Deganawida visited her to learn how to speak of peace and harmony. She listened to his words, telling him to go out and use certain terms and certain hand signs with the warring men for as a woman she was limited in her ability.

Deganawida explained to her the dreams he had for the warring people, "Peace will take the form of the longhouse in which there are many hearths, one for each tribe or family, yet all will live in one household under one chief. They shall have one mind and live under one law. Thinking of peace will replace the killing. There shall be the many who live as one. The traditional longhouse shall keep everyone safe."

Deganawida's belief in peace grew as the Mohawks, Oneidas, Onondagas, Cayugas and Seneca fought with one another. Each group lived, hunted and fished along the same lakes, the same forests and the same hunting lands. All these tribes had chosen to follow a well-traveled path known as the War Path. This specific area of travel wound along one forest trail cutting through the Mohawk Valley to Finger Lake. Here boats were sent out either for fishing or for warring.

When Deganawida was chosen to become a warrior, he had a dream. *Ha-Wen-Neyu*, the Boss of the Great Sky told him to speak to all the warring tribes across the Great Lakes of peace. *Ha-Wen-Neyu* relayed to him this message, which was for him to pursue peace and to bring a united power of the five fighting tribes. Through dreams and meditation *Ha-Wen-Neyu* taught Deganawida magic and the words needed to convince others that peace was the answer in the Great Lake region.

Deganawida followed the rules of the warrior, taking four days to purge, four days to sit in silent meditation. Then in his state of spiritual strength, he followed his vision path to a place where there lay a huge white boulder, lying at the base of a tall cliff. Taking the dried jerky from his pouch, he stuck it between his cheek and his teeth in his mouth. At this boulder, he wrapped leather around the widest area of it, dragging it day after day closer to his village. There he chiseled and sanded it with dirt and rough bark, listening to *Ha-Wen-Neyu* teachings, telling him of the People and how to speak with them. Blue Sun brought Deganawida food during the day for he had become extremely thin. She chose to keep him company as he quietly chiseled on the one large white boulder.

At times, he shared his ideas with his grandmother Blue Sun. His people stood around to watch as each day he chiseled and sanded away. Slowly, the white boulder took on the shape of a crude canoe. Deganawida was covered in white powder, his fingers calloused and blistered from his extreme labor. No one could stop him from his task for he was determined to form a long canoe out of this white boulder found at the base of the sacred cliffs that overlooked the lakes.

His brothers laughed at him, saying, "Deganawida, there is no way this canoe will float! It will sink to the bottom of any river or any waterway, why are you wasting your time when you would have a fine canoe of birchbark by now! Leave it and come war with us against the Onondaga. Stop this foolishness."

Deganawida ignored them. Every morning, he was hard at work until sunset. His hands were strong from sanding the boulder with smaller rough rocks. His chisel needed to be sharpened regularly, but he did not stop until the canoe was a fine work of art. The one seat was balanced, the rounded bottom of the canoe was smooth as glass. Deganawida was proud of his white canoe, he had faith *Ha-Wen-Neyu* would not let him sink to the bottom of the lake. Then one late afternoon, *Ha-Wen-Neyu* told him the canoe was finished. It was time for peace. Deganawida went to his grandmother Blue Sun's Long House. There he sat with his grandmother, telling her of his dreams, his ideas of peace and all of the languages he had learned over his trading on the lakes. Then he went to his mother White Frost and told her of his plans. She was worried he would be killed for the tribes around the lake were birthed on war, knew only of war and each tribe was proud of their killings.

The next morning, Deganawida dragged his white boulder canoe to the shore of Lake Huron. People gathered around him, amazed at his stubbornness to prove his canoe would float. Some of the younger men came to help him, joking as they pushed it into the water. The canoe did not sink! Deganawida stepped into it, carefully, for he was not totally convinced of this canoe's magic. It stayed afloat. Saying a prayer to *Ha-Wen-Neyu*, he stood as he floated from the shore with such joy in his heart for now he knew his quest would be a success.

Taking his carved paddle of hard oakwood, he sculled to the middle of Lake Huron. The white canoe floated with ease, gliding gracefully through the water to the opposite shore. There the *Mohawk* warriors stood, gaping at him with their spears raised in amazement. The white canoe and its owner easily coasted through the water directly to them. Once there, they separated to let him come onto their land. Their spears were laid on the ground at the warriors' feet. The chief stood proudly accepting Deganawida with humble arms. Women hurried to circle their warriors, watching this miracle of a man walk ashore.

Deganawida spoke of peace to the warriors and the tribal chiefs. The *Mohawk* listened intently, for who could disbelieve a man who paddled a stone canoe. Deganawida went from village to village. The people came to him, listening to his words of peace and unity. Deganawida spoke of outsiders who were coming soon and if the tribes were warring with one another, they would lose against the outsiders. It was vital for all the tribes to unite in peace, to form a nation able to argue for land and unity. The warriors abandoned their killing weapons, joining together to listen to his words as he sat on the shores of the Great Lakes. He didn't stay in one village for very long, for he had to convince the many tribes of peace and to abandon war. Then he moved on to the next village, paddling his way across the water. Children would meet him, wanting to wade into the water and touch his magical canoe.

One day, as he came to a quiet shoreline, stood a man alone, waiting for him. Deganawida paddled over to this huge man, standing over six feet tall with hands the size of a tree trunk's width. Hanging from this man's hand was a disjointed severed human arm, dripping dark blood onto the sand. Growling at Deganawida, this man's open mouth had torn human flesh stuck between his yellowish brown teeth. Human blood dripped from cracked lips to his crusty chin. Deganawida approached him cautiously. This man was huge, his muscles bulged, his face was covered with black char and his wild hair was filled with burrs and tree leaves. Large angry eyes, bloodshot and goopy, oozing with mucous and dirt glared at Deganawida as he had paddled closer to the shoreline.

A deep raspy voice barked out at Deganawida, "My name is *Hiawatha*. I am the strongest of all *Mohawk* warriors. They no longer want me to fight for them. How am I to eat if there is no human flesh to rip from the bodies on the fields of battle? What am I to do? How am I to live? You are destroying my life and the traditions of my father and my fathers' fathers."

Deganawida stepped from the canoe, wading onto the beach, he reached up to put his hand on *Hiawatha's* muscular shoulder. "It is a time for peace. You are not to eat human flesh again. It is time for you to find peace within your being. You could come with me to bring peace to the people, you could be my speaker for the *Mohawk* language is difficult and I am limited in understanding what your Elders have to say."

Hiawatha stared at this man who was smaller and was weaker. This strange man who was not afraid of him and did have trouble speaking the *Mohawk* language. "No, I fight to live. I live to eat human flesh and meat. No!"

Deganawida backed carefully into his canoe. He paddled away from *Hiawatha* with a sadness in his heart. *Hiawatha* threw the human arm piece at Deganawida's canoe as he growled and yelled, "War is who we are! You cannot take war away from us! My daughters will die without war! Go, go, away and do your work somewhere else!"

Returning home that evening, *Hiawatha* found his three daughters had died from a terrible illness. The *Mohawk* village was afraid of him for they believed he would carry disease to their children. The Elders asked him to leave for they no longer needed a warrior and they certainly didn't need diseases from his dead daughters. *Hiawatha* was of the Wolf Clan, therefore he turned to the Bear Clan family to help him with his daughters' funeral arrangements. Not one of either the Bear or the Turtle Clans would help him for he was known for his temper and his filthy habits. *Hiawatha* pleaded for it was of utmost importance to follow tradition. He knew he needed to mourn for them at least ten days.

Going to his father's friend who was an Elder in the Turtle Family, he begged for help. His wife and daughters agreed to take the bodies of his daughters and prepare them for ceremony. Each of his daughters was taken to the Lake to be washed, their hair was gently combed and they were dressed in their best bleached buckskins.

Hiawatha alone dug the holes in the *Longhouse of the Dead* for his daughters. Taking his bow and arrows, he went out to hunt twenty white tail deer to pay the *Roterihonto* or the Faith Keeper to give the words that would send his daughter to the place, "Across the Fire." These condolences let those, who knew and loved his daughters, give their acceptance to them, into a place where they would be embraced by their ancestors. Now, his daughters would no longer feel pain or sickness for once their bodies were brought into the *Longhouse of the Dead* over a fire, through the eastern door with their feet facing west, they were assured a life of community with their deceased families. This would only be completed once *Hiawatha* had achieved full deep mourning for ten days.

After ten days, it was the family's duty to give away all belongings of the deceased. Everything must be given away to those not related, for those people grieving while holding the deceased items would prolong the journey of the dead. At the end of the ten days, a meal with all of the deceased's favorite food must be served with a place setting reserved for each of them. *Hiawatha*'s daughters now were 'welcome' in the Spirit World beyond and once there they find peace. *Hiawatha* was the one person who was responsible for their journey since he was the sole relative surviving. This he did with great reverence and once he completed his duty, he went on a Spirit Fast vision quest. When he awoke, he knew immediately what he must do.

In the morning sun, he returned to his family's empty *Longhouse*. Everything of his daughters was gone. Building a formidable fire in the center, he took all of his possessions to burn, including his bow, arrows, hatchets and all of his warring equipment burned to ash. All of his past life was to be obliterated in his *Longhouse* fire.

Lifting his hands over the door frames at the west and east side, he pulled the posts free letting the roof collapse. At first all he could see was thick gray smoke and then flames rose high to eat away his past life into ash. His tribal people continued on their daily tasks. No one stopped to ask what happened nor did they offer to help him. Turning, away from the village he slowly ran at a fast trot. It took him three days to run all the way around the lake to find Deganawida. There they discussed how to continue bringing peace to the people of the Great Lakes. *Hiawatha*'s transition convinced more than one argumentative chief to join with them in peace. Trading and hunting became a shared duty with all of the tribes helping and surviving.

There came a rumor of one man who promised to fight to the death to avoid peace. This was an older Onondaga Chief who had lived and taught his people to fight until death in order to maintain honor within the tribe. This Chief was a tough warrior who had been pushed away from his family for he would not agree to Deganawida's peace plan. Many believed this ornery nasty man had died, having walked into the lake to drown. Eventually, Deganawida and *Hiawatha* found a young boy who led them through a dark forest path leading to a mountain.

Deganawida and *Hiawatha* found the Onondaga Chief who had dug a deep cave in a high mountain with the opening end of a long tunnel overlooking the Lakes. They confronted him, but this man spit at them when they mentioned peace. His face was contorted with vitriolic anger, giving him the appearance of an ugly monster. *Hiawatha* backed away from the Chief as he spoke of death, dismemberment and blood honor.

The Onondaga Chief's face was creased with wrinkles filled with moving worms and bugs. His eyes were red from dust and cave mites. The Chief's hair moved with two serpents intertwining, hissing, slithering and biting at one another on the top of his head.

Deganawida nodded to the Chief out of respect, "We are here on a mission of peace and will not leave until you agree to it. Please listen to what we have to say, it is important. Do not spit on what you do not know."

"Nothing you say will please me. It would be best if you leave now before I kill you and eat you!" Spit hit Deganawida's forehead.

Deganawida did not wipe his forehead, but continued with his words, "We come out of respect not to fight. You are known for your wisdom and your knowledge will help your people. We will not walk away and allow you to live alone in misery." Deganawida sat down outside the cave entrance. "We are respectful to you, would you return your respect to us?"

The Onondaga Chief sat abruptly. Deganawida nodded to *Hiawatha*, urging him to sit as well. The three men spoke, arguing and sharing ideas and concepts for some time. As they spoke, serpents fell from the Chief's head to slither back inside the cave. Slowly, the Chief's eyes cleared from the red dust and the cave pollen silt. The wrinkles along the Chief's face smoothed as the bugs and worms fell to wiggle their way into the walls of the cave.

Finally, the Onondaga Chief put his hands together as he nodded to Deganawida, "Yes, I will accept your plan for peace. You make sense. If we completely kill one another with no one left alive, there will be no one here to remember who we are or know of our ways. If the foreigners come, as you say, we must agree to be strong, united as one nation for the outsiders might be afraid of our numbers."

Slowly, standing, he continued, "Let us go and tell the people of your peace." The three men returned to the tribes at the base of the mountain. There by the side of the Lake, they had a great meeting. It was decided the different village tribes would make a union and become known as the *Haudenosaunee Nation*.

Deganawida stood, "To all of you I say, your skin must be seven thumbs thick to withstand the arrows, darts and spears of your enemies.

Stand strong together in peace for as a whole nation, you have the strength to defeat war."

Deganawida the Peace Maker Story number 2

Lifting his arms to the sky, he said, "If ever you are in need of me, call my name to the bushes and trees by the shoreline and I will return. Remember to be patient for not all the people who come this way shall know the words of peace."

Once the meeting was over, all the people buried their warring weapons. Deganawida planted a tree sapling at this meeting place by the Lake. He announced to the people, "I am Deganawida and with the Five Nation's confederation, I plant this tree as the Tree of Great Peace. It shall stand as long as you agree to maintain a peaceful nation as one strong unit!"

Deganawida walked away from the people to paddle away in his white stone canoe. *Hiawatha* maintained the peace between the people of this great Nation. Deganawida was not seen again, although many believe he is still in his white stone canoe, paddling around the Great Lakes to be sure the people retain his peaceful nation and are strong as one against the many outsiders.

Now, there is the Six Nations Reserve by the Grand River, built as a monument to Deganawida. At ceremonies, there is a chant still given, saying, "Listen my grandchildren while your grandchildren cry, because the Great League established by Deganawida has grown old. It will endure."

A Longhouse was built around this monument and this is known as the *Kayanerenh-kowa* or the Great Peace. The *Kanonsionni* or Longhouse is still there today, built by the Iroquois out of sapling and bark. Deganawida's Six Nation's Reserve by Grand River has a relationship commemorated by the construction of Her Majesty's Royal Chapel of the *Mohawks* built in 1785.

Notes:

This story is known throughout the Great Lakes area and in southern Canada. The power of motherhood and the dream quest come alive with the birth of Deganawida. Peace is a powerful tool when used properly and with the wisdom of the Creator. This story was shared by an Iroquois student at the University of New Mexico at Valencia Campus, here in New Mexico. Magical gifts are bestowed on those who believe in the unity of Peace.

Glossary:

Deganawida – Onondaga defines as Heavenly Messenger, founder of five Nations confederacy and of the Iorquois.

Ha-Wen-Neyu – Iroquois Creator of the World or Great Spirit Life Maker.

Hiawatha – Mohawk name means "He Makes Rivers." Peace keeper.

Huron People – Members of the Native American Confederacy, lived in southeast Ontario around Lake Simcoe. Today they live in Quebec and north.

Oklahoma – French word for 'Bristly.'

Jigonhsasee – Iroquoian woman helped Deganawida in bringing peace.

Kayanerenh-kowa – Title of the League of Five Nations confederacy, means 'Tree of Peace.'

Longhouse – Communal dwelling of the Iroquois and North American Indian people.

Mohawk – Native American people, one of the Five Iroquois Nations.

Roterihonto – Mohawk Faith Keeper who guards the place Across the Fire or the place of death.

Wyandot People – Lived southeast of Ontario around Lake Simcoe, also Huron.

3
MAGICAL WATER APPEARS

Eternal Holy Nanak Zara
ASIAN INDIAN

Guru Nanak, the founder of the Sikh religion was born on 15th·
April, 1469, at Rai Bhoi Di Talwandi better known as Nankana Sahib
today, near Lahore, in the Punjab province of present day Pakistan. The
small village is about fifty miles from Lahore. Guru Nanak passed away
on 22nd September, 1539, at Kartarpur, seventy miles from Lahore.

Guru Nanak possessed divine sacred abilities and was a
remarkable man. People became aware of Nanak's exceptional gifts when
he was a child. As he grew into manhood, his spiritual powers became
more apparent. Guru Nanak believed his divine gift should benefit those in
need. He gave holy guidance to those who had no hope or felt their souls
were empty.

Guru Nanak toured South India for five years from early 1510 AD
to late 1514 AD. During this journey, he visited Bidar in Karnataka state
and stayed there for a few days. He chose the foothills near the town to
camp during his stay. There he would meditate, contemplate and think. He
would remember God in all things and chant His name.

Bidar was a village in the center of the southern peninsula of India
with rolling hills of red earth landscape. This area was unfortunate for
most of the summers Bidar was plagued with drought-like conditions.
Green fields scorched, turning the fields of harvest into black dust. Dry,
hot air lifted from the burnt earth, leaving every living thing parched and
dehydrated. Trees, bushes and vines became nothing more than spindly
figures of their previous forms. Animals searched for shade around the
sparsely withered trees. Chapped nostrils on the animals bled as flies stuck
to their goopy eyes, lifeless due to heat. Many animals dug into the dirt to
sleep during this intense heat. Stray dogs hid under sheds or barren trees;
these were the only forms of animal life visible.

At this time, farmers didn't have grass or feed for the animals.
Dried twigs were chewed with effort for they splintered and stuck in the

animals' throats. Bird nests clung desperately to the bare branches. Most of the birds flew away although some stayed hopeful for rain. Feathers were fluttered to keep their hearts cool in the heat.

Drought laden Bidar burned under the ruthless hot sun. Deserted streets gave Bidar the appearance of a ghost town. Families sought shelter in their homes. Windows and doors were covered with blankets or boards to keep the heat outside and the cool inside. The elderly were kept in the darkest rooms of the house. Heat drained the life out of every living being. Just to move was exhausting.

Each summer these drought-like conditions returned. Water disappeared in the wells to leave a scummy substance in the bottom. During the heat of summer, people rationed their water, yet there was never enough to last through this blistering drought. No one was able to bathe or cook. The saline muck from the drainage streams was now blowing dust. Desperation for survival thrived in each household.

Summer crops scorched. Water became deficient. People and animals endured this misery. Babies and the elderly died from dehydration. The population chose to endure this annual anguish assaulting their land. Single men had a formidable time acquiring wives for no parent would wish their daughters to live in such a miserable environment.

Businesses suffered, *vaidya*s (ayurvedic doctors) desperately tried to keep their patients alive. People became depressed, collapsing from heat with no hope of recovery. Everyone lost money. Beliefs developed among the people that the Water Goddess had cursed Bidar. This appointed curse appeared to have no end in sight. No one knew if she would lift her curse, allowing enough rain to avoid the serious water scarcity in the summer season. Baked Bidar was in serious need of a miracle.

In 1512, the drought reached an incomparable sweltering heat. A monsoon was badly needed. Death became a friendly escape. Desperation for water brought the people outside to dig in the dirt for any form of moisture. Famine gripped Bidar as devastation choked the survival of each individual.

It was during this time, in late March and early April, Guru Nanak arrived in Bidar accompanied with his disciple Bhai Mardana. Walking along the blistering road, they perceived the desolation of the town. Aware of the plight of the people, they continued to Guru Nanak's small hut on the red foothills above the town. Mirages radiated in the sweltering air, bringing some animals out of their shelters, believing there were ponds of water nearby. Guru Nanak watched this pathetic plight of the animals and the people. He started praying.

As Guru Nanak prayed, Bhai Mardana played his single-stringed instrument. When Guru Nanak finished his prayers, both men sang the *bhajans*. Their deep resonating voices, brought hope to the people trapped in their despair. Hearing the spiritual songs of these two holy men, some were daring enough to leave their homes, walking through the searing air to arrive at the hut on the red dirt hill.

Eager for salvation the people came, giving up their sanctuaries to listen to his assurances. His teachings and religious covenants brought hope to Bidar. Heat and hunger were forgotten as followers listened to the Holy men sing spiritual songs. Raising their voices filled with eager emotion, people joined with them in chorus. Bidar became a town filled with song and graceful promise. People came to his holiness Guru Nanak and his disciple Bhai Mardana with hope.

Sitting with the distressed people, his holiness Guru Nanak listened to their suffering words of starvation, dehydration and death. Guru Nanak was saddened by their tragic existence. Their depressing situation weighed heavy on his soul.

Eternal Holy Nanak Zara

Near where Guru Nanak stayed, lived a *faqir*, a Muslim holy man in his *muth*, (monastery) along with a few disciples. One day, he heard the sweet *bhajans* sung by Bhai Mardana and Guru Nanak. The Muslim *faqir* liked what he heard. Wanting to find the source of the music, this *faqir* went with his disciples to the hut on the red dirt hill of Bidar. He and his disciples went to see Guru Nanak. When they saw the saintly Guru, they were highly impressed. Bowing to his holy reverence, the *faqir* and his followers were asked to rise by Guru Nanak. Greetings were given, which led to a conference on the desperate situation in Bidar. The *faqir* was informed of the drought, loss of water and deaths that had occurred. Conversing with the *faqir* disturbed his holiness Guru Nanak even more. The *faqir* empathized with his sorrow.

His holiness Guru Nanak joined his palms in prayer as tears started rolling down his cheeks. Closing his eyes, concentrating with all his might, he compelled the Supreme Creator to help Bidar and the people. The Guru Nanak went into a holy trance, bringing his communion into a divine glowing light. This was truly a miraculous moment.

After some time, his holiness Guru Nanak peered out at the people with his large eyes, exuding extreme compassion. He was sitting on the hill overlooking Bidar, his holiness was perched on a rock. As, Guru Nanak extended his leg to rise, his san*dal* hit a stone, pushing it up and out of the ground.

Instantly, a fountain of water shot straight up, out of the ground where the stone had been. Water soared high into the sky, flowing down the hillside, streaming beside the town. Clear liquid, sweet, divine and bountiful poured around the holy men. Water surged with force, forging a deep ravine down the hill onto the red lands. People around Guru Nanak watched this miracle with incredulous eyes. Families ran to town, yelling to others about the supernatural miracle.

Men, women, children and the elderly started chanting his praise and threw themselves at his feet in extreme joy. Hesitantly more families came out of their closed homes to sing, dance and soak in the cool, lifesaving liquid flowing from the hill. They drank the sweet, cold water to their heart's content. Truly, a miracle had taken place! They told their near and dear ones who were still hiding in the homes. Everyone hurried to the *zara* with whatever containers they could find to fill with water. Animals smelling the delicious moisture ran to drink, filling their bellies. Birds flew down from charred trees to squawk and bathe their dry feathers. This was an amazingly glorious occasion!

Guru Nanak was pleased to see life return to Bidar. He thought, 'The *zara* would now provide water forever.' He smiled, looking at the water with deep love in his eyes and heart. Then, he raised his hand in blessing to resume his worship of the Supreme Being, remembering and thanking Him.

It has been more than five hundred years since this miracle took place. The sweet water *zara* at Bidar that Guru Nanak miraculously brought out from the earth is still there and is flowing. It quenches the thirst of thousands of people in the region. Now, the sweet spring is regarded as holy, the people have built an open-mouthed pot around the exact spot of its origin. Believers throw coins in the pot hoping the holy water shall fulfil their wishes. They also believe the water to have medicinal qualities curing various diseases. For that reason, they bring along bottles and other such containers to carry the water to their homes. Bidar may have bad droughts, but now they have water to last through the summer heat.

Notes:

The miracle-tale about Nanak Zara is connected to Guru Nanak, the founder of the Sikh religion. Guru Nanak was a humanitarian and formed a new religious philosophy, Sikhism. On receiving his divine inspiration, he travelled in the four directions, both within India and beyond its boundaries like Afghanistan. The local populace has not forgotten his blessing to them for it has been preserved in the form of a legend over the past five centuries. Marathi lecturer and my research student at the time, Deepak Chiddarwar, and I recorded this narration told to us by a Sikh from the *Gurudwara*. The legend is retold in my own words. For four decades I was teaching Marathi in Udgir which is in Maharashtra state. Bidar, a city in the Karnataka state is about 47 miles away from Udgir. My wife Usha and I had visited Bidar a few times over the years. During every visit, the Sikhs at the Gurudwara would narrate the miraculous tale about the Nanak Zara that is also known as Guru Nanak Jhira Sahib or The Holy Nanak Wellspring. As a result, the tale has stayed in my mind. In 2008, when I started my study of folktales about water sources, I made it a point to visit Bidar again to gather the detailed Holy Nanak Zara folktale.

Glossary:

Bhajan – Prayers and religious songs sung by followers and *worshippers* in front of a deity and also during some special religious celebrations.

Gurudwara – The Place of worship for Sikhs. A Sikh individual follows Sikhism, a monotheistic religion originated in the 15th century, in the Punjab region of the Indian subcontinent, based on the revelation of Guru Nanak.

Muth – A monastery. A local or divisional center where a faith is preached, religious discourses are given and religious practices are performed.

Zara – Stream, a Marathi word.

Water Flows, Chiricahua and Lipan Apache
NATIVE AMERICAN

There was a time when the U.S. Army men known as the Bi'ndah-Li'ghi, or Bi'nda-li'ghi'o'yi who were the people with the 'White Eyes.' The 'White Eyes' fought against the Ndé'indaaí or Nédnaa'í *Chiricahua* known as the 'Enemy People' who lived in the Southwestern United States. They referred to themselves as the Southern *Chiricahua* or *Chiricahua* proper, also, Pinery Apache, Ne'na'i or 'Those Ahead at the End.' These White Eyed Army men offered one hundred dollars for the severed head of a *Chiricahua* warrior especially those known as *"Nde, Ne, Néndé, Héndé* or *Hen-de"* or "The People, Men."

The men wore their *breechcloths* made from a softened rectangular piece of animal leather. This was worn up between their legs and tucked over their leather belts. War shirts were washed in sand, known as 'eputitesis' made of leather with dyed red pigment around the edges. Decorated aprons were worn over their *breechcloths* and their long legged high boot *moccasins* were wrapped around the upper leg tied with woven dyed red yucca strips.

One of the larger men from the hunting camp, who was known for being terrible at hunting, decided to invite his brother-in-law on a hunting trip with him. This brother-in-law was a small sturdy man who was a swift runner. Chief Posito Moraga cherished this small hunter for his quick wit and his fine hunting skills. Everyone knew the two men were not friends, but the older brother insisted that his brother-in-law and he should go out alone. The brother-in-law could teach him and help him become a better hunter. Finally, most of the hunters agreed this would be good for both men. One would learn how to hunt and the other would learn of his brother-in-law's character to possibly become his friend.

The two men tightened their bows, balanced their arrows and placed them in the bleached leather quivers. The stone ball clubs were wrapped tightly in buckskin and their spears and knives were sharpened on flat rocks. Their women wrapped dried meat jerky, roasted ears of corn and sunflower seeds in cotton cloth, placing all in a leather pouch that would be tied around the men's leather belts. The cleaned deer bladder pouches were filled with water and tied with braided yucca leaves. It was early in the morning when the two men went out alone. They ran across the desert, studying the sand for animal tracks and cavalry movement. Following the Sierra Madre Mountains, they moved quickly soon out of sight of their sentinels on the hill above the tribal camp.

The hunters were gone for four days. Each day, the hunting camp was busy for there was a need to cut reeds, make more arrows, balance them and find sap to attach the feathers. New bows were strung after soaking the resin and leather all night by the fires. Everyone was surprised when the larger man, who could not hunt, came back without his brother-in-law. Cat-calling while laughing and pointing at four horses behind his lead horse that had fine Navaho blankets rolled on each of the horses' back, he shouted, "I am now a rich man! Where is my wife? We shall have a good life now!" The hunters watched him enter the camp. He had no kill and his bow and his arrows were clean and intact.

This was not good. The hunters knew what he had done. They knew how he achieved his wealth. It was obvious to all the hunters who were mumbling amongst one another. Walking around him, the hunters noticed the wealth of goods tied to the horses' backs. The hunters clenched their fists and shook their heads. This traitor had sold his brother-in-law's head to the Army White Eyes and bought goods from another tribe. This man betrayed his people, his woman and his honor. No one said anything, until they were able to speak with the others at the main camp.

The hunting camp was packed, by midafternoon the hunters had returned to the larger main camp. At the round fire meeting that night in the main teepee, this man nor his family came to explain his new wealth. Each person spoke in the circle of this strange event. Once the younger warriors heard of what he had done, they went after this man immediately with death in their eyes. Someone had warned him or perhaps he realized others knew of his actions. This large man had already disappeared. The anger within these young warriors was uncontrollable and in their crazed rage they slaughtered this man's wife and children and with bloodied hands they butchered this man's close friends. This killing spree was filled with mob vengeance, having a deadly revulsion at this betrayal. These young men were roped and tied, placed in a smaller teepee at the edge of the main camp. All night long, these young men screamed, yelled and stamped their feet.

One of the Elders summoned a Shaman who was visiting a neighboring camp. When the Shaman arrived, he required all the young warriors to be placed in a circle in one place, held as captives. The Shaman was dressed in his leather shirt, decorated with bright red and yellow symbols of the sun, moon, stars, clouds, rainbows, snakes and centipedes. These were beaded down the shirt's front. The fellow hunters of the brother who did not return, had their brown hair cut straight at the shoulder in mourning with headbands low on the forehead. The men's chokers, worn tightly around their necks, had strings of hollowed bone pieces mixed with shells and drilled turquoise dripping down onto their chests. The women of those killed in the massacre, wore their hair cut straight at the shoulder with their headbands tight just above their eyebrows. Their leather skirts hung to below their knees and to the top of their high leather *moccasins*. Loose topped cotton blouses of calico or gingham hung from their shoulders to flow over their leather skirts. Wearing their turquoise jewelry mixed with shells, the women watched with stoic faces of fire ash rubbed on their faces and necks.

The Shaman told the people to gather dried wood and make a huge bonfire. Lifting powders from his pouches, he tossed these into the fire, causing flames to turn colors. Rancid odors filled the air as strange popping noises burned and spit. When the bonfire burned low, he asked for the young warriors to be stripped naked and brought to him, placing them to sit in a circle around this fire. Dusk had fallen, giving each of the warriors a strange orange glow as the firelight flickered in front of them. The Shaman poured water into his black pot as it sat on the hot coals of the fire. Slowly, the pot turned from dark black to red orange with smoke lifting out of top's wide opening. Powders from another pouch were mixed into the boiling pot of water.

A slight breeze blew the raven's feathers tied to the Shaman's waist-long dark hair. The Shaman's bare hands lifted the red-orange pot from the hot coals. He stirred the mixture with a tree branch stem. Slowly chanting "*Kan*" as he stirred the boiling pot in his hand, he made his way around to each of the warriors. He tilted the pot to their lips, telling them to drink the hot mixture. Each young warrior did not hesitate, but drank the mixture put before them. When the last of the young warriors had drunk, the Shaman returned to his leather pouches where he pulled out a narrow white drum. The rhythm of the drum with the soft chanting put the young warriors into a deep sleep. They slept for two days.

The pink hue of dawn broke over the desert and the high mountain range. The Shaman broke their slumber with the clapping of his hands.

Each of the young warriors awakened, appearing to be calm yet confused. Taking a feather from his belt, the Shaman waved it over the gray coal dust, "You have awakened from a bad dream. Peace has returned to your soul and you shall return to your families as you once were."

Turning to the rest of the people in the camp, the Shaman spoke, "It is time for you to leave this camp and move. Evil has lived here. This is not a place for harmony. Gather your things and move by dusk."

One of the Elders came forward, to say, "We've good game here. There is fresh water and the mountains to the east block us from our enemies. Why should we move?"

The Shaman knelt in front of his pouches as he rolled them. Quickly, he tied them to his leather belt, "This camp has been cursed by the man who killed his brother-in-law. He sold his head to the U.S. Army. This man left before the main council meeting, by now he has probably betrayed all of you by telling them where you are camped. If he watched from the mountain, he saw his family being killed and his friends. Out of revenge he would tell the U.S. Army and they're coming to kill all of you and take this land for the White Eyes."

The Elder put up his hand to stop the Shaman, "How is it that you have this knowledge? Are you speaking with the Army to gain information?"

"No!" the Shaman pointed to his right eye, "When my right eye twitches, I know evil is coming. Last night, a vision came to me of this man who betrayed all of you. If you are wise, you will leave or die in your pride."

The Elder removed from his left wrist a thick silver bracelet. It was inlaid with Pacific coral framing a Morenci turquoise stone inlaid in the center. "This is part of our tribe's soul. It is our gift to you with appreciation and honor for saving our young hunters."

Aware of the Shaman's warning, the people hurried to gather the cooking pots, food, blankets, and poles for the ceremonial teepee. They untethered the horses and chased the corraled calves and cows out into the desert. Moving with cattle was too cumbersome and would certainly kick up dust bringing attention to their movment. Young warriors who had gone through ceremony were given the job of quickly butchering the sheep they had stolen for these animals would bleat, alarming the enemy of where they were. Wild turkeys were gathered, beaks tied with thin braided yucca ropes. Children were put in charge of herding them.

Woman rolled the sleeping palettes and blankets, binding them with leather straps to keep them tight. The round wickiups were knocked down, poles tied together with the household goods strapped to the top. Tanned hides were used to cover the teepee poles, wrapped to make one long bundle pulled behind a horse for each family. Everything a family owned was wrapped and strapped onto their individual wickiups poles to be pulled behind one horse. The branches used for the roofs were thrown about, some were dragged far from the original camp to confuse anyone tracking them.

New mothers cried while rocking their infants for they were frightened of the U.S. Army who might bring death. Older woman clicked their tongues, "Moving is a way of life for us. If we do not travel to be safe, we do not live. We have been here too long. It is time for the young people to learn of migrating to survive and to learn and live!"

The Chief spoke quietly with the elders on the desert flatland. It was decided they would move to Antelope Springs south of Chiwi Kawi, also known as Turkey Mountain or what the Mexican call Dos Cabezas Mountain. "We must travel mostly at night for the sun during the day will be ferociously hot. All must be ready to travel before dusk tonight. We will walk single file through the night until the heat of mid-day, we should be able to arrive at Wild Turkey Canyon. Our destination is Antelope Springs near our sacred Sheep Canyon."

Elders humbly listened. Feathers were tied in their long hair with leather ties. Weather worn faces, wrinkled over time from sun and worry knew the seriousness of Chief's words. Many of the men's bare chests revealed war scars from U.S. Army bullets, northern enemy tribal arrows and gouges from buffalo horns. Each man had fought death and won, earning their place in the communal circle as an elder of their group within the tribe. Those who were hunters had wide leather wristbands decorated with silver that were used for wrist protection when shooting arrows to bring down buffalo, black bears, and white tailed deer. Sharp long, curved knives strapped to leather belts were for piercing the armor of the nine-banded armadillo. Raked scars across men's legs and upper arms showed their ability to hunt and collect the ferocious armadillo who used their sharp claws to rip and tear their enemy. The people found armadillo meat a delicacy, but the hunt could be deadly. Humans have a strong odor and when the armadillo is trapped, they attack. Even though the armadillo digs into the soft sand to hide, they are easily found.

The soft voice of the Chief continued as he followed each of the Elders to their family tribal group, "You are responsible to have all your needs packed for travel. We do not have much water, nor can we attempt to get more if the U.S. Army is on its way here from Fort Bowie near Apache

Pass. Traveling at night should alleviate the need. Young men shall follow brushing away any traces of footprints with willow withes."

Studying each of his Elders' faces, he continued, "We must move with stealth and quiet. Keep newborns silent, young children must move quietly and the elderly upright and steady with the help of the younger people."

Everyone nodded in agreement. Returning to his place in the circle, Chief drew a map in the dirt, using a stick. "This is where we are now, this is where we need to be in four days' time. Here is our path to Antelope Springs. If we meet the U.S. Army Bi'ndah-Li'ghi, we move to higher ground in search of a safe canyon. There has been no rain for a long while, the water cisterns are probably empty. Watch the water jars, keep them on the horses for they should not be passed around easily." Lifting his chin, his sharp dark brown eyes closed as he said, "Go. Be ready."

In the dusk, shadows of movement were scarcely seen. Hardly a trace was to be found of human life for within hours the camp had been completely demolished. The cook fire's coals had been scraped from the earth's dirt floor, youngsters had thrown the coal dust into the air, letting it blow far away. Branches had been used to sweep the area clean of footprints and hoof marks. Now, there was a long line of people, families following families one after the other with the Chief leading. Footsteps were placed one on top of the other to give the appearance of one heavy person walking. One of the Elders was picked to be guide Chief as the people migrated south. This Chief ordered scouts ahead, watching their hand signals, noticing the wind and marking their destiny with natural known landmarks.

The tribal Shaman was last, walking behind the older people. Sometimes he chanted and sometimes he was quiet. His sharp eyes kept watch for birds, spirit signs and the sounds of the Earth. He was the Keeper of the Souls, wearing the Gila monster design on his forehead with the millipede symbol on his arms and back. Each of the scouts had their faces colorfully painted with specific designs by this Shaman prior to being sent out into the desert. These markings kept the scouts spiritually safe. Also, if one were to be found hurt or dead, these designs would tell their people of the deceased identity.

The people steadfastly walked along the base of the Dos Cabezas Mountain range. It was now the middle of summer and extremely hot. Apache people were trained since toddlers to walk, run and hunt breathing through their noses for the dry hot hair would make them thirsty if they breathed through their mouths. Soon night passed into dawn and the sun's heat beat down on them. Women pulled their wraps over their heads and tried to keep the young children in the shade of their own bodies. Wind kicked up at intervals, blowing hot dust into their faces. The scorched earth baked the thick leather soles of their moccasined feet. As the afternoon heat radiated up from the dry desert floor, runners were sent from the different families to speak with the Chief.

An older runner spoke quietly, "The old ones and the children need to rest. Is there a place to camp soon for the water jars are becoming empty and the day is far from being over?"

Grunting the Chief nodded, "There, to the west of us is a foothill. We shall find a shallow gorge there."

As the runners raced beside the families, they used a tree branch to brush their footprints from the sandy desert floor. Water jars were soon becoming empty. As the people continued to step precisely into the footprint in front of them, they slowly made their way into a shallow gorge. Children fell into their parents arms as infants suckled greedily. Grandparents squatted in the cool of the shade, knowing they would need to move at dusk.

The hot sun baked the earth as it inched its way across the dusty desert. A single hawk flew overhead. Slowly, dusk brought orange clouds overhead to follow the sun, disappearing over the linear horizon. Children were nudged awake. Babies wrapped closely to their mothers' sides. Grandparents pulled one another to stand as the younger men untethered horses. Forging across the flats, they progressed in the cool of the night to a mountain crest of the Dos Cabezas Mountain range. Their scouts found them with news that the U.S. Army was at Parker Canyon, which was not far to the south.

The Chief nodded at the news saying, "We will not fight the U.S. Army for our women, children and older ones are here in this group. Warriors are to stay close with their families and protect. The survival of our tribe depends on everyone being together in case of an outside attack."

One of the younger riders was sent only to return with worrisome news, "The Shaman was correct. There is a troop of U.S. Army studying our old location. They were given a map of where we were and where we would probably move. It is wrong for their Apache scouts spoke of our people going to the northeast to Blanco Canyon. Yet, here we are going southwest."

"This is good. Where did you find this information?" Shaman asked.

"My father's brother is a scout at Fort Sill. I met with him by the pine trees near the gully. He warned for us to stay away from the Turkey

Creek Caldera for Mexican soldiers are waiting for us there."

The Chief led his people into a small gorge at mid-day. It was quiet. No one built a fire. Smoke from the top of the mountain could be seen for miles. Scouts were sent to find a deeper gorge or even a canyon for people needed to rest. After one full day of resting, the scouts returned to tell of a deep gorge only half a day away hidden by tall pine trees and some boulders. As the Apache silently plodded with one foot to land inside another's footprints, the scouts dropped down to dismount their horses. Feathers were untied from the horses' manes as dry dirt was rubbed on the horses' fur, coloring the horse the same as the earth around them.

The first scout approached the Chief, he said, "We were not able to find water in the rock caches. Even these little guys found no water." He dropped a handful of dried millipedes into his hand. "Dust, dirt and these sad creatures were all to be found in the upper level water caches."

The Chief clicked his tongue, "Our people need water. You need to continue searching for a spring or find and dig an earth well."

Wiping dust from his deep brown eyes, the scout shook his head to smile, "Here, once we are able to cook, these will be good." Taking a leather pouch from his belt, he handed it to the Chief.

The Chief opened the pouch and poured out tightly tied agave plant leaves and stalks. The soaked stalks could be cut and sucked for sweet sap. The fat leaves could be cooked once fires were allowed and the leaves would be chewed with a taste similar to sugarcane. Mothers and grandmothers grumbled for these would not take the place of fresh water. Children's lips were dry and cracking as they were handed the stalks. Infants wiggled and cried as they tried to nurse on sour milk from their mothers.

A cautious Shaman warned of using drums or of doing any form of ceremony. Scouts from the top of Dos Cabezas Mountains sent word that they were seeing smoke from the U.S. Army fires. If the U.S. Army traveled to the north, they would pass within visual miles of them. Now the people needed to descend into the shadowed dark pass of the multi-layered sandstone gorge within the mountain range. Juniper, mesquite and salt cedar bush barely survived as they were clinging off the steep sandstone cliffs of burnished red. Rain was needed and if the rain would come, the gorge would flow with fresh water down into the flatlands.

Shaman shook his head, reminding the people as they guardedly followed one another into the gorge not to make a noise for sound would echo, bouncing off the narrow canyon walls to the miles of flatland below. Horses' necks were rubbed to be sure they would not whinny. Turkeys and wild chickens were held tightly with beaks still tied in children's arms. Newborn infants were wrapped tightly in cradle boards to sleep. As lizards raced on lifted feet across the sand, this group of people silently and steadfastly became one with the landscape as they traversed.

Two days passed. People suffered miserably from lack of water. Water jars were slowly becoming empty as they were shared. Three scouts returned carrying clay jars filled with mud-water dug from the desert floor. It was brown slush with pebbles and warm earth. The women were not able to cleanse it by boiling. They used this dirty water only for washing bodies who were dangerously hot. The Rio Grande or Big River was at least a two day ride east. If one of the warriors or even four of the warriors could sneak past the U.S. Army, they would be able to bring back fresh water in the thicker water jars.

The Mescalero Apache scouts who were used by the U.S. Army and who knew how to track their own people were the major threat. Even when the wind blew hoof prints away, the Mescalero Apache scouts used their cultural skills to help the U.S. Army soldiers discover other Apache tribes for military slaughter. Attempting a stealth ride to the Rio Grande with the U.S. Army so close would be suicide for the scouts in this tribal camp. The natural earth water dug from the desert kept the people doused with wet mud and small children were able to put the dirty water in their mouths for a time and then spit it out. At least it was moisture of one form, regardless of dirt. Mother Earth helped her children survive with her own mixture of moisture.

Early in the morning, the Shaman spoke to the Chief, telling him it was time to gather the people and travel once again. He had a vision, pointing to a canyon at the north end of Turkey Mountain, far from the Caldera where the Mexican Army was waiting for them. The mountain had two major cisterns that possibly contained water. Being able to hide in the mountain's canyons, gorges and forested areas would be good. Possibly, the people would be safe and water would be found there. It was time to get the people to proceed promptly or the hot winds would destroy them. The Chief waved in his scouts, questioning them for news. Four of the scouts spoke of the U.S. Army traveling to the northeast across the flat caliche desert, appearing to return to their fort. The U.S. Army would avoid traveling through Turkey Mountain. This would allow these tribal people the freedom to pass along the western escarpment, which was the shortest distance to their destination. Anything glistening or shiny from the sun would alert their location.

Horses' eyes were covered with leather strips and noses were reined in with leather halters. Painted haunches and rumps illustrated the personal character of each rider were powdered with dirt. Apache youths with feather roaches tied in their long black hair, crept low between the people and the mountain. The roaches gave the appearance of birds' wings fluttering around the bush on the mountain. One by one, the adults and the elderly pushed the staggering children ahead of them, huddling close to the high mountain escarpment. Moccasined feet were lifted and placed flat to avoid raising dust. Young men carried teepee poles on their shoulders as they hovered close to the ground in order to not be seen. Dust and mud covered skin and hair as everyone stared straight ahead, keeping the line steady and flowing, following the Chief.

The Chief was aware of the U.S. Army's cavalry for their military line of trotting horses, wagons and cattle drifting parallel to them elevated a huge cloud of dust as they traveled miles away in the opposite direction. Soldiers' voices carried across the barren land to the escarpment of the Apache people. Military men whistled, laughed and called out to one another. The U.S. Army had no concern of being noticed as their caravan of wagons trailed behind fat cattle herded by a double line of dusty horsemen in thick brown uniforms. Staggering Mexican slaves tied with ropes to the back of the wagons struggled to stay upright. The U.S. Army had the might and with it came their government's right to take the land.

Suddenly, the tribal Apache chain stopped. Children at the front of the line had collapsed from exhaustion and dehydration. Mothers suckled their infants to keep them from screaming. Men scrunched down to race beside the quiet people, lifting the fallen young in their arms. Many of these youths carried their wild turkeys in their arms or slung in leather pouches over their shoulders. The turkeys were easy food to nourish this nomadic group. Slowly, people began flowing moderately forward. This passage was extremely dangerous in that the Apache people could now see the U.S. Army and just as easily the U.S. Army would be able to see them. Breathing the hot dry air, stifling coughs with watering eyes, the Apache trudged across the top of the mountain range. Not even a bird or a bush suffered to venture here in this heat.

An orange red sunset radiated the parched dirt of the mountain. By late dusk, the U.S. Army was no longer visible. Squatting women, children, the elderly and the men on the path leaned against the baked escarpment of Earth Mother to rest awaiting the cool of the night.

Pre-dawn brought the quiet movement of nomads to a halt. Newborns cried wanting sweet milk from their mothers' breasts, not the sour milk they found now. Wide eyed children studied their parents' faces as no words were spoken. Elders spit on their hands to mix saliva with dirt to cover their faces with mud as protection from the sun. Father Sky remained azure blue, no Cloud People shadowed the earth. A sultry breeze blew dismay to the weary. Grandmothers whispered silly songs to the children as they plodded forever forward. Grandfathers nudged children ahead of them with reassuring calloused hands. The horses had padded leather tied over their hooves to protect the frog of the hoof from the sharp rocks and the heat, also to camouflage their tracks. Time was of the essence now that their water was low.

Soon, the Apache came to a ceremonial altar on the mountain top. Their passage was blocked by a pile of lava rock with boulders four feet high and eight feet wide with four natural holes in the center of this ceremonial shrine. The edges of this sacrificial altar pointed east and west with small to large holes facing east toward the rising sun. Here in this sacred place, each person was to take a stone, grasping it in their palms to pray to all four of the sacred spiritual corners of Earth Mother- east, south, west and north. Once the prayer was completed, the person was to relinquish their stone into one of the holes. Thus, their requests would be answered by the Spirits for the stone holes allow the prayers to be known by Earth Mother.

Each person was expected to participate. This nomadic tribe had a high population, everyone was allowed to pray, abandon their stone and wait. Since they had arrived here in late afternoon, it was late into the night when the prayers were finally completed. Babies cried loudly, even when the mothers placed them on cool sand. Children were lying down, gasping. Old ones knelt side by side, holding one another's' hands for support and emotional strength. Gray braids were tied behind the nape of their necks, crusted with dried mud. The water jars wrapped in the leather skins carried on the backs of the horses had cracked or fallen and broken. The water jars the scouts were using now had silt in the bottom of them, no longer useable for fresh water if found.

As dusk follows day, the Apache found a deep canyon to settle camp. Squatting next to the Chief an old grandmother whispered, "These families will not survive much longer without fresh water." She pointed to the men hurrying to help their children, the grandmother nodded, "The women are restless. Your men come from other tribes to marry our women. Men must live within their women's tribe. Men are sturdy, trained to be tough in war and the hunt. Our women are courageous and able bodied when they are busy. Would you allow the women to gather sumac from the flatland to form more water jars?"

Chief frowned, "The U.S. Army is at least a day away from us by now. They will return if they see smoke on the horizon. If the women make water jars, they will need to quiet." The Chief smiled at the grandmother, "Perhaps, if the women are busy gathering and weaving, they will think of other things besides thirst. Yes, remember to tell them to stay low, as low as the sumac bush itself."

Young women were sent to retrieve the desert sumac leaves. Tracking wild quail and white-tailed deer imprints in the hot sand, they found the three to five foot tall bushy trees. In the spring, animals ate the sumac berries. Small girls plucked the fruit from the lower branches. The tart flavor of crushed fruit soaked in water was a children's delicacy. Mothers and grandmothers took the gathered sumac leaves and intertwining the flexible bending leaves to form the bases for water jars. Stringy yucca leaves were sewn as the sumac took the shape of wide jars, bowing out slowly then stiffly to make the mouth of each jar. Each unfinished shape stood on the hot lava rocks to dry, the flat brown color of each jar blending with the dirt.

Long-haired young men held sharp knives as they darted from pinion tree to pinion tree, cutting and bleeding the tree trunks, gathering sap. The women rolled the collected sap into stout balls to form a sticky resin glue. These round balls of resin were dropped into their leather shoulder pouches.

News from the returning scouts related this was the last moisture from the dug earth wells. The still air was hot and dry. Sentinels softly whistled their bird calls, no movement on the desert floor. The Apache were seriously suffering from lack of water. Women made modest mesquite brush fires away from the camp down in ravines as young girls fanned the smoke, deflecting it as it lifted. Children sucked on the mesquite pods after they were baked under the fires. Women took the sun dried water jars placing them onto the small flames. Pinion pitch heated in a ceramic pot was poured into the water jar, after which a large pebble was placed inside. Calloused brown hands rolled the water jar between the palms, with the pebble and hot pitch inside the jar. This sealed the woven openings of the intertwined sumac mixed with yucca leaves. The pebble commingled the sap, water proofing the interior of the jar. Slowly, the jar was coated fully with the sap.

Wrapping a piece of buckskin on a stick, each woman dipped the stick into the hot sap jar to seal air tight the outside of the water jar. Before the pitch dried, her calloused fingers smoothed the pitch on the outside to give it a smooth and finished feel. Some women rubbed red ochre on the outside, giving the water jar a rich red color.

Families in the camp smelled the rich nutty odor of the hot pinion pitch. They knew this was a good sign. Once the mesquite brush fires were out, it was time for the water calling ceremony. The new jars with sweet grass lids were brought into the camp area. Unfilled jars sat in the center of the temporary camp. Soft whispering chants started. No drums were used for being high on the mountain, the sound would travel far. Brave young boys crawled up the side of the mountain, carrying muddy earth water in the clay jars as offerings to the Sky Father. Their knees were scratched and bleeding, but their pride was strong for being so courageous.

In the dark shadows of the canyon camp, women knelt in a circle outside of the water jars. Hands lifted with palms open to the Sky Father, begging for fresh rainwater to give to their children and elders. The charcoal teal sky with not a cloud insight, listened to the women. Men felt helpless watching their families with cracked bleeding lips, dirty faces and desperate prayers. The Shaman shook his rattle wrapped in leather strapping, studying the sky. No clouds. No wind. No rain. Children and infants would die, water was desperately needed. Chanting continued quietly. The desert heat of summer was scalding. This was not good. No clouds appeared.

More Apache women were chosen to gather sumac, cut the sharp yucca leaves and gather the pinion pitch. More water jars were formed. Shaman called to the spirits to fill the water jars. The next morning, water jars remained empty. There were no clouds. In the cool of night, there were no clouds. Dust trails were seen on the desert below, but they were from traders or stragglers. Shaman decided the people would have to move again. The curse from the man who killed his brother-in-law had followed the people. It was time to travel.

Again, the camp was taken down and the few articles were tied onto the horses' backs. Mothers were physically drained, weak infants no longer cried. Healthier Apache scurried to remove any trace of their camp. Older boys were in charge of holding or helping the younger children. Older girls stood by the women, helping with the babies and new infants. One mother pulled her older son into the line as she grabbed his hand a stone fell from his open fingers. The stone was warm from being tightly clutched by the boy for days. His mother knelt beside him as he hurriedly retrieved the stone, "Boy, where did you get this stone? Why are you holding it tightly?"

The boy stared down at his dirty legs, "This is my ceremonial stone. I wanted to keep it, not drop it in the hole. It's round and smooth, I want to keep it with me."

The Shaman was called. Again, the boy was asked where he found the stone. This time the boy set his jaw and shook his head. Men scolded him for one should not defy the Shaman, especially in front of others. Shaman unfolded the boy's fingers to take hold of the stone. Quickly, the boy grabbed back the stone from the Shaman, to say, "This was my ceremonial stone. I liked it and didn't want to leave it at the altar. It's my stone. I picked it and now it is mine." His hand was tightly fisted around the stone.

His mother put out her hand, "Give me the stone, son. You haven't done anything wrong. Give me the stone."

The boy shook his head. His fingers grasped the stone firmly. His mother put her hand on his shoulder to calmly ask, "Son, give me this stone. It is good you found this stone. It may be magic. Give me your stone and we shall see what it can do for us."

Slowly, opening his hand, the boy dropped the stone into his mother's palm. Rapidly, Shaman lifted the stone to study it in the sunlight. There were waves in it as if it held water. Lifting one of the water jars from a horse's pack, the Shaman dropped the stone into the water jar. It fell in with a thud.

"No!" The boy grabbed the water jar from the shaman, "This is my stone! I am to keep it."

As he tilted the jar to retrieve his stone, water shot out of the newly formed jar to fly up into the air, pouring over his palm, down his legs, filling his *moccasins*. Frightened, the boy dropped the jar for water continued to spurt up and out straight into the air. Everyone around the boy was now soaked in cool, clear water. Women burst out laughing, clapping and dancing around this boy. Children ran to the fallen jar, letting the water cool their arms and legs. Quickly, people caught the water in the newly formed jars. The grandparents were led to the water, allowing to wash away the dirt and grime. Dirty black hair now glistened in the sunlight with the washing of this magic water. Babies were held high in parents' arms as the water healed their bodies and filled their mouths, washing the goop from their eyes and noses. Horses pawed at the mud with their hooves as the water flowed down the ravine of the canyon to the animals corralled below.

Kneeling on the ground, wide eyed and frantic, the exasperated boy madly searched for his stone. Flinging his long hair over his shoulder, digging in the mud with his strong fingers that were now raw and bloody, tears streamed down his face, mixing with the water as he searched for his stone. Then slowly the realization came to him, the stone had become the water in the jar. His sacred stone was gone. Kneeling on the ground, the boy smeared his face, neck and hair with the refreshing mud.

Water Flows Chiricahua and Lipan Apache Story Number 3

Shaman knelt beside the boy, "You and your stone have saved our people. Spirits gave you the wisdom to bring the water. You no longer need the stone. This stone came to you for a purpose. Another stone will come to you and your purpose will come with it. Stop searching. Help the people."

Standing, watching the people around him, the boy knew his destiny had been brought to him. He would find more stones. He would help his people in different ways, but now was the time to appreciate the magical water. All the newly formed jars were quickly filled. Headbands dripped, *breechcloths* were soaked, and women's blouses were saturated as the water continued to shoot straight into the air around the people. Whistles were heard as the scouts from the Rio Grande returned. They had been attacked by Mexican soldiers. Their gathered river water was lost. Dismounting from their sweating horses, scouts ran to the fountain of water. Filling their parched mouths with water, they listened and then knelt before the dripping wet boy who brought about this miracle. The horses were allowed to drink from the stream running down the side of the mountain as they were wiped down with soaked blankets. Everyone danced in the delicious water as jar after jar after jar after jar was filled to overflowing.

A grandmother knelt outside of this happy celebration to tearfully close her tired brown eyes as she lifted her head to the sky. "Thank you, Spirits, thank you for saving my people. Thank you, Child of the Water and Ussen Boss, for bringing us a young shaman. Thank you, for allowing my people to know you!"

Sun decided to go to bed early that night. His pink and orange blessings colored the sky while he unfolded his blanket of night to cover the earth. Evening Star sparkled a benediction on his nomadic people. Satiated Apache people slept peacefully. Clean babies suckled fresh milk from their mothers' breasts. Elderly couples nuzzled close together in the cool desert night air. The moon rose over the canyon walls to shine off the horses' wet manes. Filled jars of cool water with sweet grass braided lids were sealed with melted pine tree resin. Night insects scurried around the wet lava rocks. When the gushing water jar toppled quietly onto the muddy ground there was a quiet hush in middle night.

Only the four sentinels noticed the silence for the gurgling water flow had stopped. Nodding to the filled jars nestled in the desert sand by the cliff's edge, they smiled. The people had water. They would survive this journey for they had been baptized with Spirit blessings. Prayers had been answered. Spirits be blessed.

Notes:

The Apache people migrated south from Alaska, Western Canada and Pacific Northwest from 1100–1400 CE. At the time of European contact, the Chiricahua roamed approximately fifteen million acres through southwest New Mexico, southeast Arizona and northern Sonora and Chihuahua, Mexico. They were held as U.S. prisoners of war from 1886–1914 with a population of over two thousand. Today, they number around six hundred souls.

Lipan Apache are from the Southern Athabascan group who settled in the southern Great Plans of the United States. In 1750, the Lipan were driven from their home by the Comanche raiders and their allies. They settled in the territory from the Colorado River of Texas to the Rio Grande in New Mexico and Mexico. 1875–1876, the U.S. Army and the Mexican Military joined in a campaign to eliminate the Lipan from the Mexican state of Coahuila in Northern Mexico. Both of these Apache groups were put on the federal reservations. They were weavers of baskets, hunters, scouts and nomadic bandits. The first Apache tribes knew nothing of agriculture and to survive they raided farms, pueblo people and colonists as well as Mexican cattle ranchers. Their life was all about foraging, fighting and basic survival. This is their story of creative subsistence against great adversity.

My daughters' adopted grandfather Augustine Mirabol was a Lipan Apache whose father had married into the Chiricahua. He told this story over and over again to my daughters as they grew into the fine adult women they are today. Unfortunately, he is no longer with us, but with his Creator in the sky.

Glossary:

Breechcloths – A type of loincloth made of one strip of material, a narrow rectangle passed between the thighs, held up in back and in front by a belt or string. Flaps hang down in front and back. Worn by Native American Males.

Chiricahua – People related to Native American Apache, lived in southern New Mexico, Southeastern Arizona and Northern Mexico. Relocated to reservations.

Hende or Hen-de' – Apache for People or Men.

Moccasins – A soft leather heelless shoe worn by Native Americans.

Nde'indaai or Nednaa'I Chiricahua – Enemy People.

Nde, New or Nende – Apache for people or men.

No-na-ai-te Clan – Cloud Clan of Southwestern U.S. brings rain.

Shaman – A trained or chosen person who is an intermediary between the natural and spiritual worlds, uses magic and spiritual forces.

4
REINCARNATION BY WATER

The Saviour Sea God
ASIAN INDIAN

Twenty-five years ago, in the village of Palshet, there lived two brothers who were fishermen. Neelkanth Patil and Bala Krishna Patil. They were hardy fishermen who grew up with families who fished, learning from their father and uncles to fish and were excellent fishermen. This is their story.

These Palshet fishermen are easy to spot for they are known as the Kharvi fishermen, part of the Kharvi tribe.

These tough fishermen wear *lungi*, which is a rectangular piece of cloth a little bigger than a bath towel wrapped around the lower body like a sarong. Most of the fishermen have their own style in wearing *lungi* with bright checks or squares printed on the cloth as their signature colours. Low clouds, fog or storms allow these bright colours to be seen by other fishermen if they are close enough. *Lungi* could be made short in length for the men to bring the boats in and out of the fast-flowing water and without getting the *lungi* wet.

Large earrings, one or two inches in diameter fit into their pierced ears. They wear braided black threads around their necks with a rounded or square box for a pendant. Each of these pendant boxes is personal and can identify who the fisherman is if found at sea. Another black thread is tied around their bulging upper arm muscles, as if to show off how strong they are. Usually they wear no shirt for they do not sunburn, their skin is dark, almost black, tough and dry from being out in the salt seawater and hard wind. Strong calloused feet need no shoes, which would hinder them by sliding on the wooden boat floor, also, if they needed to swim.

Their uncombed scraggily hair, long and windblown, gives them the appearance of wild men who are unruly and untamed. Their lips and teeth are red from eating large quantities of betel leaves with ground limestone powder. This food is a natural stimulant, being healthy as well, for the betel leaves have citrus juice in them. These men are fearless when it comes to taking risks in bringing in large fish. The sea is their mother and their father. The sea nourishes them, nurtures them and takes care of them. The sea is everything in this world for them. He is their God. The Supreme Being. The Patil brothers were equally excellent fishermen, brave, courageous and daring.

Fishermen like the Patil brothers, marry and have families with the blessings from the sea. All the people pray to the sea, believing the sea will always take good care of them for they have ultimate respect for the sea. His ebbing tides take away the fishermen's pain and his full tides bring happiness to them.

Neelkanth Patil and Bala Krishna Patil were loyal husbands, good fishermen and wise to the sea. As with the other fishermen, they would paddle their way home, always pleased to see the two huge rock faces, they believed to be their gods. These rocks represent the Sea God. They were sent by the sea. The strong Patil brothers taught their children the power of the Sea God. He is the saviour for in one moment the sea would rise up with high winds, ready to devour fishermen who were foolish enough to be out in such danger. The oldest Patil brother flinging back his wild black hair, would tell his sons that he was sent by the sea, tested by the sea and saved by the sea.

2 The Saviour Sea God - Bordeo Borivas

These large rocks were scrubbed regularly out of respect for these were holy. After the sacred wash, wives applied *halad* and *kunku* to these rocks to offer their respect. On special days, the Patil brothers and their families would sacrifice a chicken at the base of these sacred rocks to keep the Sea God appeased.

1 The Saviour Sea God - Bordeo Borivas

The youngest Patil brother placed his youngest son's hand against the rock to say, "These tall rocks are sacred. Your mother comes here to pray for the return of the fishermen in her family. Feel the rock, feel how rugged it is and strong. These rocks bring us home to you, remember this."

Walking to a huge boulder, taller than he, the younger Patil brother continued to teach his children. "See how near this boulder is to the twin rocks? It is spherical and similarly reddish black. I can see this giant boulder way out at sea. While fishing, way out there in the ocean stretching to the horizon, this boulder shows me the way home, where you are. At times, this sea can be turbulent and angry, yet both the boulder and the sea watch one another constantly, as if each watches the other and me."

Leading his children to the middle of the beach, the youngest of the Patil brothers took his calloused finger pointing to the sea. His reddish black lips puckered as he stared at the sea as his long circular earrings dangled from his extended earlobes. Combing his fingers through his straggly wild hair, he knelt down to be at their level. He studied the sea, "We the fisher-people pray, 'O Sea God, *Bordeo, Borivas* God, we are your children. We pray to you. We serve you. Please protect us. Let our boats come back safely from the sea storms and typhoons. Let everything be fine.'"

His wide-eyed children noticed their father's serious tone as he continued, "Remember this prayer for it will bring home my boat, your uncles' boats and me back to safety. Remember." He reached down gripping the hand of the smallest child with his thick, strong black fingers as they trudged back to their hut.

The older Patil brother was busy teaching his sons, as well, telling them, "We fishermen of Palshet are tall, strong, loud, and at times argumentative. Be careful what you say for you might end with a fist in your nose." Rubbing his crooked nose, his point was made.

He continued, "We can get a rich haul of fish if we go deeper into the sea far from Palshet. Yes, that's why we deep-sea fishermen live there on the sand. We erect huts for our homes on the seashore and make small boats by cutting and logging the trees from the nearby forest. Our boats are sturdy, like us, cut and carved with part of our soul."

Kneeling down to be even with the younger children, he pointed to the sea, "If the catch is good, we buy new boats, otherwise we are stuck repairing the old ones and make do. Out there in the sea, the boats are tested by being hit hard with fierce waves. Our strong nets have to be thrown far and wide to catch as many fish as possible. At times our nets get stuck on floating logs or hooked on something deep in the sea and tear. There are expert weavers here who weave and mend the fishing nets."

Sitting back in the sand, he smiled, showing his pointed yellow-red stained teeth, "Your mother is an excellent weaver, may you be as clever as she is. All the work force in this village revolves around the ability of catching fish. These fish feed us, feed our relatives and when we sell them at market, we make good money to support our family."

Neelkanth Patil and Bala Krishna Patil with their loving wives and strong children survived well from the catch the sea provided. As with the other fishermen, the two brothers had to be knowledgeable regarding the beach surrounding the small fishing town.

The older Patil's wife kicked sand as she reached her family on the beach, "Are you teaching them about the sea?"

Smiling she knelt down beside her husband, "These sandy beaches hold the sacred rocks. They are filled with the saviour Sea Gods. Look, see how together they are shaped in an upright V. These rocks guard the fishermen who are out in storms, hurricanes or become lost in the night. Fishing along this coastline is dangerous and many times deadly."

Holding her red and brown *saree* tight against her midsection, she pointed to the irregular shoreline. She explained, "The Palshet seashore is vast, stretching over several miles. There are some sandy beaches like this one, but see there where most of the seaside is filled with sharp rocks small and large, tall and wide, sharp and flat? Manoeuvring around these rocky beaches is dangerous for the jagged and sharp-edged stones and huge spherical boulders are the same color as the shoreline, which is as you can see are all reddish black.

"Since the beginning of time, our Sea Gods' waves have crashed against the beaches day and night, endlessly, with all their might. This is the sound that rocks us to sleep at night." Laughing, she picked up a rock to throw into the sea. "This water pounds against the rock, the waves flatten spreading a painting of white frothy bubbles along the reddish black shoreline. This combination of color leaves a backdrop of white, red and black combined."

Pointing to the far beach, she continued, "Son, there are many more huge rocks hidden in the sea. There are those inexperienced fishermen and foolish young men with no knowledge who have crashed upon those huge rocks and perished. Boom!"

"Will that happen to *baba*? Will he crash against huge rocks and die?"

Their father smiled, "Let's hope not! I have been fishing for many years, long before you were born. I'm a tough and smart fisherman, the sea has taught me well. Besides, you enjoy the fish I bring home for dinner, right?"

Nodding in agreement, the children continued to stare out at the magic of the sea and the tall rocks that protected their families. The youngest son pointed to his father's dark calloused feet that were next to his, "Will my feet be as large as yours?"

His mother brushed the sand off of her son's foot, "Let's hope so. Your father's large craggy feet hold him in the boat even if it tips over, right?"

The older Patil brother shook his head, "Strong feet help to develop a strong mind. But now I want you to listen to the sea. Our life in Palshet has a rhythm all its own, like the songs we sing. When the sea is calm the village of Palshet is quiet and peaceful. The mood of the villages changes with the ever-changing nature of the sea."

His wife interrupted him, "Remember how when you were very small how you would complain about us bringing you down to the beach at dawn? Now, you are used to our prayers as we greet the sun when it rises from the sea and then at dusk when we bow as the sun sets. This is our way, our tradition. Someday you will teach your children to say their evening prayers to the silvery, white waves as they shine brightly on moonlit nights."

Their father stood, brushing the sand from his knees, "All of us villagers grew up witnessing the rhythmic dance of the tides while listening to the deep, sombre sounds of the sea when we slept in our huts on the beach. We are as one with the sea, the sand, the fish and the sky."

His wife lifted the smallest child into her arms, "Yes, now it is time for bed. Did you say your prayers to the sea?"

The Patil brothers and their fellow fishermen survived well off the sea and most of the fish they caught was kept, preserved for their own consumption by drying and salting them. Their life was tough, but the Palshet fisher-residents were content and lived happily under the aegis of the sea. Fish were sold in the markets, which were nearby or the bigger markets found along the shoreline further away.

In the year 1992, on the 23rd of May, the Kharvi fishermen went to pay their obeisance to *Bordeo* as per their tradition. They broke a coconut to *Borivas* as a sign of respect. The sea on that day was stormy. The Neelkanth and Bala Krishna Patil brothers knew they needed to get these fish to market before the storm worsened for if they did not, the fish would spoil. The money was needed and a storm had never stopped them before, why should it now?

Their wives came with them to *Borivas*. "Take care for the wind is hard. Even the waves are growing taller. Be careful," they warned. Not wanting to show disrespect to the sea, they added, "*Bordeo* shall take care of you. *Borivas* will bring you back safely, don't worry!"

Bowing to the sea, the wives' colourful *saree* dresses flapped in the hard wind. The women had their hair tightly wrapped in buns to keep it in place. The gold post earrings in their ears and on their noses glittered in the sunlight as heavy clouds moved in overhead. The Patil brothers, too, bowed to the sea and paid their obeisance. Three more fishermen were accompanying Neelkanth and Bala Krishna Patil. They, too, with their families were praying to the gods. Blustery winds filled the sails, rocking them back and forth, jostling against the anchors, trying to push the boats into the sea.

Everyone shouted, "*Jai Bordeo! Jai Bordeo! Jai Borivas! Jai Borivas!*" Anchors were lifted, boats were pushed away from the shoreline. Blistering winds channelled them quickly into the sea's turbulent waters. Their craft was well made to withstand even the roughest of waves. People on the shore could hear their men's voices singing out as they disappeared into the wind blowing them directly over the waves to their destination of Mangaon Dock in Mumbai. They made record time and the fish were quickly unloaded.

As the fishermen thought of returning, they found the wind was now blowing against them. The sun was hidden in the sky by thick dark clouds. Waves rose higher and higher, becoming stronger and stronger, making the crafts unmanageable and impossible to maintain direction or current. The fishermen knew they would have to hurry if they were to leave for a severe storm looked imminent. Three of the fishermen chose to remain in Mumbai. These fishermen were not in a hurry to return.

Neelkanth and Bala Krishna Patil decided to return home as they wanted to reach Palshet in time for dinner. They did not want their children and families to worry. They prayed to *Bordeo* and to *Borivas*, pleading to the gods to protect them and help to return home safely as they set sail in their boat. Both of them boarded their boat, holding a paddle with one hand, pushing with a pole in the other, they challenged the storm. Their boat was well equipped with strong sails, sturdy sides, bases and ropes. Each fisherman was muscular from years of hard work. Gusts of wind pelted them with seawater. Whirling round and round in their boat, they both lost direction.

25th May, 1992, this was the day when the sun did not shine. The hard-blowing wind kept the boat bouncing on the sea like corks. The sails were stretched to hold forceful winds, both taught to the point of tearing. The boat fought to stay upright as chaotic waves smashed into its sides. Soon, dark clouds blanketed the horizon, deadly thrashing winds whirled the boat about and crashing tall waves slammed down on top of it. A cutting rain suffered these two brothers who were flung about in their craft.

The fishermen were jolted as ferocious waters hit them hard. Dark clouds vibrated with crashing thunder. Hurricane winds accelerated ripping their sails, spraying stinging water into their faces, burning their eyes. The sea was incensed with rage. Turbulent waves crashed, slamming one against the other as if they were fighting. This was the onset of the destructive Fyan hurricane.

The tropical gale overpowered the sea. Its mountainous waves threatened to engulf everything in sight. Darkness descended on the sea surface, making visibility zero. The sails of the boat gave way to the combined forces of wind and rain, shredding them into small pieces. The sturdy boat was entirely at the mercy of the ravaging waves. Swaying wildly, moving directionless. These two men were twirled, drenched and swirled round and round, as the boat took on water.

Neelkanth and Bala Krishna Patil no longer saw the other, nor were they able to hear the other call out for direction. There was no horizon, no direction to follow. Exhaustion engulfed these strong, fearless brothers for they were no longer able to fight against the wind, the waves and the darkness. Their courage was no match for this typhoon. Surviving the storm appeared to be impossible. Humbly, they surrendered themselves to *Bordeo* and *Borivas*. They prayed to the gods. Their gods were their last and only hope now. Their solid boat had filled with seawater and the waves were determined to smash them into pieces. Thinking of their children, wives and families, they tied the cracked broken wooden slats to their bodies with rope and plunged into the sea. Perhaps, the Sea God would save them and *Bordeo* would protect their lives. Pieces of their boat disappeared only to be lifted to the surface, to be hit again with waves, being smashed over and over again.

The Patil brothers were thrown deep into the sea with no knowledge of where the other was or if still alive. Their bodies churned in the water, stinging salt water burned their eyes, noses and throats. Splintered wood smashed against their bodies as the undertow of the waves pulled them into the depths of the chaotic sea. Nature had gone berserk in the catastrophic wind. The rains were apocalyptic. The wrathful sky, it seemed, had developed a looming syphon furiously pouring flood water through it. Lightning strikes zigzagged, bouncing off the silver turbulent sea only to be applauded by a deafening explosion of thunder, causing the earth to tremble. Suddenly, in all of the chaos, the world lost all light to become pitch dark above and below the hurricane sea.

Fisher-residents of Palshet had always read the sea and its messages. The typhoon brought a new lesson to the fisher people of Palshet. Winds ripped through their village with pelting rain. Quickly, the swollen sea rose above the shoreline. Trees bent double to kiss the flinging sandy beach. Dark swirling clouds hovering on the horizon with poor visibility brought a feeling of dread. Where were the fishermen who had gone to Mumbai? Were they battling the storm at sea?

Serious waves tore at the rocky shoreline. Sandy beaches easily surrendered to the violent rising tidewater as waves smashed harboured crafts to shrapnel. Fishermen and their families were not ignorant of the sea and its ways. Generations had lived in harmony, dancing on its watery ways from season to season. Death was not a stranger, but this tempest was extreme and dangerous. These people were intricately bound to the sea for survival, but this was disaster. News had reached the families of Neelkanth and Bala Krishna Patil of their seafaring venture to return home. Worry and fear enveloped their families. Would these men survive? Would the boats made by strong men be able to survive this storm? Had they been blown out to sea to disappear forever? How would they return? Would they be hurt?

Neelkamal and Shantabai, the respective wives of the two men, stared out at the rampaging sea. They thought of their fine, strong men whose lives were possibly taken by this storm. How could their children grow wise without their fathers? What would become of them? Why did *Bordeo* do this? *Borivas* would not allow this to happen for they believed with all their being of His protecting the fishermen. Screaming out over the howling wind, "This cannot be, *Borivas*, you love and care for all of us and our husbands!"

The children wanted desperately to be with their mothers, but were told to stay put in the village with their grandparents. Neelkamal and Shantabai wrapped their *sarees* tightly around their bodies and their heads as they stood strong in the pouring rain to confront the rocks representing the watchful gods on the seashore. Tree branches snapped from thick tree trunks to be blown and roll dangerously out onto the beach. People scrambled to protect their homes, their children and their boats. Wind whipped across the land to kick up dirt and whistle under doorways and window cracks, tearing down loose walls to threaten life and lives.

Neelkamal and Shantabai only thought of their husbands out in the dark raging sea. As they neared their seashore sacred boulders, an extreme emotional pain flowed through them as they went into a hypnotic delirium. The wives beat their breasts and wailed uncontrollably. Neelkamal and Shantabai had believed their fine husbands to be invincible and now they realized how vulnerable they actually were. Some of the villagers desperately tried to pull Neelkamal and Shantabai away from the sacred boulders to get them into shelter, but these women would not be deterred. Most of Palshet was in a widespread panic. Everyone was fearful of loss.

Bending into the high wind, Neelkamal and Shantabai staggered their way to the rock called *Borivas*. Lying prone before Him, they banged their foreheads at His feet, reproaching Him for not guarding their husbands. Crying out above the storm, they questioned Him as to why He allowed this to happen. They pleaded with Him to protect their husbands. "O Sea God, our husbands took their boats out into the sea relying on you! How could you put them into such danger?"

As they wept, *Borivas* remained calm and erect as usual for He was the stoic boulder who watched over the fishermen. He studied the cresting mammoth waves. He observed the grieving women. He was aware of Neelkamal and Shantabai with their desperate pleas.

Having relayed their fears to *Borivas*, the wives were certain in their minds *Borivas* was aware of their distress. Neelkamal and Shantabai helped one another to stand as they pushed against the wind, returning to the large sacred rock called *Bordeo*. Again, they prayed to *Bordeo* with all their might for Him to bring their men home to them. *Bordeo* stood there calmly, assessing the stormy sea. As a holy rock all He was able to do was to evaluate the frothy, giant waves and witness their wild, menacing dance of destruction. The women threw themselves at the smaller rocks that represented god's feet.

They paid Him their obeisance and began interrogating Him, "We believe in you, how could this happen? How is it that our husbands are in such terrible danger? Oh, go! Go, yourself, save their lives. Bring them back! Keep them safe! Bring our husbands back, O *Bordeo*, bring our husbands back! We beg you!"

The storm continued to rage. Hours passed as the grieving women became exhausted. There were no more tears to shed. After screaming for so long, their throats were parched and dry. As night began to settle upon the land, the air cooled. The women's muscles became stiff and cramped lying on the wet sand at the base of the sacred boulders. Their *sarees* were soaked through, their hair filled with sand, eyes were swollen from staring out at the sea and their energy was drained. The pelting rain continued to fall ceaselessly. Roaring waves continued to deafen all other sounds.

Physically and mentally the wives were fatigued, yet they held fast to the hope of their husbands being well and soon home. They were only thinking about their husbands. Where were they? Were they all right? Were they even alive? These thoughts wrenched at their hearts. They still had faith in their sacred Sea God as they continued to desperately pray to Him again and again. He wouldn't deny them for He sees everything. He knows everything for He can do anything. He saves lives. He solves the problems. He will surely help. He can save and bring the husbands home. How can He let His children drown? He would not let His children die! He will save them and bring them home! The children will see their fathers again! *Bordeo* will set everything right!

Evening fell, as darkness grew the hurricane winds started to relent. The sea waves slowly calmed. The Kharavi fishermen and villagers of Palshet begged Neelkamal and Shantabai to eat or at least try to drink some fresh water. Their families pleaded with them to return home but the wives would not leave the seashore. People brought them warm blankets and tried to console them, telling them about the love the Sea Gods had for their husbands, perhaps the Sea Gods took them since they were the favorite fishermen.

Quietly, Neelkamal and Shantabai became confident of their husbands' wellbeing. Feeling numb and emotionally distraught, they didn't eat or touch the fresh water, but became resolutely stubborn. Blankets were put aside as they sternly whispered, "We will not leave *Bordeo*. He won't disappoint us! He won't let our belief in Him be proven wrong!"

Continuing with their silent prayers for the return of their men, they kept searching the sea's horizon for sight of their husbands. This continued for two days and two nights. Both Neelkamal and Shantabai were lying on the seashore before *Bordeo*, praying to Him with unshakable belief. They believed *Bordeo* would bring their husbands home. Refusing food or fresh water in the firm belief that their husbands were without as well, they stayed put, waiting. Patiently waiting.

On the third early dawn, as the warm rays of the sun spread over the sea and a soft breeze flowed, golden hued waves caressed the seashore tenderly. Suddenly, a shrill cry echoed out from a lookout at sea. A Palshet fisherman noticed something unusual floating on the water in a distance from the shoreline. Everyone hurried to the shore as boatmen pushed out to sea. Two substantial objects were floating toward shore. The volume of such was believed to be a good sign. Boatmen paddled back to shore as the sizable forms came closer to shore. Barefooted fishermen rushed forward, wading cautiously to retrieve two human bodies tied to wooden slats!

Neelkanth and Bala Krishna Patil had come home! They were barely conscious! Their bodies were ice cold, their feet were bleeding from fish bites and their eyes and lips were chaffed and crusty. Dragging their cold stiff bodies through the water, wild haired fishermen lifted them onto the sandy shore. Sharp knives cut the thick ropes that they had used to tie the wooden slats to their bodies. The Patil brothers' fingers were bent and stiff from grasping tightly to the rope around their chests. Both of the brothers tried to speak, but they were too weak to form words.

The villagers were all asking them questions at once. The exhausted brothers just shook their heads as if they did not understand. Being too weak to lift into a sitting position, the older fishermen helped them by patting their backs to expel the water from their lungs and abdomens. One of the helpful villagers ran to his home, returning with water, sugar and milk. They mixed the sugar into the water, slowly pouring into the mouths of these dehydrated brothers. Slowly, Neelkanth and Bala Krishna Patil became more aware, shaking uncontrollably as they remembered the horrors they endured in the sea.

Milk was poured gently through the brothers' lips. Carefully, they drank the protein, feeling stronger. Everyone was amazed these men survived for it was truly a miracle. Finally, a fisherman by the name of Mohan Patil ran to Neelkamal and Shantabai who were still praying before *Bordeo*. He called to them, "Get up! Get up! Your husbands have come back! Look there!"

The two women slowly turned their heads to see a group of people surrounding two men. They sprang to their feet with some unknown strength as their eyes filled with tears of joy. Reaching to the tall boulder rock containing the Sea God, they whispered, "*Bordeo*, you heard our plea. You and *Borivas* protected our husbands. You sent them back alive. You didn't disappoint us. You didn't let our faith prove us wrong. You have blessed our husbands and brought them home!"

After their grateful moments to the Sea God, they ran quickly to their husbands. "O dear husband, O dear husband! You have come back. *Bordeo* and *Borivas* brought you back safely. He saved your lives!" They spoke in unison as they knelt beside their recovering husbands.

The fishermen of the village were overwhelmed in seeing the joy on Neelkamal's and Shantabai's faces for it was these women's strong conviction and unshakable faith that had helped bring their husbands home. To this day, the villagers of Patil continue to join hands around these sacred Sea gods, showing them respect and obeisance. The sea listened to *Bordeo* and sent their fellow fishermen safely home through that deadly storm. Faith and strength brought Neelkanth and Bala Krishna Patil home to their families. This was truly a miracle.

Notes:

The Borivas god and the Bordeo save the fishermen from the storms at sea. Even today, people believe if one surrenders himself to the gods with complete faith they will be saved. Bordeo saves the life of such a devotee. Many women narrate how they have experienced this first hand. Even the fishermen who return from the sea relate their experiences. They believe in the power of these gods. Palshet Village is in Maharashtra state. Traveling about half-a-mile from the seashore near this village, there are two separate Sea Gods named Bordeo and Borivas. Palshet Village is a more than four miles or eight k.m. from the Guhagar Taluka in the district of Ratnagiri, India. Bordeo is a huge rock abutting the sea standing in front of a tree called Bori (Jujube or Indian Plum). The name Bordeo comes from the tree's name. The Borivas, on the other hand, is a set of two high rock faces near the seashore.

I visited Palshet in June 2017. During that time, I spoke with Mr. Balasaheb Labde and fisherman Mr. Mohan Patil and was introduced to Bordeo and Borivas. This story is considered part of the Palshet village's oral history. It was told to me by Balasaheb Labade, PhD. The legend is retold in my own words.

Labade PhD is a lecturer of Marathi at Shringartali in Guhagar Taluka in Ratnagiri district. He is a compiler and researcher of folk literature. A writer, poet and critic. He has received many awards at the State level.

Glossary:

Baba – Father.

Halad – Turmeric powder.

Jai Bordeo and Jai Borivas – 'Jai' in Marathi means 'victory.' In this case, this word is used as "hail to" so as to indicate praise or admiration.

Kunku or kumkuma – A red powder made from turmeric or any other local materials. Women put red colored kunku on their forehead. It looks like a red spot. It has a cultural significance. It represents prosperity. It is also widely used for worshiping the Hindu gods and goddesses. It is a sign of respect in social life.

Stone Boy Saves Uncles, Brule Sioux
NATIVE AMERICAN

Brule Sioux's Stone Boy story also has a version told by the Cheyenne.

There were events that occurred before history was recorded that belonged to the Seven Great Council Fires. The tribes were the Yankton and Yanktonai, Sihasapa or Blackfeet, Oheno'pa or Two Kettles, Itazipco or Without Bow, Minneconjou, Sitca'gu or Burnt Hip *Brule*, Santee, Unepapa, and the tribe of Oglala, Hale, Gallatin and Riggs. The Sitca'gu or *Sicangu* tribal people were living in a well-established *teepee* village on the flatlands of the Dakota.

During one summer of a bad drought, a prairie fire started near the drop-off at Flat Canyon's ravine. Fire raced across the prairie, engulfing dried grass in its wake. As the flames lapped up the flatland grasses, it raced straight toward the *teepee* village. Men, women, and children screamed in horror as the ten foot high flames flew straight at them. Horses pulled free from stakes and many that were hobbled at the edge of the village broke free to race away. Mothers grabbed their babies as they tried to out race flames. *Teepees* were burned within seconds for no one was spared within the camp. Fast runners carried smaller children in desperatation to outrun the deadly heat.

A father returning with his six children from a rabbit hunt noticed the flames ahead. He hurried them to a cliff. He rolled the children down the sloping sides of the canyon drop. At the base of the canyon was a deep spring of fresh water. Finally, he jumped. Both of his legs were broken, but using his elbows he dragged his body and his crying children into the water. Death pursued them, flames dropped down the canyon walls, eating grasses, plants and small varmints in its path. In the water of the spring, the strong father's arms shoved his children down under his main body, under his broken legs to keep them beneath the water. Not able to get his neck and head beneath the wet, he held his breath and prayed to Mani'tou for his children's lives. Water churned around him as it tempted to boil.

All became quiet. The raging fire roared away to the southeast. The father's burnt soulless body rolled over to allow his children to lift from the water. Leaping into the air was a small girl followed by her five brothers. They were all gasping for breath. This was the Dakota prairie fire of the 1770's.

The older brothers carried their little sister to their *teepee* village. All they found were scorched bodies, charred *teepee*s, blackened stone weapons and cracked ceramic pots. The smoking hot ground was all that was left of their home. The oldest brother of fourteen years took his siblings down a steep path to the spring. The girl was four years old. Oldest Brother waded into the spring to carry his father's body onto dry land. Setting him on a plateau of rocks, Oldest Brother began to chant. The other siblings knelt down around their father's charred body to join in the chant. Middle Brother held his little sister in his lap, helping her to clap the rhythm. They believed Mani'tou had saved them for a purpose. None of them knew what the purpose was to be, but they believed, for they were alone. No one else from their village had survived.

Leaving their father's body on the rock plateau, the children returned to the charred village. The brothers found the remains of their family *teepee* along with their father's stone-ball club, hatchet ax, lance spear and knives. All were burnt, but the brothers repaired the metal pieces as best they could and sharpened the blackened stones for use. Most of the clay water jars were cracked, but a few were only blackened from the heat. The chert stones used in removing fur from skins and some black cooking pots were gathered by the six survivors. The children spent the night away from the village for the toxic odors of burnt flesh made them ill. In the morning, the children moved to the east with what little they had scavenged.

Years passed and sister became a young woman with her older five men brothers of the Burnt Thigh, or *Sicangu* Tribe. They now lived in a tall, round hut on the flatland. Sister built the permanent hut from mud and prairie grass. Small stones placed in a thick mud plaster covered the pole roof of leafy branches, twigs and more mud mixed with prairie grass made for thicker protection. Traditionally, she could have made a temporary *teepee*, but growing near them in this place were wild corn plants for grinding into cornmeal and other natural vegetation. Her brothers learned how to press and heat the green corn sprouts and stalks to make a ceremonial beer. Nearby, berries and fruit trees grew at the edge of an oasis of trees. Sister had planted wild turnips, potatoes and wild herbs in the shade of the dusty brown foothills to the north. The plateau had regular herds of migrating buffalo for her brothers to hunt. Life was good here in this little hut for the six of them. Their mother had died giving birth to her and their father had died during the prairie fire, but these six had been well trained as small children to hunt, gather, and cure food.

Now, as it happened this one particular fall brought hard constant winds. The drone of the piercing hot air was endless for day and night it battered everything in its path. The southwest side of the mud hut was hit the hardest, drying the mud wall and breaking it down. Branches and leaves on the roof were ripped off, leaving the permanent hut open to the sky. It was decided a move was necessary if they were going to have a dwelling that would survive the harsh winds and cold winter snows. Sister gathered the cooking items, bedrolls, feathers and blankets, to follow her youngest older brother down into the shelter of a canyon. Her five brothers had stretched worked buffalo hides around deeply placed poles packed in dirt. This solid *teepee* was large, tall and had a firm foundation. It would not fold in the harsh wind. The smoke hole at the top, where the poles met, was tied with buffalo leather. Now, they were shielded from the winter weather.

Twenty yards down into the base of the canyon walls was a narrow stream. This was convenient for Sister to gather water for cooking and cleaning. A large boulder had rolled down the mountainside and had landed directly in the water's pathway making a small pool for fish. It was here Sister placed her water jars to fill and her oldest brother set his fishing net.

One morning, Sister awakened to stare at the buffalo hide wall next to her sleeping pallet of thick furs. Brother Four was moving around, rolling his bed pallet to place against the inside of the *teepee*. She heard him go outside and start the cooking fire. This was his habit. Brother Two and Three were still sleeping. Her oldest brother was already by the stream with his fishing net, catching their breakfast. He liked to brag about being the fisherman who provided the first meal of the day. Listening carefully, as she pulled her buckskin dress over her head, she could hear her Brother Five chipping away making arrowheads for the day's hunt.

Outside, sitting next to the cooking fire, Brother Four was wrapping his long hair in leather straps. The men parted their hair down the middle, having two long hair wraps, one over each shoulder. He already had his headband firmly around his head, down low on his forehead to his eyebrows. This kept their hair from getting caught in trees or flying about in the wind, scaring away the game. Sister combed her long hair with her fingers, quickly making two braids wrapped with beaded leather bands.

Her ankle high moccasins were shoved over her feet, tied with leather straps. Beaded leggings were wrapped around over her moccasins onto her legs to the upper calf and tied with leather strips to be tight. As she stood to poke the cooking fire, her oldest brother climbed the slope to them, carrying a net filled with cleaned trout. Laughing and greeting them, he carefully placed the large trout on a flat stone beside the cooking fire. This was a good morning, a morning to remember.

After the trout had been eaten and the fish bones left to bleach in the sun, the five brothers set off to hunt their main staple for winter, the buffalo. This was their way. Five brothers would hunt and sister would gather berries still available and sweet grasses with some herbs found down by the stream. Together they had food to survive well. Sister kept the cooking fire going all day. As the sun began to set, she studied the flat horizon for her brothers. This one particular evening, only four brothers returned to their sister. Their oldest brother had somehow separated from the others while hunting. Sitting outside, around the cooking fire they watched for their oldest brother to return home. They waited all night.

In the morning, there were no fish for first meal. The oldest brother never returned. The four brothers set out to search for him. They took their spears, bows and arrows, and plenty of cleaned and dried deer bladders filled with water. Sister stayed close to the *teepee* all day. At dusk, she walked out onto the flatland. Loudly moving toward her were three brothers. They were arguing, shoving and yelling at each other.

Youngest Brother stood in front of her, "We were all together, running after a lone buffalo. Sandy foothills with diverging canyons went everywhere. We decided to divide to scare the buffalo out into the clearing. When we reached the other side, there were only three of us!"

Second Youngest Brother interrupted him, "This was your idea! We had planned to stay together."

Younger Brother continued, "We searched, backtracking our steps. We were side by side. We only found dirt! There was no sound, he didn't call out or shoot his arrow for us to find him. Nothing, he disappeared!"

The Third Brother shook his head as he handed his sister two killed and skinned opossum. Quietly, he went inside the tent.

As the sun set, there were only three brothers with Sister at the cooking fire. Brothers Four and Five were now gone. Second Youngest Brother took his sharp knife and cut off the tip of his little finger. As blood spurted, he drew a blood-red small circle on the outside of the *teepee*'s buffalo hide. Then he added larger circles around it. Each outer circle was larger and larger until the last circle had an opening skyward. Careful to not drip blood on the circular symbols, he drew two blood red rainbow shapes. "Now we know they are alive, but unable to return." The three brothers were exhausted and slept. Sister stayed awake outside the *teepee*, listening for the death call of the owl. It was quiet. The lost brothers did not return.

The next morning, three brothers decided to search for their older brothers. The hunt had separated them, now they were not going for meat, but for locating their lost brothers. Three brothers promised their sister to return as five. Sister filled her cooking pot in the stream's flowing water. Putting her hand on the large boulder that detoured the water around it, she sang loud and long for her five brothers to return. Sister let her tears silently fall into the stream. "Please, please, bring my brothers home. Please, Spirits, hear my prayers."

A loud splash, startled her from her deep meditation. Scurrying away from her was a black-footed ferret with a small fish in its mouth. Large jay birds squawked around her, hunting for their evening meals of grubs and worms. A single squirrel stood tall as a sentinel at the top of a glorious pine tree, grasping the last rays of the setting sun. Off in the distance a coyote howled and yipped searching for its pack. Cottontail rabbits scurried under canyon trees as Sister hurriedly returned to the *teepee*. Prairie dogs hunkered down into burrows as the night breezes blew dirt close to the earth's surface.

Evening darkness brought two brothers to sit in front of the cooking fire. Youngest Brother shook his head as he jerked his headband off, "We traveled all over the flatlands. We returned to your old broken hut, no one had been there. We searched for tracks by the round of trees. Only pheasant, grouse and chipmunks there and they told us nothing. Raccoons are plentiful beyond the tall ash tree at the end of the canyon, but there was no sign of our brothers."

Second Youngest Brother stared into the fire, "We didn't have the energy to hunt. Even the big rabbits stared at us amazed as we ignored them. There were no vultures anywhere to indicate death. We found mule deer tracks, antelope, elk and big horn sheep, but nothing to show us where our brothers were being kept. Nothing to be found. Somehow we were separated."

Youngest Brother put his hand on his sister's arm, "We were careful! We called out to one another, we were close to each other. We were searching for tracks, following one another and calling out or whistling to one another, but somehow, somehow, our brothers are leaving us."

Second Youngest Brother jerked his chin upward as he spoke

softly, "We were all together! Were they picked by the Spirits? Where could our brothers have gone?" He pulled his wrapped hair free, combing it with his long fingers. "The three of us knew how dangerous it is to separate. We knew, we knew! Yet, now we keep disappearing."

Standing, he went to the outside of the *teepee*. There he cut his third finger to draw the sign of a large circle, open at the top. Turning to them, he said, "We are not giving up on them. Their souls are still with us!" Bending low, he went into the *teepee* to bandage his finger and unroll his bedroll.

Younger brother stared out at the night sky, "No owl calls of death. No vultures circling death. There are no signs of them or where they might have gone. Somehow, they are still alive. We will find them and bring them home." Leaving her alone beside the cooking fire, he went into the *teepee*.

Another new morning, with the two brothers who departed again without their usual fish breakfast. They had been quiet for there was the fear of not returning. Sister had begged them to stay with her, to wait for the others to return. Her brothers insisted on searching, they would not sit and do nothing. They would find their brothers! She had held onto their arms, begging them to stay, to be safe with her. The brothers held their heads high, "It is our honor to find them. They may need help in finding freedom."

Sadly, Sister watched as they ran across the dry powdered earth of the flatland edged with high sandstone formations. Buffalo herds grazed in the east. Rubbing charcoal on her face and arms, Sister slowly walked down to the stream. Sitting on the large boulder, she lifted her palms skyward, "Great Spirits, watch over my brothers. Mani'tou, these are your children. Wherever they are, keep them alive, and let them be found. Your power is great, mine is small, yet I pray to You for help. Mani'tou, let my brothers live. Let them be found."

Sorrowful tears fell onto the black lava basalt boulder, staining them then disappearing into the pores of the rock as the sun heated the air. Sitting with her feet under her with her loose hair billowing around her shoulders in the wind, Sister prayed until the orange sunset. Her large brown eyes searched the fading blue sky for an answer. Eagles flew high above her, hunting for snakes and prairie dog pups. At dusk, there was a loud plop in the stream below her. Two small black eyes peered at her. The black footed ferret swam below her in the stream. His short black tail-tip wiggled as he moved. Sister smiled for this was a sign that she was not alone. Watching the ferret hunt for grubs and small fish, she suddenly remembered to return home.

Waiting at the *teepee*, Sister searched the horizon as purple-blue darkness descended. Sister built up the fire as a beacon for her brothers. Standing, searching the flatland's horizon with expectation, she waited. Calling out to her was one lone voice. Youngest Brother returned, haggard, his face drawn with grief. He collapsed, exhausted next to her, "No good. It's no good. We were shoulder to shoulder, not touching, but that close. My brother disappeared as we ran through the gorge by the ash tree forest. One blink, he was with me and in the next, I turned and he was gone. Not even a moccasin mark in the sand."

Youngest Brother shook his head as Sister offered him some stew meat. "You know that tomorrow I shall go searching for all four of my brothers? This night may be my last night here with you. Sister, if I do not return, you must be strong for all of us. Stay here, we will find you. Believe this, we will return and we shall all be together again. You must be strong and believe. Stay here, this place is our sanctuary and the only home we know is with you. If you believe in us, we shall believe in you and return." He stuck his hand into the hot ash, turning he drew five men and one woman on the side of the *teepee* in charr. "Mani'tou will help us return."

Sister stayed awake all night. The crackling cooking fire became her friend in waiting for her brothers' return. Her youngest brother slept alone in the *teepee*. Night birds flitted around them in the dark. Dawn came with sadness. Light pink clouds dotted the horizon as desert swallows flew above the *teepee*. Prairie dogs raced from burrow to burrow as the predatory birds watched winging on high.

Youngest Brother stood with his spear, "I am going to find our brothers. Don't worry. Don't be afraid. You're strong, we will return." He touched her shoulder and was gone. Sister had no need to get fresh water, the water jars were still filled, but she decided to walk to the stream. Climbing to be on top of the large black boulder, she realized she could no longer cry. Her body ached with the loss, for she knew, she knew her youngest brother would not return.

Palms lifted skyward as she knelt on the large boulder. Her large brown eyes studied the clear blue sky. Clouds were on the horizon billowing toward her, then dissipating into nothing. Sister felt the heat of the large boulder under her. Her heart pounded in her chest as she silently called to all the Sky Spirits to help her brothers. As the boulder cooled with the days waning, she jumped at the sound of something dropping into the stream.

Leaning forward, she saw her friend the black-footed ferret. He was lying on his back with his stubby black feet straight up in the air. Twisting, he flipped onto his stomach, doing this over and over, he churned the water to bring smaller fish to the surface. His sharp teeth caught a fish, gobbled it and then he flipped with another fish in his mouth. His small black eyes peered up at her.

Staring down at him, she said, "You survive well in the water. Is the water the answer?"

He did not answer as he dipped into the flowing stream, disappearing between the rocks.

Hurrying back to the *teepee,* Sister waited at the built up cooking fire until the dark of night. She watched the cooking fire flames burn down to cold grey coals. No one came back to her that night. In the morning, as birds hunted overhead, she rolled her hair tightly behind her head to wrap a leather thong around it. Pulling on her tall moccasins, beaded leggings and plain buckskin dress, she ran down to the stream. Climbing the large boulder, she patted it as if it were an old friend. "We need to do something. I am a woman, I'm strong. I refuse to accept that my brothers are gone. Earth Mother, this boulder is from your being. Sky Father the heat of the day is from your being. I am calling to you for guidance."

Sister knelt on the boulder as it heated with the day, cooled in the evening and was silent in the night. Her ferret friend arrived at sunset. Ignoring him, she remained on the boulder, praying. The golden pink fingers of dawn reached across the sky, as Sister opened her eyes. Tears fell upon the boulder. Wiping her cheeks, she jumped down from the boulder and returned to the *teepee* with a handful of dried firewood. The *teepee* flap had not been opened. No one had returned. Going through her brothers' bedrolls, she searched for a reason as to why they would leave. The extra bows and quivers hung side by side on the inside poles. Shaking her head, she knew the brothers would not leave her alone on purpose. This was a testing, perhaps.

Anger filled her solitude. Lifting the water jars, she let her feet take her down to the flowing stream. Screaming in anger and frustration, she shattered the water jars. Her fists pounded against the boulder, "Where are my brothers? Where are they! Where are my brothers?" She fell, kneeling in the cool water. Her knees jabbed into the broken water jar chards at the bottom of the stream. There in the flowing stream, she noticed a glistening opaque stone. When she was small she had heard stories of the old ones who chose to end their spirit life by swallowing a stone only to choke and quickly go to the other side.

Her wet fingers grabbed the glistening stone from under the boulder. Rubbing it between her palms, she felt how warm it was and how round. Wishing to join her brothers, she shoved the large stone into the back of her mouth, praying, "Spirits of Life, let me be with my brothers. Please, let me be with them."

The stone jammed between the top of her tongue and her throat, frantically gagging, she fell backwards. Gulping for air as her fingers tried to retrieve the stone, it painfully worked its way down her throat and into her body. "Ow! Ow!" Coughing, Sister crawled out of the water. The black-footed ferret's teeth held onto her big toe as she dragged him with her ashore. "Off, off, get off me! Go!" She smacked him with her hand. Quickly, the ferret let go, sliding into the water to disappear.

She bent over, rubbing her pained midsection. Crying out, her voice echoed down the canyon walls, "What have you done, Spirits? Take me! Take me!" Kneeling on the grass beside the boulder, she fell onto her side to accept her fate. Sister slept there all night. The warm morning sun, woke her. Standing, she felt strange, but she was alive. Weeping as she rubbed her midsection, she returned to the empty *teepee*. There she fixed herself a small meal, but after eating it, she threw up the food. Her abdomen was swollen as if she had eaten a feast. Unrolling her bed palette, she slept for four days. At the end of those four days, she awoke refreshed. Her body was large, her legs swollen, but her spirits were light.

Going down to the stream, she waded in the cool water. Her big toe healed in the flowing water. Cupping her hand, she drank to quench a desperate thirst as she watched the birds come nearby. Deer and grouse cautiously watched her from a close distance as she sang. Turning to the rustling tall trees beside the stream, she said, "I am not alone. The Spirits have you to be here to be with me. Spirits, I believe in you!"

She spent the remaining day standing in the stream, cooling her swollen ankles. Soon, her abdomen felt sharp pains at different intervals. The stabbing hurt traveled up and down her back. Hurriedly, she returned to the *teepee,* only to collapse outside the doorway. Crawling inside to her bed palette, she cried out, "Finally, the end comes. Now, I will be with my brothers!"

The brilliant sunshine awakened her. There beside her on the bed pallet was an infant boy. Her pallet was wet with blood and moisture. Pain was fresh between her legs. Hugging the infant to her bare breast, he suckled quietly. The infant boy was beautiful. He didn't cry. His sparkling brown eyes made her laugh. Knowing she had not been with a man, she named this baby boy Stone Boy. Spirits would keep an eye on this little one.

Sister watched him constantly. When they went to gather berries, he stayed beside her. When they went down to the stream, she had him sit on the boulder to watch the black footed ferret. Eventually, the ferret was brave enough to allow Stone Boy to pet him. Sister filled her water jars with water, saying, "Stone Boy, this boulder in the stream is your father. He will teach you of laughter, net fishing and of pain."

Patting the boulder, she grimaced, "Yes, he will teach you of pain. When you feel you cannot hurt anymore, he will save you and bring you joy." Taking her little boy's hand, she had him pat the boulder, "This boulder will be your friend, remember and pray to him always." Stone Boy jumped off the boulder to stand in the stream, watching the ferret roll, catching small fish in his mouth.

Stone Boy grew quickly. Being born in the early spring, he was walking by early midsummer. The late summer monsoons found him talking and racing around the *teepee*, playing with his uncles' bows and tomahawks. Leaves in the forest were turning red, golden and rusty brown as Stone Boy was now a young man. This strong young man wished to use his uncles' bows and arrows to hunt and explore. As he helped his mother carry firewood in the falling snow, Stone Boy asked about his uncles and their abilities. Alone at night, Sister quietly cried and cried, desperate to keep Stone Boy closeby her.

As winter's cold nights grew longer, her son studied his mother's sad face in the firelight. Finally, he asked, "Mother, what is it that you would desire more than anything anyone could give you? What would bring you joy?"

His smile warmed her heart. Shushing him, she whispered, "What I would desire is not possible."

Stone Boy poked at the fire with a long stick, "Yes, but if what you desire were possible? What would you desire?"

Shaking her head, she frowned, "In my heart, I wish your uncles were here to train you in the hunt, to show you how to weave and net fish. I think of how honored they would be to know you for you would bring warmth to their hearts." Wiping a tear from her cheek, she added, "But they are not here. There is no point in discussing a desire lost and never to return. Let us sleep. It's late."

One early spring morning, after they had eaten, Stone Boy took his mother's hand, "Mother, today I shall go and find my five uncles. Don't worry, I shall find them." Patting her hand, he smiled, "I need uncles to teach me how to live as a man. Therefore, I shall go and get them."

Sister screamed as she tightly gripped his hand, "No! No! You mustn't leave me! Your uncles went in search of one another and they never came back. No! You must stay with me. I am your mother!" Grabbing his arms with all of her strength, she stared into his charcoal brown eyes, whispering, "No. Please. Stay!"

Leaning to her, he held her shoulders, "I'll not ever leave you. I shall return with my five uncles. I'm your son. I will return to you. Stay by the *teepee* until we return." He lifted her hands from his arms as he turned from her.

Sister collapsed, gasping for air as she tearfully called to him, "Please! Please, stay with ME! Spirits, bring my son back to me!" Lifting on all fours, she lifted her head to watch as her son trotted off to the north. He was now a man with one of his uncle's bows and a quiver filled with arrows. Gasping with pain, she whispered, "No. No. No. Please, please, Spirits bring him to me. Spirits, do not let him go."

Sister ran to the stream. Tearfully, she crawled onto the boulder. Yelling at the Sky Spirits, she raised her tight fists, "You! You, spirits! You, bring him home to me! You watch over him and you keep him safe!"

Shaking uncontrollably, she screamed until her throat was dry. Misery enveloped her, cold anger shook her bones, "No, No, no, no...do not take my son from me, no."

Stone Boy felt secure for he had his uncle's bow. He had made his own arrows and had learned from practice how to stretch a bow if this one snapped. Traveling at a good steady run through the morning, he felt free. Flatland led him to the forest. Fat, tall trees reached skyward. New spring growth was forming. Winter's dried leaves of orange, red, gold and dark brown crunched under his moccasins. Small animals hopped, ran and hid from him as he aimed his arrow to hunt for his dinner.

During the day, he stopped to eat berries for a noon snack. Birds squawked as he reached into their nests for eggs. Muddy slippery snakes slithered into the undergrowth. Sun peered down through the open branches of trees as he continued. Each night, he asked the Spirits for a dreamquest as his mother had taught him, but none came.

Late in the afternoon, on the fourth day, he noticed a man-made structure in a state of decomposition. This was part *teepee* and part mud hut. *Teepee* poles were askew, buffalo skins were rotted and ripped, and stacked dried mud had sloppily replaced both. Rocking back and forth in the sun, sitting outside of this sad building sat Old Woman. This woman was as ancient and decrepit as the fallen mud structure behind her.

Seeing Stone Boy staring at her, Old Woman called out, "Come. Come inside. Eat dinner with me for I am lonely. Come, I have good food."

Stone Boy felt sorry for Old Woman. His mother had taught him to be polite to older persons, if he ever came in contact with such. He was uneasy about her invitation, but he was hungry. Inside, her home there were spears, arrows and bows, cracked lances and bloodied leather strips. Behind the cook fire, he noticed six tall bundles leaning against the far wall. They were upright, wrapped in dried, cracking buffalo leather robes. He studied them, wanting to ask about the bundles, yet, being afraid of her answer, he was quiet.

Old Woman was bent sniffling and snorting over the stew pot. She had loose skin, wrinkled and discolored. Dropping chunks of meat into a hanging cooking pot, she stirred the mixture. Sticking one long yellow fingernail into the boiling pot, she stabbed a piece of meat to taste. Her stringy, dingy hair fell into the pot as the disgusting smelly mixture boiled. Curly long whiskers randomly stuck out from her chaffed chin. She cackled when her eyes met his. Clicking her black cracked teeth together, she spooned the brown foaming stew into a discolored wooden bowl. Gnarled calloused hands handed him the stew bowl.

Stone Boy attempted to eat this rancid smelling mixture if only to be polite, although purposely most of it landed in his lap. The flavor was awful, making it difficult to swallow. Choking on the meat, he spit it into his hand and then dropped it down his beaded leather shirt front.

Greedily gobbling down the stew, she smirked at him. Her black teeth glistened in the firelight, "You must stay the night. Tradition requires that you stay with me until dawn." She unrolled an old buffalo robe for him similar to the buffalo robed bundles leaning against the far wall. This made him suspicious. Lying quietly upon it, he stayed awake for he sensed danger.

When Old Woman noticed he was awake, she cackled, "Would you walk on my back? I'm old with terrible back pain. You are light. If you walk on my back, this will release some of the pain."

Stone Boy cautiously stood on her back as she lay in front of the fire. At the edge of one of his feet, he felt something sharp sticking up from her buckskin robe covering. "Ah, this could be what killed my uncles. This could be a spear or poison on a knife." Having thought this, he began jumping up and down on the center of Old Woman's back, carefully avoiding the sharp object. He jumped higher and higher, longer and longer, harder and harder until he heard her spine snap. Kneeling, beside her head, he listened for her breathing. She appeared dead.

Carefully, he pushed aside her thick buckskin robe covering to find a sharp spear coated in black resin. He tossed this small spear into the corner. Wanting to be sure she would not come back to life, he dragged her outside. Stone Boy dug a deep hole, gathered kindling, and built a huge fire that lit up the night sky.

Lifting her frail body in his strong arms, Stone Boy threw her lifeless body into the hot fire. At first her buffalo robe burned. Flames sputtered and spit as her dry skin burned to ash, billowing away in the night breeze. Sitting beside the fire, he chanted for her soul to be saved by Mani'tou. Once the fire was completely out, he scattered the ash onto the flatland, leaving it to disappear with the wind in the darkness.

Stone Boy ducked into the decrepit mud house. Shoving the bows, arrows and broken lances and spears out of his way, he went to the long bundles leaning against the wall. He patted them. Something soft was contained within them. Hugging the first one, he lifted it with all his might to carry it outside. Cutting the tied leather thongs with his hunting knife, it gently unrolled to reveal a man's body not much older than himself. He returned inside to bring out another long bundle to cut the leather straps, leaving it to unroll by itself. Another man's body was inside. Going in and out of the mud hut, he carried each of the bundles outside to cut the leather straps. A man's body of about his height and weight was found within each bundle. The last bundle contained a man's body missing an arm and some muscle from one of his lower legs.

Returning inside, Stone Boy found a wooden board with a piece of solid meat chopped by the cooking pot. Studying it closely, he realized this was human flesh. Old Woman was eating human stew. Turning away from the cooking fire, he carefully picked up the hunting weapons on the floor to take them outside. As he walked out of the hut, he mumbled, "Evil, lived here."

Once outside, he gathered more firewood to build a great bonfire. The firelight showed all six of the men to be stiff, dry as jerky with their eyes and their mouths sewn shut. Stone Boy knelt before each man to cut the thread around their eyes and mouths. Kneeling by the fire, he asked the Spirits as to how he could bring these men back to life.

Far away to the south, Sister suddenly sat upright on the huge boulder by the stream. Night stars had shown down on her as she had been sleeping. A soft wind blew her hair around her face. There was heat radiating from the boulder underneath her. Closing her eyes tightly, a vision came showing her of her son sitting around a fire with her brothers and a stranger who was wounded. Opening her palms on her knees to the night sky, she began to sing to the Spirits, "Give Stone Boy wisdom. Stone Boy is strong and wise, he is our son. Bring wisdom to him, let him find his path!" She sang over and over again with joy in her heart as the boulder became warmer and warmer.

Stone Boy lifted his head to the night sky, calling, "Spirits, bring a vision to help these men live. Spirits, bring a vision to help these men have life." Standing without thinking, Stone Boy moved to the side of the mud hut. His eyes were closed, his breathing slow as he picked up six round stones covered in gray-brown moss. The moss stones were carefully placed at the feet of each man. Then he lifted each of their feet and crossed them at their ankles. Stone Boy knelt in the one open space before the bonfire. His eyes were still closed as he heard a voice saying, "Stone Boy, you are one of us. You come from us. You are us, listen and pay attention."

Following the voice's instructions, Stone Boy found a flowing stream nearby. From this stream he cut pliable willow. He returned to the fire to weave a round dome lodge frame of interlaced wet willow branches. He covered this framework with the buffalo robes. Inside the willow frame lodge, he built a small fire in the center. Setting six flat rocks against the flames of the outdoor fire, he left them to heat. Then, carefully, he carried each of the six dried-up men to lie side by side around the small fire within the closed lodge. Using a forked deer antler, Stone Boy lifted the red hot rocks, one at a time from the outside large fire to be placed by the inside smaller fire. Finally from the outside, he closed the lodge by lowering a flap of buffalo hide.

Cautiously, he re-entered Old Woman's mud hut to gather the filled water bladders. Carrying as many as possible, he returned inside the willow lodge to hang them from a willow branch. Pulling the buffalo hide closed, the willow lodge filled with hot smoke. Staying inside, Stone Boy took each of the water bags to place one by one of the burning hot rocks lying inside the small fire pit. He had six water bags at his side. No air was able to escape. Taking a water bag, he dribbled the water over each of the men, starting at their head and working down to their feet. Praying, he thanked the water, saying, "You brought me here, you brought them here, and now with this water bring them back to life."

Four times, he poured water onto the heated rocks near the fire, four times he waited until he could hardly breathe and then he opened the flap to let in fresh air. At the start of this ritual, he saw only white mist in the dark. When he poured water a second time, he sensed a stirring. When he poured water the third time, he began to sing, "Fill this presence with life! Fill this presence with life! Spirits, fill this presence with life!" When he poured water the fourth time, those who had once been dead, sang with him.

Seven men's voices filled the willow lodge. A chorus cried out, "Fill this presence with life! Fill this presence with life!"

In the thick steam, one man after another sat upright. Fingers moved, toes wriggled, eyes blinked as the breath of life entered into each form. Stone Boy's eyes teared in the mist. Living men were there, gasping for air. Stone Boy shouted out, "They have come back to life!"

Realizing the men were standing in a circle around his pit fire, Stone Boy reached behind him to lift the buffalo leather flap. Smoke poured out of the willow lodge into the night sky. Moonlight and the light from the fire showed five men spiritually brought to life and a sixth man lying on the ground groaning in pain.

Stone Boy softly said, "You must be my uncles for you are as good looking as I am." The uncles laughed, pleased to be alive again. The wounded man was older and his wounds had started to bleed. Stone Boy hurried to his side, "How can we help this one? What can be done to complete his arm and repair his leg?"

The tallest of the men cleared his throat to say, "We need to go out into the air. Let's take him outside and let the Spirits see his wounds."

Crying out in joy for being alive, yet in pain, the man was placed on the ground by the outdoor bonfire. Stone Boy knelt, lifting his palms upward to the night sky, "Spirits, thanks to you this man is alive. He is hurt and in pain, can you heal his wounds?" As Stone Boy prayed the five men around him were busy.

They found a long willow branch, heated it to flame. Blowing on the red hot branch, they cauterized the leg wounded of the hurt man. He bellowed out in severe pain, collapsing into unconsciousness. Again, the burning hot branch was used on the open flesh wound where his arm had been ripped from his shoulder. This time the man did not move, he slept. Stone Boy prayed, his eyes closed, not listening. Two of the men brought gray-green moss from the forest trees, firmly packing it around the cauterized wounds. The men knelt beside Stone Boy to pray with him.

Clouds floated over the tall forest trees, coasting to the flatland. Sun rose illuminating the sky with soft pastel pinks mixed with golden rays. Trees rustled with the morning breeze. Birds flew eager for worms and seeds. From the edge of the forest, deer, mountain goats, bighorn sheep, elk, turkeys, woodchucks, squirrels, rabbits, mink, muskrats and beavers peered at the kneeling men. Slowly, the men rose to stretch. They spoke among themselves of Old Woman who had tricked them. Each told of how she asked them to jump on her sore back and afterward they remembered nothing. Nudging Oldest Brother's arm, Youngest Brother asked, "Do you think he's our relative?"

Stone Boy lifted his hands to the sky, saying, "Water saved you. *Mani-tou* thanks tunka-rock-Tunka-Stone Boy, Tunkashila, Grandfather Spirit thanks the rocks covered in water. This little lodge, the rocks and the water and the fire, these are now sacred. We will use these from now on as I have done here for purification, for life, for health. This has been given to us as a way we may live. Water is life. Earth is our Mother. Now we shall live."

Sun reached high in the sky, as the wounded man awoke. Rolling away from his wounded side, he spoke, "The Evil One took me from my family. My sons and I were hunting buffalo when she stepped out from behind a sandstone formation to ask for help. When I followed her here, she took my mind, then she took my body." Shaking his head, he continued, "Where are my people now? They probably have forgotten me."

Three of the brothers had been busy whittling him a long wooden crutch. Stone Boy sat with the men, telling of his life with his mother, their sister. Oldest Brother, went down to the forest's stream to catch fish. The two other brothers came back with berries and a squirrel. Oldest Brother nodded to Stone Boy as he laughed, "I am the fisherman of this family. Breakfast is my doing, without me, you'll not have food in the morning."

Sharing stories over the cooked food and fresh berries, the brothers decided the wounded man should return with them to their family *teepee* in the canyon. As the evening brought warmer air and his wounds healed well enough to move, the men destroyed Old Woman's hut

Brule Sioux Stone Boy Saves Uncles Story Number 4

and the willow lodge. They were eager to return to their sister, each of the brothers took turns carrying the wounded man on their backs or over their shoulders with another carrying the crutch. Joy shrieked from their mouths when in the distance they first saw the *teepee*. As they neared, they noticed the outdoor cooking fire was cold dry ash.

"No!" Cried Youngest Brothers as he fell to his knees before the *teepee*. "Where's our sister?"

Stone Boy hurried down the path to the stream. His uncles followed as they called out to her. There next to the boulder was Sister's unconscious body. The right side of her body was on the sand and her left side was in the cold water of the stream. Stone Boy lifted his mother into his strong arms, putting her face close to his cheek, he whispered, "She lives, she's cold. She's alive."

Carefully, her body was carried to their *teepee*. Brothers built up the cook fire to warm flat stones around it. Once the flat stones were warm, they cautiously took them into the *teepee*, placing them under Sister's buffalo wrap. Shivering, she awoke to find her five brothers, her son and a stranger sitting around her, singing. Shivering, she listened to their stories while more heated flat stones were brought to warm her and fresh water was forced on her to drink.

Since time began, water, fire, rocks and stones have saved our people. The large boulder next to the stream remains there, even today. *Sweat lodges* are made today to heal the sick, bringing life to those almost dead and hope to those in need. Water from the sky falls to the earth. Earth water flows to feed the body. *Sweat lodges* bring the water from the stream to heat the body, releasing body water to bring life. Spirit songs are heard. Such is the way. Stone Boy went on to do great things for our people with his magical ways. His ways are not forgotten as the ways of water are with us today.

Notes:

The word 'brule' is French for 'burnt.' They call themselves Sicangu or Burnt Thighs. There are two branches of Brule Sioux, the Upper Brule and the Lower Brule both of which live on the Rosebud Indian Reservation in southwestern South Dakota and on the west bank of the Missouri River. They were divided in the late 1700s to be united by Chief Iron Nation in a treaty he signed in 1868 to establish the Great Sioux Reservation in South Dakota. This story includes the traditions, customs and the belief systems of the Sioux people. Jodi Whitesides explained this story to me at a truck stop near Gallup, New Mexico in 1998.

Glossary:

Brule – Adapted French word, means burnt.

Manitou or Mani-tou – Native American Ablonquian word for supernatural being or Great Spirit who controls nature.

Nadowessi – Little Snakes.

Sicangu – Burnt Thigh People.

Sweat Lodge – Hut or dome shaped lodge of natural material used for ritual cleansing or purification as a steam bath.

Teepee – A housing structure in the shape of a conical tent, made of skins wrapped around poles with an opening in the upper center for a smoke hole. Easy to transport, move and carry. Set teepees can last for many years if the poles are set deep in the ground to be well anchored.

5

EVIL THREATENING MEDIUMS

Well and the New Bride
ASIAN INDIAN

There is a village Wadanage in Maharashtra, India, famous for its high aquifer. The fields have an elaborate irrigation system, allowing farmers to grow fertile fields of green. There are wells on every farm. Some wells are wide. Some are deep. There are step wells others are waterwheel wells. Here in Wadanage the hot summers do not dry out the wells. Some of the popular sayings are, 'Be water rich like Wadanage' or 'Go and drown at Wadanage.' There is the belief Wadanage is a blessed village with a Water Goddess who provides water for each well. Others speak of ghosts who live in the wells. Wadanage wells are known for their legends and stories.

A hundred years ago, there was an exciting wedding celebration of Suman and Asaram. This elaborate affair was planned to take place in a village near Wadanage. Every village and farm were filled with excitement and joy. Everyone was busy sewing new clothes, fixing celebratory food and cleaning the roads. Men worked hard together as the women were busy cooking, sewing and sharing ideas for decorations. Everyone was in a hurry. Finally, women called the men to put up the decorations on the *Mandv*, an arbor made of wrapped red cotton draped around bamboo pillars. Red cotton wraps lifted high were then placed along the border of the roof.

The *Mandv* was divided in two parts. One side for men and other side for women. Hundreds of invitations were sent out to all the people in the area. Everyone came to enjoy the ceremony in the *mandv*. Men wore white *dhotars*, colorful shirts and *phetas*—the typical Maharashtrian turban placed firmly on their heads. The women dressed in their elegant *sarees* of different colors. Each woman wore their best bangle bracelets, gold necklaces and post gold earrings. Eyes outlined in black kohl gave each woman a youthful glow. Petty gossiping, smiling, and laughing made the women the center of the scene. Taking in the festive mood and melodious words of the laughing women, the men relaxed not realizing they were happy as well. Their children were dressed in newly sewn beautiful clothes, also.

The rich sound of a musical instrument similar to the oboe, called a *sanai* or *shehnai*, livened the mood with the drum or the *chaughda* or *nagara*. The traditional Indian music played by professional musicians had the children dancing to the rhythm. As the men smoked their tobacco, they sat on carpets to share ideas on planting seeds, harvesting techniques and family life. Standing in anxious anticipation, the women asked one another about designs and prices of *sarees*, inquiring about ornaments and bragged about their children. This huge population gathered for the union of these two families in this marriage of the two people. The pomp and splendor marked this occasion as a relationship to last forever.

The beautiful bride arrived. Suman was elegantly tall; her glossy dark skin was painted with turmeric-paste on her hands and feet. The red spot *kunku* was placed perfectly on her forehead. Her deep set brown eyes were highlighted with black kohl, her hair was pulled back in a tight bun wrapped in a wreath of aromatic flowers. The softness of her traditional green *saree* and green blouse swayed with her movement as the green and golden bangles jingled on her wrist while her necklace and golden nose ring of pearls glimmered in the sunlight. Glowing in her joy, she walked proudly to the decorated *mandv* arbor.

The proud groom arrived at the gate of the *mandav*. Asaram's forehead was decorated with san*dal* paste, turmeric and vermillion. Handsome Asaram was tall in stature and distinguished in his traditional attire. The radiance of his dark skin was contrasted by his white *dhotar*, a long silk shirt. How grand his red coat was with his red designed *pheta* or Maharashtrian turban wrapped around his dark hair. A golden ring glistened on his ring finger.

The guests were eagerly awaiting for the new bride and bridegroom. The maternal uncle walked Suman into the Mandav where she stood upon the *paat*, a twelve-inch-wide wooden bench. Staring down at her feet, she awaited the ceremony to begin. Then the maternal uncle walked out to the bridegroom Asaram. The two men moved to the *paat*, where Asaram and Suman stood face to face. The Brahman priest started the rituals by chanting the *manglashtka*. When the chanting stopped, they each took a garland and carefully put it around the other's neck. Then a long yellow thread was placed around the wrist of the groom Asaram only to be wrapped in union around the wrist of the bride Suman.

The feast for all was made of steamed rice, spicy *dal*, and *sweet bundi* made from Gram Flour, Ghee and Sugar. Every guest was given a leaf plate filled with this delicious food. After all the food was gone, each person stopped and gave their blessing to the bride and groom and then they returned to their homes. Close relatives and friends stayed late to celebrate with the bride and groom.

Following the traditional custom, after the wedding the new bride Suman had to leave her *maher* or her parents' home for the period of a lifetime to go to *sasar* or her husband's home and live permanently there. Of course, leaving the *maher* and her beloved parents and all other family members was very sorrowful for her. Tears were in her eyes as she said good-bye to her relatives who were crying as well. It is assumed that marriage is the second birth for an Indian bride.

Going to *sasar* allows the bride to enter into a new life, being married with a new home. Yet, she bears the grief of leaving behind the people and life she has loved and known since birth. During the time period of Suman's marriage, it was traditional for her younger sister or *karawali* to help her adjust in her new *sasar* or husband's home for the first few days. This helped with the extreme separation and emotional stigma of living with new people in a new environment.

The new bride Suman, her sister Malti, bridegroom Asaram, his parents, all family members, relatives, and invited guests sat on bull drawn carts, loaded with their luggage to travel to their village Wadanage. Fifteen bull drawn carts traveled in a line. They enjoyed the journey for their village Wadanage was not far from bride Suman's village, which they reached safely that night.

Early the next morning, there was *Satyanarayan puja* or the worship of Lord Vishnu in their home. Thanks to Lord Vishnu, the wedding had gone well without any problems. After *puja,* they enjoyed a delicious breakfast. Then Asaram's father made a declaration, "Please listen for it is our family tradition that every new bride and groom must go to each of the village temples and pray to the village deities. Then their marriage will be blessed by each of the village deities."

Asaram's father gave them a detailed account, "Tomorrow morning after your bath, you must first visit the *Bhairoba* temple. He is the village deity and our local guardian deity for he is the incarnation of Lord Shiva. Traditionally, then you visit the *Vitthal-Rukhmai* temple for they are the incarnations of Lord Krishna and his wife Rukmini. After prayer there, it is important to visit the *Goddess Laxmi* temple as she is the wife of Lord Vishnu. In each temple pray for a happy and healthy married life, healthy children, good prosperity, and peace of mind. Remember, every time the deities bless us, they show us a good life path. When their blessings are with us, we can overcome every difficulty and calamity. So, keep this in mind both of you should visit these temples to worship and pray. We will have lunch ready for you when you return."

Asaram heard his father's instructions. Early the next morning, Suman, *karawali* Malti and his two sisters left their home in a bull drawn cart driven by a cart-man from Wadanage. First, they reached the *Bhairoba* temple. The newlyweds worshipped the village deity *Bhairoba* by putting their palms together in front of Him and shutting their eyes. They broke open a coconut and offered it out of respect for this fruit is sacred. Special food, brought from home, was placed in front of the *Bhairoba* as they prayed for his blessings and a happy married life.

Secondly, they visited the Vitthal-Rukmai temple. It was not far from *Bhairoba* temple. Suman noticed how the beautifully carved *Vitthal-Rukmai* idols were of black stones. The idols had their hands on their waists. Again, the newlyweds offered the special food brought from home and prayed for blessings. There they noticed a worshipper sitting in front of *Vitthal-Rukmai* idols. He was an old man with his eyes closed and a saintly expression upon his face. He was playing a *veena* or a stringed musical instrument even though he was in a trance. The constant rhythm of his instrument matched his chanting of the Lord Vitthal. The new bride and the bridegroom bowed reverently to him, although he was not aware of their presence.

The temple of the *Goddess Lakshmi* was thirty-five minutes away by bull drawn cart. When they arrived it was almost noon. The bullcart was put under the shadow of a tall tree. The path to the temple was a distance from where they dismounted the bullcart. As they walked, they felt the heat from the sun. The path twisted and turned with no shade overhead. It was hot, very hot. They met some men pushing their carts, some stray dogs and every now and then another worshipper.

Finally, reaching the temple, they went inside. As tradition prescribed, they were to offer a red *saree* to the *Goddess Laxmi* along with the special food from home. They had to make this offering through the priestess. They waited a few minutes for the priestess, but she did not appear. Another person went to search for her.

When the priestess arrived, she asked, "Why are you here so late? I was planning to go to my farm. We close the temple at noon and open at four in the afternoon. It is not wise for a new bride who still has the turmeric paste on her body and still wearing her new green *saree* and green bangles to go outside of her husband's home in the noonday sun."

The priestess shook her head at Suman, "High noon with hot sun is a bad time for a new bride. Evil forces are attracted to the high sun and a new bride is easily affected for you are emotionally vulnerable. After your prayers, please, go directly home. Don't go anywhere else."

Taking the red *saree* and the special food, she added, "Give me offerings, I will give them to our *Goddess Laxmi*, but then go safely home."

Suman and her sister Malti placed their offerings in the hands of the priestess who then placed the red *saree* on the idol of the goddess with a fold of the *saree* flowing over the goddess' head. The red *saree* was beautiful on the idol. Finally, the food was placed in front of the goddess as Suman and Asaram put their palms together, shut their eyes and paid obeisance to her. After that they asked for the priestess' blessing.

As the priestess was closing the temple, she again warned Suman of the importance of her going directly home without stopping. As they departed the temple, Asaram assured the priestess that they would go directly home. Then all of them left the temple of *Laxmi*.

Words of woman priestess resonated with Asaram as he hurried everyone onto the path back to the bullcart. Also, he was worried for his family was waiting for them to share lunch. Walking the path, Asaram was in the lead, trying to get the rest of them to move along for it would be the middle of the afternoon before they reached home.

Suman was in a good mood for they had prayed at each temple and all had gone well. She was excited to experience this new area. Noticing the different shades of the green fields, rich with shimmering crops in the sunlight with the clear blue sky overhead for there were many different colors all around them. The bright yellow sun, the light green of the crops in the field, dark green leafed trees, shades of gray in the shadows with the black bark on the tree trunks. The farmhouses were of different colors, mixed with the colorful laundry drying on the clotheslines.

As the path turned, there was a large well. Excited and enthusiastic Suman asked her sister Malti to go with her to look down the well. Asaram was way ahead of them, certainly he wouldn't notice if they both went quickly and hurried to catch up with him. Suman and her sister leaned over to see how deep the well was, only to find the water close to the surface.

Suman was thrilled for she was hot and thirsty. The greenish-blue water in the well had overflowed and in the pond around it were frogs, guppies and birds.

"How lovely, look! Isn't this beautiful? Feel how cool and refreshing the water is!" Jumping back, Suman pointed, "Oh, no, look! A large green snake is slithering toward us!"

Asaram turned to find them by the well. He ran to her, "Suman,

Well and the New Bride

no! We need to go, it's late! Remember what the priestess said? We need to hurry home. Come, please, we need to go!" Suman followed him frowning, behind her was her sister.

Walking behind Asaram, Suman felt the heat. She started to perspire and feel weak. The temperature was easily about one hundred-and four-degrees Fahrenheit. Heat radiated from the dirt path. The birds were napping in their nests for this was the hottest time of the day. Staggering along, Suman noticed the dogs sleeping in the shade of the trees. Her face felt as if it was burning, her feet felt swollen and tired. She noticed her sister's face was red as was Asaram's sisters'. As she walked, Suman squinted her eyes for the trees were changing shape, the ground was moving around her. She knew something was wrong for there was a long black shadow following her. The green colors of the crops lifted up to zigzag around her head. Green bangles flew at her as golden ankle bracelets danced in front of her eyes.

Trying to call out to Asaram, her body lifted off the ground and then a voice was calling to her. Hands grabbed her ankles and jerked her down to the ground. A hot wind was blowing on her, lifting her, soaring up up up. Closing her eyes, Suman could feel her body spinning round

123~

and round and being unable to balance, she fell unconscious on the hard ground, foaming at the mouth.

Asaram watched in terror. His sister-in-law Malti ran to Suman. Kneeling beside his new bride, Asaram gently spoke to her, trying to get her to regain consciousness. His sisters dismounted the bullock cart, hurrying with the bullcart driver to the fallen woman. Lifting Suman onto his lap, he rocked her in his arms. "Suman! Suman! Please, Suman!"

Malti frantically looked around her for a container. She asked the bull-cart driver, "Do you have anything to hold water? We need to get her some water!"

He ran to the cart, returning with a round brass bowl. Malti ran to the well to fill it with fresh water. Hurrying back to Asaram, she handed it to him. He washed Suman's face with the water and moistened her lips. She remained limp in his lap, her eyes closed, barely breathing.

Carefully, he carried her to the bullcart, "We need to take her home. It is hot here and she needs to rest in the shade where it's cooler." Malti placed her *saree* over her sister to give her shade as they lifted her into the bull-cart. Asaram stared straight ahead as the cart moved slowly home. His sisters were quiet. No one knew what to do or why this had happened. Malti sat beside Asaram watching Suman.

As they neared Asaram's home, Suman opened her eyes for a few seconds. She stared at Asaram then her eyes closed. He felt her forehead, which was hot, her face flushed. Asaram's parents were waiting for them since the time for lunch had long passed and they had become worried.

When the bullcart came pulled in front of the house, the parents rushed to the cart. His father called out, "What has happened? What's wrong?"

Asaram carefully departed the cart, still holding his bride, he said, "Something terrible has happened to Suman. She had a fit and fell to the ground unconscious. She's hot, feverish and weak. What should we do?"

His mother calmly led them into the house, "Put her down here. Now, son, tell me exactly what happened, be precise."

Malti and Asaram explained how they had arrived late at the last temple and the warning they had received from the priestess. Malti told of Suman's interest in the well and wanting to see the frogs and birds near it. "There was a large green snake that slithered toward us. It scared us and we ran away from it. After we were back on the path, Suman became disoriented, she called out in fear then she fell on the ground and started foaming at the mouth. Her body was shaking for a short time and then she became quiet, still, asleep. We couldn't wake her!"

Asaram's mother and father spoke quietly together and then asked one of his sisters to go for the *vaidya*, the Ayurveda doctor. Silently, the sister returned with the doctor. He knelt beside Suman, studying her pulse and he noticed her body temperature by touching her forehead and examining her pulse. Reaching into his medical bag, he handed Asaram's mother some powdered medicine, "This will help her. Mix this powder in water, lift her head and slowly give her teaspoons of this. She will sleep, but when she awakens, she should be back to herself."

Asaram helped his mother gently pour teaspoon after teaspoon into his bride's mouth as she slept, she swallowed. Asaram stayed by Suman's side as she slept for several days. He was anxious for her to awaken, and at night he sat by her side crying quietly. His mother stayed by him during the day, saying, "Asaram, my son, don't worry, everything will be all right soon. She has had the medicine, it will work when she wakes."

In the afternoon, his father paced in the doorway, saying, "This is not good, but we have to face the situation. The doctor is very intelligent and he is an experienced *vaidya*. He has checked her. Given her medicine. We think it might be a heatstroke for it was very hot the day you went to the temple. It feels as if the sun is intent on burning the earth."

Asaram did not hear their calming words. All he could do was remember the beautiful wedding and his happy bride. He couldn't believe how his life had radically changed in only a few hours. Yesterday Suman's face was glowing, she glowed in her flowing green *saree*, her bright eyes filled with joy and the life they had planned together. Now she was here, lying quiet, unconscious.

Standing, Asaram grew restless. Turning to his father who stood in the doorway, he asked, "How did this happen? What did we do wrong? How could we be happy one moment and then in the next have our lives destroyed by something we couldn't see?"

Walking to the window, he stared beyond the yard to the fields of crops, "We worshipped *Satyanarayan* and prayed to Lord Vishnu at our home. We offered the special meals to *Bhairoba*. He is our village protector. Our protector. We offered the red *saree* to *Goddess Laxmi*. What wrong did we do? What was our mistake? Now, what can be done?"

Someone behind him cleared his throat. Turning quickly, Asaram found an elderly man sitting beside Suman. He wore a Maharashtrian turban on his head. The cataract laden eyes stared with white pupils at the sleeping woman. His face was grim, his lips covered by his long white moustache. He nodded to Asaram to come and sit beside him.

Clearing his throat, he spoke slowly, "My son, you are correct.

You are not to worry about the gods. They are pleased with your prayers, your gifts and your obeisance. They have accepted your loyalty. You are blessed, both of you, for the gods are guarding your bride. If you had not visited the temples and prayed with your gifts, she would be much worse, much, much worse."

Bowing slowly to Suman's sleeping body, he added, "Your new bride will be all right soon." Turning to Asaram, he continued further, "I have answered your questions. Now listen, you were told by the priestess to go directly home, yet your new bride walked out into the bright sunlight and away from the path to visit a well. Wells hold evil spirits, certainly you know this for you live here, in the land of wells."

Waving his hand toward the window, he said, "There is evil in each well when the noon sun is high in the sky. This is the time evil spirits and monstrous powerful curses reach out of the well to the vulnerable. Your new bride still had turmeric paste designs on her hands and feet. She wore her green wedding *saree* and her jingling green bangles. Both of you were tired from the long wedding and she was emotionally drained from this experience as well as moving away from her family to a new life. She was an open vessel for evil to enter."

The elder stroked his mustache from his lips, "More than forty years ago, performing here in our village was a traditional form of Marathi folk theatre where only men were allowed to attend. Every show was full of exciting, energetic entertainment. The singers and dancers performed the *tamasha*. Villagers from far and wide came rushing every day to see this magnificent show."

Clearing his throat, he went on, "There was a female dancer who was the main attraction of the *tamasha*. The men were especially interested in this dancer for she was a temptress. Her flirtatious manner, bright blue eyes and delicate hands moved with her rhythmic dancing steps, jingling with her ankle bracelets."

The elderly man's voice grew quiet, "Then she disappeared. A week later, her body was found floating on top of the well near the temple of the *Goddess Laxmi*."

Shaking his head, his voice whispered, "No one knew what had happened. There were some who believed she was murdered. Others thought she had committed suicide. Both of these were ruled out for she had no wounds on her body. The other dancers knew she was not a happy person and her work left her exhausted, spent and tired. Perhaps it was suicide, which is terribly sad. The spirit of this unsatisfied dancer may still be in the well." Putting his hands together, he nodded to Asaram, "Perhaps hearing the melodious sound of ankle bracelets while your bride was passing the well in the noon sun, this may be what happened." Shaking his head, he said, "So, it happened." All of Asaram's family was sitting around this elderly man as he had spoken.

Asaram's mother was sitting behind her son, turning to one of her daughters, she said, "Go, and call the exorcist. She lives at the edge of the village. I know her, she lives south of our village. Go, my daughter, I will give you the address."

The elderly man carefully stood, holding his back as he moved to the doorway, "This is good. The exorcist may be the one to help your bride, Asaram." A younger man helped the elder out of the room.

The magic was felt in the room prior to the arrival of the woman. Quickly, people stood as she entered the room. Her cloudy eyes studied the room as she entered. She gave Asaram a bucktoothed smile, pushing back her gray hair from her high forehead. The red spot on her forehead was larger than most. Her red *saree* was wrinkled and torn in places. Noticing the body, she went directly to Suman sleeping form.

Shoving Asaram back, she spouted, "Move, out of my way!" Bending over Suman, she felt her forehead. "She's burning with fever!"

Moving her calloused hands to Suman's eyes, she lifted her eyelids, "Hum!"

Then she slowly waved her hands over Suman's body, stopping at her chest. The old woman closed her eyes, humming. "Ah, the woman is possessed by the spirit. Was she near the large well?"

Swallowing hard, Asaram answered, "Yes, it was the day after our wedding. We went to the temple of *Laxmi*. My bride visited the well there. She wanted to see the water."

Clicking her tongue, the old woman shook her head, "She needs to be treated. I know the spirit. It is the spirit of the dancing woman."

Asaram's father asked, "Tell us, what to do? We are ready to do anything! Our daughter-in-law should be saved."

The exorcist woman stared at Suman. Turning she studied the faces of the others in the room. Everyone was afraid and worried. They were waiting for her direction.

Pointing to Asaram's mother, she gave her orders, "Hear me carefully, you need to cut a lemon. Stuff it with vermillion and turmeric, secondly, you will need some curd and rice. Third, have a blouse piece of any color and a whole coconut with husk."

Walking to the mother, she continued, "You will need to take a bath, be very clean and rested. Take this material with you to the well early in the morning as dawn is breaking. Then with obeisance and closing your eyes offer the material to woman spirit who lives in the well."

Putting her palms together, the exorcist woman, smiled, "This will work. After the offering you may get results. Slowly, your new bride may recover. But it will take a minimum of three days. Now do not disturb her. Let her sleep calmly." The old woman exorcist bowed to Asaram's mother as she walked out of the house. Everyone quietly left the room, leaving Suman to sleep with Asaram by her side.

The mother did exactly as she was ordered to do by the exorcist. The next morning, the mother reached the huge well before the sun rose. Kneeling beside the well, she offered the gifts as she prayed, "I beg you spirit, please do not trouble our new bride Suman. Bless her." Bowing away from the well, she returned to the bullcart and home.

Malti was waiting for the mother with a bowl of water by the front door. As Asaram's mother-in-law came to her, she stopped to let Malti wash her feet. "The water feels good. The gifts were given to the well and I prayed for Suman."

As she dried the mother-in-law's feet, Malti smiled, "This is good. Now maybe Suman will awaken and be as she was before this happened!"

Slowly, over the next few days Suman awoke. When she asked for food, they knew she was going to recover. On the fourth day, she recognized everyone as Asaram helped her to stand and walk to another room. Asaram and Suman then enjoyed a happy life for many years.

Notes:

This myth is about a *hadal*, otherwise known as a female goblin who is fourth from the top in the hierarchy of ghosts.

Deep wells and the blackish-blue water often evoke fear in one's mind whether it be at night or in daylight. In that situation, if someone who is not mentally strong goes near such a well, he or she is bound to come under the spell of an unknown terror. Such a person may allow themselves to become 'possessed'. Such an experience can be really terrifying and gives rise to various tales. The legend here is one such tale depicting a very scary experience.

In East Indian society, there is a belief that a new bride is vulnerable, easily possessed by a spirit. This superstition has been held in the last centuries and is still prevalent even today, especially in rural areas. If a new bride, having the wet turmeric paste applied on her body and wearing a green *saree* and green bangles, goes near a well at high noon, her spirit can be possessed by a *hadal*. In such a case, it was the belief that if the bride is not treated by a mantric or a recitation of the divine, she may either lose her mind or may even die.

This legend was made available to me by Smt. Savitri Jag*dale*. She is an author and poet. She shared with me some of legends. The following legend was one of them. The legend is retold in my own words.

Glossary:

Breaking of a coconut – It is believed in India that coconut is a sacred fruit. So, one of the most common offerings in a temple is by breaking a coconut. Coconut plays a vital role in all *puja* rituals as well.

Manglashtka – Holy verses of blessings sung for the wellbeing of bride and groom as a part of wedding ceremony. The priest prays to all the planets, gods, goddesses and holy rivers to bless the couple with a happy and healthy married life.

Sanai-Chaughda – These two are different types of musical instruments. Both of them are played at festive events or special occasions. *Sanai* or *shehnai* is a musical instrument similar to the oboe and the chaughda or nagara is a membranophone instrument that is considered to be the lead instrument in ceremonies and weddings.

Satyanarayan puja – A religious worship of Lord Vishnu.

Tamasha – Traditional form of Marathi folk theatre. A grand show of entertainment with singing and dancing. Marathi is a language spoken predominantly by the people of Maharashtra state in India.

Stolen Wife, Cochiti Pueblo
NATIVE AMERICAN

There was a time when the Pueblo migrated to avoid intruders from the south. Then strangers arrived from the east to push the Pueblo northwest. The people moved, again and again. Once, there was a time when the pueblo was being built at a new location. An elderly man and his woman grew tired of working on making *adobe*s. There half built home was in a state for the elderly man was not good at building and his elderly wife was not able to complete the mudding on the outside. The clan chief ordered the granddaughter White Cloud and her husband Majestic Deer to live with them. White Cloud and Majestic Deer moved into her grandparents' home. These two were young and White Cloud had just given birth to a baby girl.

The grandparents' *adobe* home had holes in the walls where the mud chinking had fallen onto the dirt floor. The cold winds brought winter warnings to this family. As was tradition, the women of the Pueblo houses were to seal the *adobe* walls with fresh mud usually every spring. White Cloud wrapped her baby in a woven cotton blanket and tied the baby into the cradleboard leaning it against the inside wall of the home. White Cloud rolled her own waist long hair around two of her fingers and with yarn tied her hair into a *chongo* or circle eight bun at the nape of her neck. Gathering tightly woven willow baskets, one under each arm, she carried them to collect river mud. At the home she stood on a cut tree trunk as she shoved and packed the mud into the gaping holes between the *adobe* bricks of the wall. White Cloud made trip after trip to the river for mud, stopping only to nurse her hungry baby girl when needed.

Food was scarce in their small home. Majestic Deer stretched his bow, cut wild oak saplings to whittle into arrows, as he watched his woman work mudding their home they shared with her grandparents. He had offered to help her, but she was stubborn in her traditional role as a Pueblo woman. In the Pueblo, the men built the mud brick *adobe* walls for the homes and the women chink and seal the *adobe* brick walls with mud. White Cloud was not to be deterred from her womanly duty. Soon her white cotton dress was covered with the mud as were her arms and legs. The short work moccasins had clumps of mud on the tops of them with layers of mud under her feet.

Majestic Deer lifted the cradleboard with his sleeping baby girl inside it, telling White Cloud, "We are off to gather raven feathers or at least crow feathers for my arrows and to find a long shaft for a spear. We shall return soon."

White Cloud flung mud at him as he danced away, she laughed, "Yes, find your light fluffy feathers while I do hard work!"

Majestic Deer shook his head, calling back to her, "We'll bring you back a special feather if we can find you under all that mud!"

As White Cloud's hands muddied one of the walls, other women approached to help. They brought their baskets filled with mud. Grandmother watched from a safe distance near the outdoor rounded oven or *horno*. She was baking bread for the women helpers. Grandfather mumbled as he wandered in circles outside of the house. The women's hands filled each open hole in the wall with mud, smoothing the mud generously across the walls until by evening the mud mixture coated the building to give it a glowing golden-brown color in the sunset.

Majestic Deer returned with his hungry baby girl. His pouch was filled with long black raven feathers with blue tips. Showing them to his grandfather, he said, "These are magical and will bring down many elk and deer. We'll have a good winter. This house will be warm and soon I can go on the hunt for food." Majestic Deer lead his grandfather inside their home. The solid walls held the heat from the cooking fire in the corner of the main room. Now the home smelled of wet earth and peace. White Cloud rested with her baby girl while Grandmother and Majestic Deer cooked a meal of beans with squash and corn, fresh acorns and sage.

At dark dawn, Majestic Deer whispered to his sleeping wife and baby who shared a palette bed on the floor with him, "I'm leaving now to go with the other hunters. Please, take care of the grandparents and our baby girl. You don't have to do anything for you're allowed to relax now that the walls are strong and finished."

Majestic Deer woke Grandfather, asking him to not go wandering away from the home for this would worry White Cloud. Majestic Deer spoke with Grandmother, asking her to help White Cloud with their new baby girl. Once he felt everything was in place, Majestic Deer met with fellow hunters to search for herds of game over the horizon in the early dawn light. He felt his family was safe from harm, being in a strong walled home. They could help one another. The hunters had to travel far to the east to find game.

Several days after Majestic Deer had been gone, White Cloud asked Grandmother to care for her baby girl while she went to the spring to fill the water jars. Pointing with her index finger at White Cloud, Grandmother clicked her tongue, "Remember to stay away from magic! You're still recovering from giving birth. You've worked hard fixing the walls and your body and your spirit are weak. Stay away from magic!"

Smiling, White Cloud lifted water jars by their leather loops. These she tied to her cotton woven belt. She greeted the other women on the path who were returning to their homes with filled water jars. The fresh spring was surrounded by cottonwood trees with lovely green grass framing the perimeter. White Cloud dipped the jars into the water of the spring, filling them with fresh sweet water. After filling four of the smaller jars, she noticed a shiny item glistening under the surface of the water. Not knowing this was magic, White Cloud lifted the object from the water to inspect it. Her hand glowed with light as she held a colored twig. Colors of silver with red, black, and green circles were geometrically painted on it. The magic in this colorful twig belonged to the Governor of the Yellow *Kachina* People. His great powers were within this twig for using it, he was able to bring rain, thunder and clouds to the four directions. Yellow *Kachina* People Governor watched White Cloud as she held this magic twig for he had planted it for her to find. He was impressed with her beauty.

In a split second, he flew through the air to stand beside her. Putting his hand over hers, he tried to jerk the colorful twig away from her. "This belongs to me. You certainly may not take it or have it."

White Cloud laughed at him as she jerked it from him, "You forget I am a woman! I mud homes, I give birth to babies and I carry water from this spring. You certainly cannot have this for now it belongs to me! I found it!"

As she laughed, she raced around the spring to carefully jump over and around the bushes. She appeared to fly as she leapt from one side of the spring to the other. White Cloud's wild laughter scared the birds as they squawked in the trees. Holding the magical twig high in the air, her hair came loose to fly around her head. Yellow *Kachina* People Governor flew after her, admiring White Cloud's beauty and her strong body. Finally, White Cloud stopped to hand him the colorful twig. "Here, this is yours, I wasn't going to take it even though I found it."

"White Cloud, may I have some of your water?" He asked as he pointed to one of the smaller water jars near her feet.

She handed him the water jar. He took a long drink and handed the jar back to her. Smiling, she put her hands on her hips to smartly say, "Hey, no, you didn't finish drinking all of the water. Once you start to take a drink, you have to drink all of the water in the water jar!"

Yellow *Kachina* People Governor stared at her, "And if I don't drink all of the water what will happen?"

White Cloud tilted the water jar to toss water onto his face. He jumped away from her to run and leap over the spring. She chased him this way and that way, laughing and having fun.

Yellow *Kachina* People Governor asked White Cloud, "Would you like to see where I live? It isn't far from here and you would like it, I'm sure."

White Cloud frowned, "I am Majestic Deer's woman. It would not be right for me to go to your home with you."

Yellow *Kachina* People Governor shook his head, "He need not know. You can trust me after all I make this pledge of honor while standing here in the water of your spring. Water is a sacred source. I will take you there and bring you right back here to the spring."

Being in a good mood after days of hard work and believing he was a man of his word, White Cloud agreed. Yellow *Kachina* People Governor blew upon the colorful twig and it expanded into a flying canoe. No sooner did they both sit in it when it flew up into the sky. White Cloud's hair flew behind her and her eyes were wide with amazement. In no time, the canoe settled on the roof of Yellow *Kachina* People Governor's house at the top of Flint Mountain. White Cloud stepped from the canoe to descend a wooden ladder placed from the roof to the ground. As the Yellow *Kachina* People Governor stepped out of the canoe, it shrank back to being a colorful twig, which flew into his hand.

After he climbed down the ladder to the ground level, the Yellow *Kachina* People Governor clapped his hands at the blanketed door frame. As he stepped inside, he held the blanket open for White Cloud, saying, "This is my home and now it is yours."

White Cloud tried to go back to the ladder, crying out, "Oh, no! You're to return me to the spring! Water was at your feet when you spoke of returning me. You, yourself stated that when one speaks with honor when near water one must keep their promise. You clearly stated Majestic Deer would not know of my being here with you. You are the Yellow *Kachina* People Governor of the Spirit World. The Spirit World will not be pleased with you if you dishonor their trust! Your word is to be trusted!"

Pulling back the blanket hanging on the door frame, he growled, "You are the thief! You, who took my magic without my permission. Therefore, you are not to be rewarded. You are mine and it is here you shall remain as my property."

Collapsing on the floor in defeat, White Cloud shook her head, "I have responsibilities to my baby daughter, to Grandparents and to my man! You have no right to take those away from me or from them. Your word should be honorable!"

Waving the colorful twig over her head, Yellow *Kachina* People Governor chanted, "You are here. You shall remain here. You are now my woman."

Days later, Majestic Deer returned home from his long journey. The hunt had been good. The hunters had returned with ten poles of fresh meat. They had butchered and prepared the meat at the hunt site in order to keep the weight lighter upon return. They had rolled and dried the fresh meat each day of the hunt to wrap it in skins and tie the bundles on long horizontal poles to carry home.

As Majestic Deer entered their home, he called out to White Cloud. He was anxious to show her his bounty, but he found only her grandparents and his baby girl sitting inside. Grandmother was rocking the baby girl who was sucking on a cloth that had been soaked in honey water. Majestic Deer asked, "Where is White Cloud?"

Grandfather shook his head, "She went out one morning to get water for the family and she never returned. We found the water jars by the spring, but she seems to have disappeared."

The baby spit out the cloth to cry and cry. Majestic Deer lifted his baby girl into his arms. "She needs fresh milk. I will take her to White Cloud's aunt for she just had a baby. Her aunt can nurse both babies." Turning in the doorway, he added, "We need to find White Cloud." As he walked to the aunt's home, he sang to his daughter. There were women returning from the spring with water jars. He asked each one if they had seen White Cloud at the spring. Some of the women reported seeing her at least ten days ago as she entered the trees with her water jars. Since then, no one had seen or heard from her.

White Cloud's aunt was pleased to care for the baby girl. She had a home filled with three boys and her new baby boy. The aunt rocked the baby girl in her arms, "White Cloud is not one to leave her duties. She is a stubborn woman and she is traditionally loyal to her family. Something must have happened to her or she would have told someone where she was going."

Over the next few days, Majestic Deer searched the land for White Cloud. He questioned everyone he met. Camping at night near the *Rio Grande*, he called to the Spirits to help him find the mother of his child. "Where is my woman? Why won't you help me find her? Is she safe? Is she alive?"

Majestic Deer became angry as he travelled from Pueblo to Pueblo, mountain top to mountain top. After a time, he became sad and wept. Returning to his home, he collapsed into a deep sleep. When he awakened, Grandmother was kneeling beside his bed palette. "Grandson, there is a path you have not taken. Your daughter needs you to be strong and healthy. We are here for you and for White Cloud. Your baby is safe in her aunt's care."

Majestic Deer leaned on his elbow toward her as she continued, "White Cloud is a woman who challenges life. Wherever she is, I am certain she has not given up trying to return to us. Now is the time for you to be courageous and work with the Spirit World."

Falling onto his back, Majestic Deer closed his eyes, "How? I called to the Spirits on the mountains, by the *Rio Grande* and in the forests. They did not answer. How does one find a Spirit Guide to help? Grandmother, I need help."

Grandmother pushed his long hair from his forehead, "Today, you rest and eat well. We shall have a feast of a meal and then you will learn the ways of the old ones. You have been anxious, angry and mixed up inside of your soul. It is time for you to find a place of harmony and peace. Only then can you reach your woman."

Majestic Deer bathed in the river north of the Pueblo. Wrapping his hair into a *chongo* at the nape of his neck, he closed his eyes to feel the cool water gurgling around his ankles. Stepping onto the soft dirt, he pulled his buckskin shirt over his head. Wiping the dirt off of the bottom of his feet onto his calves, he tied his waist belt, tightening it. Shaking the rectangular leather hide, he tucked one end of his breechcloth under his leather belt by his back to pull it through between his legs and tucked it under the front of his belt. Moccasins were turned out to release dirt from inside and then slid onto his feet and tied at the ankle. He felt balanced and clean.

Rich aromas met him as he entered his home. Grandmother stirred hot posole, a stew of cut meat mixed with corn, squash, beans and hot chili peppers. Fresh bread cooled on a blanket and a wooden covered bowl of golden honey was placed beside it. Grandfather was kneeling on the floor with his old ceremonial drum. Duck and pheasant feathers were placed in Grandfather's *chongo*, tied with a cotton yarn dyed red and black. Grandmother filled a wooden bowl of posole, handing it to Grandfather. She said to Majestic Deer, "Today is the day, you start a new journey to fulfill your goal. Majestic Deer, we may be old and we may be bent from time, but up here," she patted her forehead, "there is such knowledge. Listen and you will learn wisdom."

Taking a bowl of posole from her, Majestic Deer noticed Grandmother wore her black *manta* dress tied only over her right shoulder. Her moccasins were beaded, wrapped high up to her calves. Turquoise and silver bracelets jangled on her wrists, a rolled turquoise necklace mixed with soft red orange coral hung around her neck. Her hair was loose with a headband embroidered with colorful fabric to hold her bangs against her forehead. Majestic Deer turned to Grandfather who had on his large squash blossom necklace. The *naja* at the end of the necklace had been recently cleaned. The upside down *naja* in the shape of a horseshoe represented the safe place for the souls of the family. Souls were able to leave the open part of the *naja*, but if threatened, they were able to return to the sanctuary at the top of the *naja*. Grandfather was the oldest member of the family; thus, he was the keeper of the squash blossom necklace.

The three of them ate in silence as they scooped up the posole with the fresh bread. Dessert was bread with honey. Majestic Deer felt the peace of his family surrounding him. Grandmother removed the bowls and the wooden bread board. Grandfather took the honey bowl, placing it in a wooden box. Then he started to beat the drum. Majestic Deer closed his eyes to chant with Grandfather. The drumming became louder and louder as other men entered the room, kneeling behind them on the floor. The floor began to vibrate as Grandmother's feet pounded the floor. Vibrations became stronger as more women joined her, each with a ceremonial *manta*, and each with their ceremonial jewelry.

Majestic Deer remained kneeling, chanting and listening. Drums echoed in the room. Heels of women's feet pounded harder and harder in time with the heartbeat of Mother Earth. Suddenly, he felt a hand on his shoulder. He didn't move, but waited as someone placed red paint on his cheeks, chin and forehead. Feather talons were stuck into his *chongo* and a headband was tightly tied around his head. His heart beat in the rhythm of the drum, the pounding of the feet and the chanting of the men's voices. Then there was silence.

Grandmother's voice spoke to him at his shoulder, "Grandmother Spider is waiting for you. It is time. You must go and speak with

Grandmother Spider for she has the power and the wisdom to guide you to White Cloud. She will help you."

Turning his head, Majestic Deer heard the sound of people shuffling out of their home. Grandfather said, "Open your eyes, my grandson. It is time for you to go on a dangerous journey. There is death waiting for you. There is success waiting for you. It is for you to decide if you are strong enough to go."

"Grandfather, what if White Cloud is gone from us, from this world? How would life be then?" Majestic Deer touched Grandfather's arm.

"Grandson, it is not for you to project. This is dangerous. None of us know what lies ahead in our lives. We must trust the Spirits to guide us. Do not try to believe something you do not know. Believe in what is here, inside of you." Grandfather poked Majestic Deer's chest. "Do not put thoughts in your mind if those thoughts are not proven. If you follow those unproven thoughts you will live in sadness. Believe in what you know and you will succeed."

Grandmother handed Majestic Deer a water jar, "Grandmother Spider will know where White Cloud is. Grandmother Spider will know because she weaves her web to all parts of the earth." She handed Majestic Deer a bundle. "These are gifts for Grandmother Spider. The most important is the leather sack of blue corn meal ground down to almost powder. This cornmeal was finely ground by White Cloud."

Majestic Deer walked for four days, remembering the path told to him by Grandmother. Finally, he came to a tiny hole in the side of a sandy hill that glittered with hundreds of silver webs. Sprinkling some of the blue corn meal around the hole, he called, "Hello? Grandmother Spider?"

Jumping from the doorway's opening came a black fat spider. Majestic Deer stepped back, watching fearfully as the fat spider grew in front of him. Her eyes were large, mirroring his image. Her wiry eight legs lengthened as tree branches with clippers at the end. Spindly legs, bent backward at the knee held a plump woman in a black *manta*. She had no hair or ears and her nose was only two small holes in the front of her face. The open mouth was filled with sharp pointed teeth and a hole under her upper lip revealed a spool of silver thread.

Majestic Deer stayed calm, asking, "Grandmother Spider, please, can you help me? I bring you gifts out of respect for your wisdom and I am grateful for any help that you will be able to give."

Saliva dripped from her mouth as she answered him, "You must come into my home for there are lessons you must learn before I can be of help to you."

Studying the tiny hole behind Grandmother Spider, he wondered how he was going to be able to enter her home. A sharp pain was felt on his upper arm and then he began to shrink as wet thread wrapped around him, bundling him into a moist cage. Closing his eyes, Majestic Deer envisioned his baby girl sleeping. Within a heartbeat, he was lifted, rolled and released from the tight sticky threads.

Grandmother Spider ordered him to sit, saying, "Tell me, my son, why you have come to interrupt my day."

He explained, "My woman White Cloud has gone away. She is missed by our small daughter, her grandparents and myself. Would you be gracious enough to listen to my story?"

Sitting beside him, Grandmother Spider put one of her hands on one of his hands, "Majestic Deer, do not worry. White Cloud didn't leave you. She's being held at the very top of Flint Mountain or our sacred *Daodyuma* Mountain. She wishes to return to you, but she cannot."

Majestic Deer studied Grandmother Spider's face, "She is alive? She didn't leave us by choice?"

Frowning at him, Grandmother Spider answered, "You're not very smart are you? Don't you know your own woman?"

He had no answer to give Grandmother Spider. Being respectful, he stared at her lower feet as she continued, "I will give you instructions as to how you may bring her back, but you must do exactly as I say. Water will be your powerful helper. First, you must go home. Gather water from the spring where her water jars were found. Wash with this water, using a particular water jar. Be certain that you are completely washed. Are you wise enough to wash your complete body? Remember use only the water from that spring using a water jar of hers. Do you understand?"

Majestic Deer nodded. She continued, "Once you have washed, gather your arrows, your bow and come to me. Do not stop along the way. Be sure you are clean, seriously wash your body all over! Take this blue cornmeal that you brought for me. In the morning, before you come back to my home, offer this cornmeal to the Great Spirit. Then come quickly." She studied his face, "Can you remember all of this? Do you need me to tell you this again?"

Smiling at her as he continued to look down, he shook his head, "Grandmother Spider, I will remember what you have told me. I'm smart and I can do what you require."

Shaking her head, she whispered, "Let's hope so for you woman's sake."

Hurrying home, Majestic Deer took one of White Cloud's water jars, filled it with water from the spring to wash. Carefully, he cleaned every part of his body. Gathering his arrows and his bow, he went outside to respectfully lift the blue corn meal to the Great Spirit who greeted him with the feathers of the morning sunrise.

Grandmother Spider was waiting for him at her doorway. This time he was ready for the pain in his upper arm from her magical bite. When he opened his eyes, he was kneeling on the floor in her main room. Her mirrored eight eyes reflected his image, "You did well, my son. I watched you." Dipping her clawed segment into red pigment, she painted symbols on Majestic Deer's cheeks and forehead. With a different claw segment dipped into blue and then yellow pigment, she drew different symbols on his face. Her dexterity in design and drawing was impressive to him as he saw his reflection in her many eyes.

"The designs on your face are those of the *Woi'oca* or duck for these will show respect to the East the place of passage to the Above. Your face of sea-blue represents water and around your lips is the same sea-blue. The snake with a red head and alternating red and yellow body segments represent eternal life moving from this place to the Above. The dragonfly painted on the upper right of your forehead represents strength to move above water to a place of safety in the spirit world." Grandmother Spider braided his hair at his forehead wrapping a twig of Kwiraina blue-spruce into the folds of his hair. "This braid is tight, keep it so for you do not want to lose this small branch. This shields you from evil deeds."

In one of her fur paw-like claws, she held a carved stone tube. "Take this stone tube, this bag of tobacco and this medicine stick. Just before you enter the Yellow *Kachina* People Governor's home, bite a piece off the medicine stick. Wash it around in your mouth until it is mush. The taste is bitter and awful. Take this brown saliva mush from your mouth and rub it on the flesh of your body. Be sure to rub it on your head, your hair, your face, the bottom of your feet, and the back of your hands, rub it all over your body."

"Grandmother Spider," Majestic Deer quietly asked her, "Yellow *Kachina* People Governor works with helping those who are ill or in battle go the Above World, why is he holding my wife in such a way?"

"Ah," Grandmother Spider smiled showing her many sharp teeth, "Our people and our spirits like to play tricks as a testing to the people. Your woman was not wise and she was trapped and now must pay her price. This punishment will be placed on you as well if you confront the Yellow *Kachina* People Governor. People are here as a blessing and are tested to earn their right to be here in this place. Remember his strength comes from water. Do not allow him to get you anywhere near water for he will then have his power four fold."

Majestic Deer held up the reed tube with magpie feathers inserted into it and the tobacco. She smiled, "The tube *Wic'Bi* and the tobacco, which is not 'Sa' but is '*Qwaep'e* from the Spirit Stick Plant. '*Qwaep'e* is from the flatland far from water and will help you win against the powers of the Yellow *Kachina* People Governor. This magic stone tube *Wic'Bi* has *Dyami cpaik* short eagle feathers in the front of the tube as well as the magpie *crowakaiya* or eastern bird feathers. These with the spiritual tobacco '*Qwaep'e* will guard you and get your woman home to your daughter and grandparents. Once you're outside it will become the correct size for you."

Grandmother Spider rested one of her appendages on his shoulder, "Bless you, my son, be strong, be courageous, but most of all, work at being clever. Yes, be clever or you will lose miserably." Leaning to his left ear, she whispered spirit song words from the *Winock yunyi* song or words to strengthen his heart.

Thanking her, Majestic Deer put the stone tube *Wic'Bi*, the spiritual tobacco '*Qawaip'e* and the prayer stick *H'A'Tcminyi* deep inside his quiver. Flint Mountain known as *Daodyuma* is tall with many steep cliffs and rough rock slides. His journey up the eastern *Daodyuma* Mountain took several days. Finding his way through the canyons that shared gorges with *Daodyuma* Mountain were hazardous and difficult. Finally, Majestic Deer struggled to reach the top of *Daodyuma* Mountain. His breechcloth was brown with dirt, his legs scratched from yucca spears and cactus spine injuries. The sun had tanned his bare chest and arms, while his face retained the symbols of strength painted with pigment.

Majestic Deer had no problem finding the Yellow *Kachina* People Governor's home for it stood large on the landscape with smoke rising tall from the stone chimney. The land around the home had been scraped clean of all living plants. A scorched path lead to the front of the building with a branch ladder leaning against the outer mud wall from the ground to the roof of vigas with mud-growing grass. Flocks of vultures perched on the gnarly branches of nearby dead trees. A murder of crows cawed loudly as they flew hurriedly about warning him of danger. Majestic Deer approached the front of the building.

As he neared the Yellow *Kachina* People Governor's blanketed doorway, White Cloud came running out to meet him, "Oh, Majestic Deer, how I have missed you, but you should not be here! The Governor of the

Yellow *Kachina* People is cruel and horrible. He will try to kill you!" Frantically, White Cloud wiped her flour covered hands on her bleached *manta* dress embroidered with symbols of lightning, clouds and death sewn on the front.

"Don't be afraid," Majestic Deer told White Cloud, "I've come to take you home!"

"No! No!" White Cloud whispered cautiously as she looked behind him, "He will destroy you! Something terrible will happen. Please, oh, please, he will kill you! My foolishness brought me here!"

Shaking his head, Majestic Deer put his hand on her arm, "I have come to take you home to your daughter and to your life as my Pueblo woman."

Stoically he examined the area near the building for signs of the Yellow *Kachina* People Governor's presence. There was a pile of bones with deer horns to the east of the house and lightening spears of different sizes leaning on the east wall. There wasn't any energy coming from the area. Majestic Deer reached out to his wife, "White Cloud, the Yellow World is the place where people ascend to the upper world. The Governor is referred to as *Dapop* the eastern governor or *Awahiya* and is not known for evil. This *Dapop* is only involved with bringing water to the people. How is it that you were brought here against your will?"

White Cloud sobbed, "Oh, yes, then you believe you must wait for him? He tricked me into picking up his magical twig in the flowing water of the spring and now I am his woman. He tricked me, Majestic Deer! He won't let me go! If he finds me gone, he will track us down and kill us!"

Majestic Deer studied the pain in her face, asking, "Did you agree to come here with him? Were you in the water in the spring when you agreed to come here? Where has he gone? Why does he leave you here alone if he wants you to be his woman?"

"Yes! Yes, Majestic Deer, he tricked me with his colorful magic! Yes, I was in the spring collecting water! He knows I'm frightened of him! He scares me. His powers are everywhere! He has gone to the south to bring rain and thunder to the people there. Once he returns, if he finds me gone or you here, he will kill us!" White Cloud fell on her knees, "Please, take care of our daughter! Majestic Deer, the Yellow *Kachina* People Governor has me! Please, go!"

"No, I will wait for him to return." Majestic Deer was firm in his conviction. "Do you have some food? I have climbed for days and I'm very hungry."

"Come." White Cloud shook her head, "There is some food you can eat and other food that will make you sick. I have learned what to eat and what to leave. Come."

White Cloud prepared a fine meal for Majestic Deer. After he had eaten, Majestic Deer climbed the ladder to the roof. Biting a piece off of the *H'A'Tcminyi* prayer stick, he mashed it between his teeth. Grandmother Spider was correct, the taste was horrible. Eagerly, he spit the brown gooey saliva onto his palms and rubbed it down his front. Using his breechcloth, he rubbed the nasty stuff on his back and all over his flesh. Now, he stank of dead skunk oil. Lifting the pipe and tobacco from the bottom of the quiver, he placed them at his feet. The H'ATcminyi prayer stick was shoved into his kilt belt. Placing his arrows back into the quiver the tobacco and *Wic'Bi* reed tube were laid firmly between them for an easy reach. His quiver was hung over his left shoulder and his bow was held in his right hand. Touching the small blue spruce branch braided into his hair, he smiled.

As the sun reached the highest point in the sky, a hard wind blew with growling thunder and the door blanket of the home flew up then slammed hard against the far wall. Yellow *Kachina* People Governor had arrived. Pounding the floor with his feet, Yellow *Kachina* People Governor stormed through each room of the home, "I smell ashes! Someone has been cooking and it wasn't for me!" Roughly grabbing her arm, he yelled, "White Cloud, who is here! How dare a stranger come into my home when I am not here?"

Trembling, White Cloud stood tall, "There is no one here. Yes! Who would dare come into this house if you were gone?"

Yellow *Kachina* People Governor snorted fog from his wide nostrils, "Someone is here! Someone has been in this house!" He growled thunder at her, "You! You brought someone into my home!"

Yanking her arm from his hand, tears fell from her eyes, "Yes, there is someone here. It is my man. Majestic Deer has come for me. He is going to take me home."

Yellow *Kachina* People Governor glared at her, "Where is he?"

Cringing, but standing tall White Cloud hesitated to answer. Behind her, Majestic Deer entered the doorway, holding his bow tightly in his hand, "Here, I am, right here."

Laughing his deep thunderous laugh, Yellow *Kachina* People Governor mocked him, "Majestic Deer is here! Hah!" Stomping over to him, he smirked, "Oh, you are the great hunter who leaves his wife alone while he goes off to hunt! Now, we shall find out who is the stronger! Is it the hunter or the all-powerful Yellow *Kachina* People Governor?"

Majestic Deer bowed to him, "You are the one with magic. We the people respect you for your gift to bring us rain and and water. You have great powers to maintian life and I have none. Yes, I must do as you say."

Yellow *Kachina* People Governor pointed to the corner of the room, "You, sit on top of that tall stone *Ku'pi*. The one sticking up from the floor. Be careful not to hurt yourself, hah!" Turning his head, Yellow *Kachina* People Governor snorted, "You stink of *Tsu'in*! This will not protect you, hah!"

Doing as he was told, Majestic Deer sat on the red coral stone *Ku'pi* strategically placed in the corner of the small room. Yellow *Kachina* People Governor held White Cloud by the wrist, "You must stand beside me. You are not to help him!"

Rigidly, White Cloud stood beside Yellow *Kachina* People Governor who took a cane pipe from a bag that hung from his belt. Carefully stuffing the cane tube with tobacco, using his thumb and index finger, he blew on the tube's slit open bowl. Fire filled it to become red hot. Puffing until it was going strong, he tossed in in the air to Majestic Deer, "Here, smoke this!"

Majestic Deer caught the hot tube in his coated his hands of *H'ATcminyi*. Putting the cane tube to his lips, he toked on it. Inhaling the smoke made him dizzy, he rocked this way and then he rocked that way, but he did not fall over. Somehow, he maintained his harmony and balance.

Yellow *Kachina* People Governor fiercely thumped his foot down on the floor. Pieces of mud fell from the ceiling. The *Ku'pi* stone cracked as he yelled, "You must know something for you have powers! No one can survive my tobacco!"

Majestic Deer held the cane tube in his hand near his knee, "I don't have powers. I don't live by the night. Everything I do, I do in the daytime. How would I know or understand magic powers?"

He stood to return the cane tube to the Yellow *Kachina* People Governor. Yellow *Kachina* People Governor studied Majestic Deer, then said, "If you are not magic, then once I sing this song, you can take your woman home with you." Governor grabbed White Cloud by her shoulders. His fingers dug into her skin as he nodded for her to sing with him. They sang together:

Majestic Deer Man, if you are a man,
Your beautiful woman you can take
Home with you, with you.
Majestic Deer Man, if you are not a man, here,
Lightning will take you,
Home with you, with you.

Lifting his hand quickly, Yellow *Kachina* People Governor threw a bolt of lightning at Majestic Deer. The lightning whirled around him to dissipate into the room's mudded wall. It would not strike him. Four times Yellow *Kachina* People Governor threw a crackling bolt of white-hot lightning at Majestic Deer and four times it detoured around him to be absorbed into the wall. Heaving a sigh of dew, Yellow *Kachina* People Governor shook his head.

Bowing to Yellow *Kachina* People Governor, Majestic Deer spoke softly, "Now, that you have tested me, it is time for me to test you. Please, sit on the *Ku'pi* stone, there in the corner of the room."

Yellow *Kachina* People Governor giggled as he sat on the *Ku'pi* red stone. Majestic Deer whispered to White Cloud for her to tighten her belt and the laces of her moccasins. Yellow *Kachina* People Governor watched her crouch to tie her moccasins, "Now what? You have no powers! What do you wish for me to do?"

Majestic Deer filled the cane tube *Wic'Bi* with the tobacco Grandmother Spider had given him. Carefully the feathers were kept in place as he prepared the *Wic'Bi* tube. Lighting it with flint from the fireplace, his head was bowed in respect, he handed it to Yellow *Kachina* People Governor, "Here, now it is your turn to smoke this."

Jerking the *Wic'Bi* tube from Majestic Deer's hand, Yellow *Kachina* People Governor burst into a fit of laughter with tears streaming down his face. Yelling short blasts of lightning, he jeered, "Hah! Hah! You do not scare me! What can this little tiny cane tube do to me? I can smoke this in one breath!" Yellow *Kachina* People Governor toked one huge intake of the *Wic'Bi*. His face turned bright red, his body shriveled into a small white cloud as he fell off the *Ku'pi* red stone onto the floor. Majestic Deer and White Cloud stood together and sang:

Yellow *Kachina* Governor Man,
You are a *Daodyuma*,
My beautiful woman,
You shall have, you shall have.
If you are not *Daodyuma*,

Lightning shall strike you,
Lightning shall strike you and
Daodyuma, take this lightning!

Lifting his hand with his open palm facing the Yellow *Kachina* People Governor, Majestic Deer held his breath to shoot a bolt of red hot lightning at the small white cloud resting on the dirt floor of Yellow *Kachina* People Governor's room. Four times he did this. All four times the lightning hit the Yellow *Kachina* People Governor's cloud body, splitting the small cloud into four pieces. Majestic Deer and White Cloud sang this song four times and each time the Yellow *Kachina* People Governor's body split and split and split again until only a small puddle of water was left to wet the mud floor. Lightning flew from Majestic Deer's open palm, burning each of the Yellow *Kachina* People Governor's wet pooled body pieces into yellow colored dust.

When they were done, White Cloud fanned the pieces of yellow dust with a blanket, billowing them outside into the wind. Majestic Deer lead White Cloud down *Daodyuma* Flint Mountain. His tied feathers on bushes showed them the way to the flatland. The descending path had been treacherous. At times lions had followed them, rattlesnakes had slithered around them. As they traveled the flatland at night wolves howled. White Cloud's embroidered moccasins tore and her feet bled, but she didn't complain. They both held their heads high as they continued to reach Grandmother Spider's cave in the side of the mountain. Magestic Deer stood in front of White Corn as he saw the spider figure crawl from the tiny hole. Meeting them at her doorway, Grandmother Spider spoke proudly, "You have done well. Do not lose your woman again."

White Cloud closed her eyes as she hid behind Majestic Deer. Grandmother Spider stung each of them with her magic. Once inside her home, Grandmother Spider warned, "You have not

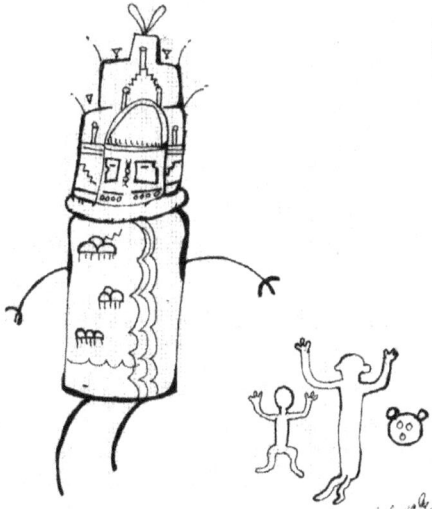

Stolen Wife Cochiti Pueblo, N.M. Story Number 5

defeated Yellow *Kachina* People Governor. His powers are beyond comprehension. It will take a short time for him to regain his strength for he is a magical spirit. He will come after you both with intense anger. Be advised, hurry to your home, use your *H'A'Tcminyi* prayer stick and bathe in its magic, both of you. If you are able, stay away from water for it will only help his magic. Now go, go quickly."

As they raced across the chamisa and rabbit bush landscape toward their home, dark clouds whirled above them. Dust devils blew dirt in their faces. Majestic Deer shouted to White Cloud, "Don't stop, whatever happens, don't stop!" They ran to the *Rio Grande*, stumbling into the fast-flowing river, they turned to watch a ten foot wall of water move directly at them. The flashflood tore against the river's sides as the rain fell hard and fast. Hail shot down from the clouds overhead. Hard, stinging balls of ice stung ceaselessly plummeting their bodies.

Majestic Deer grabbed White Cloud's hand, "Run! Run away from the river! Come on, we must get to higher ground!" He pulled her frantically up and over the sandy beach of the *Rio Grande* to the flatland now deep in running mud. Stooping as he ran with her right behind him, they crawled to a caliche ridge of dirt. The hard hitting hail followed them, pummelting down, bruising and tearing at their skin.

Hundreds of birds flew frantically overhead, desperate to cover the two cowering people who were trying to dig into the dirt for shelter. Majestic Deer pulled White Cloud under him as the hail tore at their bodies. Quickly, more and more birds flew to become a thick umbrella between them and the dark clouds of shooting ice. Feathered wings flapped, shielding them from the hail. It came to be that the birds who were hit the hardest with the hail now have spots. The bird's underneath, such as the crow and the raven, are solid in color. Finally, after what felt like an eternity, the hail stopped and the dark clouds dissipated, letting the sun melt the pellets of ice. Slowly a figure rose into the sky, it was a *Gacdyats* rainbow, a sign of remission.

White Cloud and Majestic Deer crawled out of the muddy earth. Water dripped from their scarred bodies and clothes. Each had bloody tears on their backs and arms. Leaning on one another, they made it home with the guidance of the birds. Once at home, Majestic Deer promised the birds he would bring them four of his deer kills to eat. He kept his promise to these birds who later would help him in his hunting.

Majestic Deer kept the *H'A'Tcminyi* prayer stick well-hidden and always near him in case Yellow *Kachina* People Governor came after White Cloud again. Their daughter was soon joined with a brother and as the family grew, Grandparents shared their wisdom with a humble ceremony. Majestic Deer, White Cloud and their children cared for their grandparents. All lived a good long life. White Cloud taught her daughters that it is important for a woman who is a new mother and has a good man and a home, not go out alone especially around water. White Cloud was firm with her daughters, saying, "Never dance or play around a stream, spring or an area of water! Do not make promises near or when in water! Remember to accept the love you have and not ask for more!"

Notes:

Pueblo traditions in New Mexico are strict with defined mores and rules. If a man marries a woman from a different pueblo, he must go and live with her in her family's pueblo. It is important for the family to keep a close eye on her for her husband will be responsible for hunting, fishing and maintaining the fields. After a wife has given birth, she becomes spiritually vulnerable and is susceptible to strong spirits that may be hovering around water and the pueblo. It is important for the husband to find spirit strength from magical beings, such as Grandmother Spider who saves Native People in all of her stories. Cochiti Pueblo moved several times once outsiders threatened their people. Today, their pueblo is near Santo Domingo Pueblo north of Albuquerque, New Mexico. This story is told to warn young mothers of the danger of being tricked by powerful spirits who by all means are good, but do testings.

Glossary:

Adobe – Made from wet earth or mud, mixed with leaves, twigs or straw to be a hard clay brick once sun dried in wooden frames. Not kiln fired. Stacked, staggered used as bricks to make walls for houses.
A'wae'tsa'nwae'I'I – Magical blue green spider.
Awahiya or Dapop – Eastern Governor
Chongo – Hair wrapped around fingers into a circle eight, tied with yarn behind nape of the neck. Done by both men and women.
Cochiti – Spanish name for 'small girl' given to a Pueblo northwest of Albuquerque, New Mexico.
Crowakaiya – Eastern bird feathers.
Daodyuma – Mountain south of Cochiti Pueblo

Dyami – Short eagle feathers.

Gacdyats – Rainbow.

H'A'Tcminyi – Spirit stick, can be used in healing or for protection.

Horno – Traditional beehive shaped oven, formed with mud. Used for baking and roasting in the pueblos. A fire is built inside allowing the thick adobe chamber to absorb the heat.

Kachina – Southwestern Native American supernatural being believed to be acestors of the living. Dancers can take on the spirit of a Kachina after special steps.

Kat'suna – Rain Society of the Southwestern Pueblos of New Mexico.

Ku'pi – Red coral colored stone.

Ku' – Stone

Ku'n – Skunk bush

Kwiraina Society – Can do communal curing. Has an altar and their own ceremonies.

Manta – Textile dress worn by women, tied over right shoulder to fall to knees. Woven belt with colourful embroidery around hem of dress. Also, a cloak.

Naja – Part of a squash blossom necklace worn by men. This is the center piece resembles an upside down horseshoe, elder of family wears this necklace and the naja protects the spirits of his family.

Ob'I – Wild duck

Qwaep'e – Spirit plant stick made from mountain mahogany.

Qwae'n'pu – Rrattlesnake

Rio Grande – Spanish for Big River, river flows from Colorado to Mexico through New Mexico and a small portion of Texas.

Sa' – Natural Native American tobacco, known as Spanish puche. Smoked in a 'ku' or stone.

WaBanyi – A feather bunch consisting of one long eagle feather, two or three short turkey body feathers and a feather from some other bird is tied to the neck of a stick. Short turkey and fluffy eagle feathers are tied near the talon. Used in prayer and ceremony.

Wa'Buny'I – Shell choker worn around the neck for protection.

WiC'BI – Made from a piece of cane commonly called 'istoa' or arrow. Hollow, segmented stalk, the top end is cut on a slant, narrow strip is cut, or scraped down one side of the stalk. Painted with black pigment or ma'nyi. The tube above the segment near the bottom is filled with wild tobacco, tamped in until the tube is filled almost to the top. Used for ceremony.

Woi'oc – A domestic duck.

Yaya'kapc'awae – Grandmother spider sitting down place.

6
MEDICINAL HEALING

Dangya Lake and Whooping Cough
ASIAN INDIAN

Once upon a time long, long ago, the Sahyadris forest was rich with wildlife and profound in natural beauty. The valleys were filled with dense trees and the overhanging foliage prevented the sunlight from entering the valleys below. Bears would loiter around the trees, being lured by the buzz of the bees in their hives that hung overhead. A multitude of birds fluttered around in the high branches, chirping, calling to one another as below them the rivers flowed with a steady rhythm of music. Sahyadris was beautiful in full natural splendor.

Sitting in solitude of this gorgeous landscape was a *faqir*, a holy man who had left his family, his home and had abandoned all worldly pleasures in his quest for social good and to find the Creator. This *faqir* meditated, contemplating on all that was around him in its magnificent glory. His dark brown eyes appeared to see beyond the obvious to another world as he began to chant God's name while he felt his string of rosary beads in his hand.

This *faqir* had a long beard with a white cloth that covered his head, wound around his body and was tied behind his back. The old cloth was faded, worn and in some places torn. In his free hand, he held a small black bowl that was usually empty. His body was thin, his feet bare and his legs scratched with his skin burned dark from being in the sun.

This *faqir* was in search of his Creator, He who made the blue in the sky, He who made the birds' feather glisten in the sunlight, He who made all the natural beauty in this world. Renouncing his parents, leaving home and all the comforts of his youthful life had not been difficult for his ultimate goal was to find his Creator. Yearning and searching and not having found Him, this one had not felt comfortable anywhere. There was no enjoyment for there were no answers to his never-ending questions: Who is He? Where is He? How can I find him? Why does He not speak to me? When will I see Him? How can I find Him?

The *faqir* traveled all over India, constantly searching. Now, he sat still, meditating in the Sahyadris forest, begging for an answer. He had not eaten for several days or hours, he couldn't remember. His large brown eyes stared straight ahead at the thickness of the tree trunks, the bending of the grass, and the flittering of the baby birds. Yet, he found no answers. Somehow since he was a child, he had believed that the sky and the sun would guide him to the Creator? But the sky was not telling him what he needed to know.

Looking up as he was tilting his head, he studied the clouds in the sky. They drifted away from the dense forest filled with life. Walking, he followed the movement of the clouds to arrive at the top of the mountain clear of trees. There below him was a green meadow. Focusing on the horizon, the forest was behind him and before him were two tall mountainous pinnacles. One was placed in front of the other and at the base of the first pinnacle was a lake. The water in the lake was crystal clear, reflecting the pinnacle mountain. The *faqir* stood in amazement, "The pinnacle is pointing skyward. It must be here that the Creator resides."

As he struggled to walk down the side of the sloping forest's mountain, a calming energy filled him. Speaking to himself, he said, "The Creator must be pure and clear like this lake's water." Studying the pinnacle as he neared the lake, he spoke to the sky, "Why does this mountain have a pointed pinnacle? Is it a pinnacle or is it used as a guide to point above? Yes, yes, it is a guide pointing, it is showing me, and it is telling me something. What is it? What is it?"

The *faqir* walked across the sloping land to the lake. Smiling, he spoke to the air around him, "The pinnacle is showing me what I am seeking. It is saying here, "He is! Up and above in the fathomless sky! Look Carefully! He is there!"

Words were whispered in his ears and kept ringing in his mind. His body filled with warmth as he neared the lake, staring at the pinnacle's reflection. The mirror image in the lake was majestic, the sky was chalk blue and there was no wind. His quiet voice asked, "Why didn't I see this earlier? Why didn't I feel this earlier? Why? I think this great pinnacle points to the Creator."

Suddenly, the *faqir* felt relaxed for the first time in his life. He felt peace with his new perception. His mind calmed, his eyes regained life and focus. No longer did this *faqir* feel an emptiness of never-ending frustration. His eyes softened as he studied the clear water with the reflection of the pointing pinnacle. Sitting abruptly at the edge of the lake with his empty black bowl in one hand and his rosary in the other, he

151~

stared at the top of the pinnacle. His face relaxed as he thought aloud, "This is the place, no more travel and no more searching. I will stay here near this mountain and be near this lake. I will search for Him in the clear blue sky. This is where He will be remembered until finally I will go and be with Him." There was no longer a need to search, for he had found his peace.

In the evening light, the *faqir* gathered dirt from close to the base of the forest mountain to mix it into mud. He carefully mounded it into a hut. This hut kept the cold winds from blowing on him in the night. In the morning he would get up at dawn and would watch the sky brighten gradually. Focusing on the dark water turning bluish white with the sun rising in the sky brought a great peace within his spirit. In the afternoon, he would notice the hot sun's reflection blazing on the still lake's water. The gleaming water brought about a pure transparency as he watched the colorful ripples in the lake with the evening breezes. In the evening, he sat with his rosary beads, praying and meditating to the Creator. Then he would watch the reflection of the starry sky above the lake while standing in the water to wet his body. In the night, he would lie on the soft ground in his small hut, closing his eyes with the memory of the pinnacle's reflection in the lake.

There were times when the *faqir* would go down to the hutments or area of small huts at the foothills. There he would talk to people and they would gladly offer him some food. People began to recognize him as a holy man by his attire and his countenance. They would bow to him in reverence, offering him milk and fruit. Some would offer him tubers and touch his feet. There were those who asked for his blessings whenever they saw him and once he had spoken to them, they felt better and would go away feeling blessed. There were those who spoke to him of their illnesses. Since he had traveled far and used many natural herbs over time, he was able to help them with cures for he was a compassionate man and could not ignore their pains.

During his travels, he had gathered certain herbs, grasses and mosses to be used in healing his wounds. These he was able to recommend to the sick and to help them along with their healing. Some afternoons, he would go into the Sahyadris forest and gather needed materials for some of those who were not able to find items on their own. This *faqir* never expected anything in return for he never needed anything and all he wanted was for every child of God to be happy forever. Constantly, he chanted God's name as he believed God would want him to do His bidding since he was here and he could help. Gradually, his reputation for curing spread far and wide. Nearby villages and tribal settlements became aware of his abilities. More and more people would arrive each day to have him help them recover from horrible pain. Those who he healed felt blessed and spread the word to others.

Once, an epidemic of cough spread through settlements. It was not an ordinary cough, this was severe and life threatening. The people referred to the cough as *Dangya khokla*. Small children coughed so violently, causing death. Older children coughed and coughed, sometimes coughing up blood. They spoke of the cough feeling as though something was stinging their throat and once they started to cough, their chest hurt. Those of an advanced age died and children lost their vitality due to this debilitating disease. Families hurriedly wrapped their children and elderly into blankets and went to the lake. There they found an empty hut.

Able bodied people searched in the Sahyadris forest but did not find the *faqir*. Others walked around the pinnacle mountain calling his name. Each passing day was becoming worrisome for people were dying in pain and despair. Poor people and tribal people were desperate for all one could hear was the sound of coughing, coughing and more coughing. No one knew where the *faqir* had gone or when he would return.

One day, suddenly, the *faqir* appeared in their midst. The weak, the frightened, the seriously ill threw themselves at his feet. Recognizing their pain, the *faqir* was himself struggling. Studying the sky, he walked away from them to enter the Sahyadris forest. Walking through the jungle, he tore off branches of certain trees to carry them over his thin shoulders to the lake. Throwing them into the lake, he made sure they sank by putting large rocks on the branches. The next day, he pulled these branches from the lake, placing them to the side, he built a fire. All around him people were coughing, choking, and crying out in pain.

Now, he lit a fire as he invoked the God of Fire, holding the wet branches over the flames. One branch after another was held over the flames, sparking and spitting as he constantly murmured words, requesting guidance from the sky. Occasionally, he sprinkled the pure lake water on the branches and would throw some invisible substance from his fists into the fire. After a while, the branches started to drip a silvery substance, which he collected into a *tumba*, a dried hollow pumpkin bottle. This appeared to be a shiny liquid. Gradually the *tumba* was filled. The *faqir* held the *tumba*, and looking intently at it, muttered some incantation. Slowly, he lifted the *tumba* and poured the liquid into the lake only to begin again in collecting this shiny silver liquid into the *tumba*. This went on for two days. The *faqir* did not eat or sleep but continued on in his mixture.

Dangya Lake and Whooping Cough

People came seeking the *faqir* for they were terribly ill. They watched him as he soaked the branches, held them one by one over the flames of the fire to take the dripping silvery liquid and pouring into the *tumba*, watching it become a shiny liquid. They were not sure what he was doing, but they knew he should not be interrupted for this was very holy and magical. The *faqir* was moving as if in a trance, each movement was precise, each murmur was definite and each time he looked into the sky there was a movement he did with his hands to collect the mixture. The oozing of the branches, the chanting, the murmur, the fire flames, the spitting and collecting all was done with a certain rhythm, a calculated trance brought this to happen. More and more people arrived to sit and watch, staring at his actions. Slowly, the coughing was forgotten for the people themselves were hypnotized by his actions.

At the end of the second day, the *faqir* appeared to be calm for he had accomplished his goal. Staring into the evening sky, the *faqir* had a quiet smile on his face as if he had heard what the Creator had asked him to do and he had done it! Now, he had the medicine ready for the *Dangya khokla* epidemic and this medicine was ready for the masses. The cure was in the lake's water.

Dying, coughing poor people ran to the *faqir* and fell at his feet. Crying and begging, they threw themselves at his holy feet. Compassion filled his eyes. Turning, he acknowledged the pinnacle mountain and the beauty of the lake's water. Kneeling, he filled the empty *tumba* with lake water as he drew it out, he turned to the nearest person to him and handed the cup to the man's extended palm. The man stared at him as he spoke, "Drink! Drink and be cured! Don't worry, leave your worries to Him. You will be cured and won't cough anymore. Drink!"

The man drank the water eagerly. His cough stopped. The *faqir* turned to the people, "I may not be here, but this lake will be here. Drink from this lake and you will be cured. You won't cough anymore and this lake water shall always be available to you. Whenever any of you suffer from the *Dangya Khokla*, come here to the lake, surrender yourself and tell it your problem. Close your eyes and drink this water and you shall be cured."

People stared at him then rushed to the lake to gather water. Drinking water, putting water in containers and carrying water to those who were too weak, the curing process began. The *faqir* smiled, "I have found Him now. My search is over. I do not need to stay here. This Pinnacle Mountain has shown me where He is. It has helped me see Him. This crystal-clear lake has enlightened me where He is and I shall now go to Him. I have decided to take a *Jal Samadhi*, the death by drowning in this water of my beloved lake. Yes, I shall embrace my death with my own free will to be spiritually united with Him."

Saying this, the *faqir* was quiet. An eerie silence fell surrounding the lake's water. There was only the faint sound of tiny ripples on the lake water as if they were inviting him to surrender to them. The *faqir* watched the people with loving eyes, then turned his head to gaze upon the pinnacle mountain and the lake. Finally, he lifted his head to the sky and before anyone could say or do anything, he walked into the lake. His calm conviction drew him deeper and deeper into the lake's water until in the end, he disappeared.

This was a great shock for the people. They could hardly comprehend what had happened. Many waited for him to walk back out of the lake, but he was never seen again. The people realized what they had witnessed, grieving, weeping and sobbing in sadness. This *faqir* would be greatly missed for he had taught the people so much about herbs, medicine and healing. Those who were afflicted with the *Dangya khokla* remember the *faqir*'s advice and drank water from the lake. Soon everyone felt better and eventually they recovered. As the news of the lake's curing waters spread across the land, people came to the lake, drank its water and carried it back with them in whatever containers they could find. The deathly sick were cured.

It has been many years since this took place, however, people remember, people tell of the *faqir* and his abilities to cure. The people will never forget him, but will keep his memories alive as the only person who cured the *Dangya khokla*. The pinnacle mountain is called Dangya Pinnacle and his beloved lake is known as Dangya Lake. These names are prevalent to this day. Even in this time of modern science, people who become ill with *Dangya khokla* go the Dangya Lake and with great faith, drink its water or carry it back with them to those who are ill. They bless the *faqir* and remember him for his importance and his advice spreads further and further, shared with more and more people who come to drink these medicinal waters to be cured.

Notes:

This is a miracle story about Dangya Lake and how the lake acquired a medicinal quality. Even today it is believed that this lake works in curing the Dangya khokla or persistent cough. Now over time, much of the lake seems to be filled by soil and overgrowth. However, today in the place of this lake there are a few puddles fed by some underground springs. The water of these pudddles is also believed to be medicinal in curing the Dangya khokla or persistent cough. Even though the lake itself is not present today, this area is still well known with the traditional name of 'Dangya Lake.' Many people are unaware of the natural healing mysteries of the medicinal lakes. Healing becomes a matter of faith for the people living near them. Perhaps that is the reason why they also are a source of various legends.

In these modern times science has explained the logical reasons behind many of nature's mysteries. Yet, the human mind remains inclined toward beliefs and superstitions and cannot forget the traditional legends and cures. The legends are told and retold over generations and this legend about the Dangya Lake refers to a superstitious belief.

Shri Hrishikesh Wakadkar told me of this legend. He is an engineer and has his own business at Nashik, Maharashtra. Being a mountaineering enthusiast, he knew of the Dangya Pinnacle near Nashik. Shri Dattu Lahanu, a villager living near the lake narrated this story to both of us. This has been retold in my own words.

Glossary:

Faqir – A Muslim or Hindu man who is regarded as a holy man. Faqirs are itinerant. They never shave nor cut their hair.

Tumba – Tumba is a Sanskrit word. Literary meaning of tumba is 'the gourd' (calabash).

Tumba is also known as a Kamandalu.

Jal Samadhi – To embrace death in a natural water body on one's own for spiritual reasons.

The Lake of the Beginning, Tsimshian
NATIVE AMERICAN

Baboudina and his family sat around the longhouse *dex-q!aowu'lk*. This is a longhouse with two doors, one at each end. The three fires that were lined along the inside center of the building were burning bright. He nodded to his father as he entered and his grandfather who sat around the largest of the middle fires in this long room. Baboudina had been away from his family and especially his wife for two weeks as was traditional when going to hunt sea otter. He and his two older brothers had lived in a *tack'ku'di-hit* house or eagle's nest house to watch for the sea otters. On their way to the house on the hill, they had hunted beaver and fat martin. Since the weather was cold the meat would keep until the skins were pulled and the meat separated and put in a hole in the cold ground.

At the *tack'ku'di-hit* eagle's nest house, they each had kept a chamber box near the door to use for urinating until they had finished their four week fast and were prepared to hunt. No one else was allowed to touch the each personal chamber box for it held part of who they were. At the end of the four weeks, each of the men had found an eagle's nest and killed one. Taking a sharp knife from their ankle belts they had cut off one of the eagle's talons.

This talon then had a *dji'yanasac nak* or flower tied to it. Once this was done, each of the brother hunters separated to make a miniature canoe with a figure of themselves sitting in it. This was his prayer in finding the sea otters. The eagle's talon was tied to the small canoe's seat with the flower wrapped around it. Once standing at the edge of the water, he blew urine from his chamber box onto the canoe for this would ensure his aim and ability to hunt the sea otter. This act would confuse the sea otter as to direction and the otter would swim directly to him. It was vital to stay away from his woman for if he had been with her at anytime in the last four weeks, his arm would shake and his aim would be wrong.

Each of his brothers and Baboudina had secured many sea otter for the winter months. The sea otters had been skinned and placed on high racks to dry while they fasted once again for seven day prior to returning home. Each of them was eager to be with their families for the heavy winter skies were showing snow was on its way. On the eighth day, the men took their skins and rolled the sea otter meat. Some of the meat was cooked in a mutual fire and eaten. A box of charms was opened to spread over the collection of meat and skins. The two small boxes of grease placed near the fire was used to feed the fire and the rest of the grease was used to coat their hair. As the charms were placed in the grease box near the fire, Baboudina blew on each charm quietly praying, "Let me be wealthy with children and with the hunt."

Putting the charms in the box mixed with beaver skins amd martin skins, the men returned to their village longhouse. All of Baboudina's family lived in one cedar longhouse *dex-q!aowu'lk* with a door at each end. Upon their return there would be a huge feast to celebrate the excellent hunt prior to freezing cold winter weather. Many times snow would fall, rising over the doorways, keeping the large family locked inside until the warmer weather melted the snow and allowed them to go back out for the collection of firewood and to hunt.

Baboudina and his brothers' families were staged around each of their own family areas near the two long fires within the huge house made of cedar wood and bark, chinked with mud. Communal living kept everyone safe and everyone fed. Sitting on painted animal skins with his children and his mother-in-law, his woman passed around cedar wooden bowls filled with hot salmon stew. His newborn baby girl was sleeping peacefully in the cradleboard beside her. Baboudina was tired for once he had returned home in the late morning, he had worked the rest of the day gathering fallen cedar bark with his four sons. The deep snow above them on the side of the mountain had made it difficult to find dead and down tree branches and stumps. They had managed to drag a large pile of thick branches into the inside of the longhouse to dry before the winter thunder was brought by Raven calling.

Baboudina rubbed his calloused hands together. His thick palms were sore. Pulling layers off of a *lqa'tul tcin nak* root that hung from the ceiling, he pocketed the root inside his mouth by his cheek. As it liquefied with his siliva he spit the juice into his hands, rubbing them together for healing medicine. Then he spit it on the animal skin placed on the dirt floor where he sat. This root traditionally keeps a person who chews it healthy and safe. Turning to his eldest son, he listened as his boy eagerly spoke of the large tracks they found under a grandfather cedar tree high up in the deep snow on the mountain above them. Baboudina felt truly blessed to live with his warm loving family on the land between the ocean's edge and the big river filled with salmon.

Deep wet snow still weighed heavy on the mountain above their village. Winter thunder was heard approaching, but in several months spring sunshine would melt the snowy land to bring an abundance of flowers, herbs, vegetables and greenery. Their hunters netting and trapping of salmon and candlefish had been successful with the first frost, but the meat from the otters and land game would ensure there was plenty of food for the long winter months ahead. The women had been busy making *chilkat* blankets formed from cedar bark and mountain goat hair. This would be a good winter with food, family and fine blankets.

Suddenly, there was a deafening roar. The longhouse shook, mud chinks from the high ceiling rained down on top of them. Children screamed. His woman quickly glanced at him as she grabbed the baby's cradleboard to her chest. His mother-in-law threw herself over his youngest son of four years of age. Huge bark planks crashed from the ceiling, allowing the high protective cedar beams to give a deafening crack then slam down on top of the people. In a heartbeat, all of the northern wall of the longhouse fell forward into the room, landing hard on top of his family. Suddenly, Baboudina's body was catapulted through the air, smashing to roll against the far fat cedar posts on the remaining south wall. The wall fell outward, allowing his body to quickly sink and be buried into the deep world of freezing snow.

Having no time to think, Baboudina with his eyes closed, scrambled using his muscular legs and hands to desperately swim his way to the open air. His thoughts were of his beautiful woman and his five children. Holding his breath, his strong fingers ceaselessly clawed their way up and out to the top of the wet stiff snow. There was no sign of the longhouse. Blinding white snow filled the world around him. It was freezing cold. Shivering, he screamed out the names of his family. Baboudina tried to stand only to collapse into the wet beneath him. Finally, lying flat, he crawled to the highest area. Desperately digging at the snow mound until his hands were bloody and his knees were numb, he realized no one would be able to breathe this long under the suffocating wet. Closing his eyes, he prayed to have his family go to *Kiwa'a*, the Place of Happiness, but all he could see was darkness behind his eyelids.

Crying out, Baboudina shook his bloodied hands to the sky,

yelling, "Take them to *Kiwa'a*, to the Place of Happiness! They do not deserve to be in *Ketl-kiwa*! Do not send them to the Place of Torment!" Exhausted, he fell onto his side letting his numb body shiver in the snow. All he had on was his soft cedar breechcloth going between his legs and wrapped over his thin leather belt. His feet were bare and his black hair, long and loose was frozen stiff in the cold.

Sucking on his bleeding index finger, Baboudina stared at the evening sky, searching for *La'aya'k* of the Milky Way rainbow that bring the dead to the *yek* world to live with *Nas'caki'yel* or supernatural spirits above earth in the sky vault. There were no stars, no clouds, and no colors in the sky only a hard wind blowing from the north to the south. How was it possible for him to be the only man to survive this deathly avalanche that destroyed his longhouse? Turning, he scanned for the other longhouses in the village. Nothing. There was nothing to be found. The tall totem pole he was carving with his eldest son was not to be found. The creaking and crackling of the thick snow was the only sound. Grabbing his clan emblem *Tane'di* or Otter carving was held around his neck by a leather strap, he prayed to *Nexa'di* for his people to live strong in the spirit world of *Nas'caki'yel*. He missed his family and was beyond cold.

Swinging his arms by his side, Baboudina slid flatfooted with his bare feet, careful to not pierce through the snow's crust, forward to the south where the land would be flatter and warmer. His people walked barefoot in snow and the soles of their feet were thick and tough as was Baboudina. His only clothing was his breech cloth and his mountain goat and soft cedar woven leggings that he had kept on until the fires had warmed his legs. Now these were frozen to his skin. Layers of muscle and fat kept his short body from freezing as he quietly moved to the south from the thick snow land to a land of brown frozen land.

As the black of night gave way to the soft glow of dawn, Baboudina heard the sound of a fast moving river. Not knowing how far he had traveled, he proceeded through a dense forest with low overhanging tree branches. Gathering fallen dried wood, he made himself a small fire under a tall spruce tree. The thick trees within the forest had protected the ground from the snow. Baboudina was thankful he was able to keep moving, keep his body warm and now with the fire, he finally felt he was able to rest and find warmth. The stoked fire radiated heat as he slept on the dry ground until the end of the day. Baboudina heard twigs break above him in the trees as the smoke lifted in the night sky.

Whispering softly with his throat sore from the cold, Baboudina said, "*Yek*, please care for my family. You are the spirits who live between this flat earth vault and the sky vault. I hear you. *Hayica'nak'*, you are the Old Woman Underneath who guards the earth vault with a frozen beaver leg, you shook the earth and caused the avalanche to fall on my people. *Hayica'nak'*, do not let my people go to the Above Vault! Do not give them passage to go with *Lq'aya'k* to make the journey across the sky!" Exhausted he fell back onto the soft dirt covered with stiff dead leaves.

Hunger woke him. Baboudina knew he had to eat to survive. Breaking thin twigs from a red cedar tree, he chewed on the ends to make sharp spears. Continuing to chew on these small spears, he ran toward the sound of the flowing water. Some of his toes had turned black, amazingly his feet felt no pain. Baboudina's hands were scabbed and swollen, but he was able to continue making small spears. Carefully as he walked to the flowing stream, he studied the ground for animal tracks. Birds flitted above him in the trees, snakes slithered into the underbrush and the rustle of small rodents was heard under the trees.

Baboudina leaned against a tall tree. Before him was a dead tree dripping with black bark. Tears fell from his eyes to roll down his cheeks as he prayed, "Family, keep you *qatuwu* and *wasa'tu'wati* within you, somehow I shall save you. Family, do not let 'what feels' leave you, 'keep your shadow' for somehow I will keep the ghosts from your souls." He began to shake, his hunger increased, but the cold within him seemed to grow inside his body. Pushing off from the tree, he was amazed at how colorful the world appeared around him as if for the first time he was able to see each item before him in a panorama of bright shades. Remembering his need for food, he continued along his way to the sound of the water.

Stooping beside a stream, he noticed human footprints with small feet, possibly a woman. Squatting, as he studied them, his mind filled with rage at the loss of his woman and his children. *Tu-kina-jek* was his spirit guide. How was his spirit guide not there to protect them? There must have been a *Nukw-sati*, an evil witch who had come to the village and no one had offered her food. Baboudina grimaced in his intense emotional pain. Extreme rage riddled his body as he chewed his sharp spears to follow the small footprints to the edge of a small tributary that fed into a substantial lake.

Baboudina noticed the lake had no snow anywhere around it. The air was warm and calm. Kneeling, he dipped his fingers into the water. It was tepid. Wishing he had his long spear, he examined the lake for fish. There was a ripple at the far side of the lake. Studying the water, his vision lifted to notice a woman sitting on a log at the water's edge. Gritting his teeth, his anger returned, filling all his senses for how was it that this woman lived and his fine woman had been taken from him? This woman should not be able to feel or breathe. In his mind he could see his own loving woman with their newborn baby. She had been smiling at him in their longhouse. Breathing hard, his memory returned to the terror he had survived. A dark evil grew inside of him, filling his being with a hot burning desire to kill this lone woman. Baboudina silently squatted at the lake's edge. Lowering his body into the water he quietly submerged. Swimming deeply underneath the surface to the opposite side of the lake, he leapt out to attack this woman with his bare hands. No one was there!

In disbelief, Baboudina studied the area beside the log, staring for her tracks in the mud. Then he knelt beside the log, realizing she must have been a ghost for there were no footprints. Turning this way and that, he searched for her. Turning away from the lake to gather twigs for spears since he lost his when he dove into the lake. It was then that he noticed footprints going away from the water. While he was swimming underwater, the woman must have retreated into the forest. Rubbing a scabbed hand across his forehead, he wondered where she had gone. Deciding he needed to eat for certainly *Tu-kina-jek* his spirit quide was testing him. Baboudina returned to the thick trees to retrieve small branches. This time he wove smaller branches together to make a fish net. Placing thin cedar bark at the curve of the net to help keep its form, he returned to the lake. As he knelt down to throw the net into the water, he saw the woman, again. She was kneeling at the lakeside across from him.

Madness filled his conscious mind. Tossing the net into the lake, he dove quickly, swimming with his powerful arms, he leapt out of the water ready to strangle her. Once again, he was alone. There was no woman to be found. Baboudina roared out in anger, he lifted a log and threw it, letting it roll to the edge of the forest. Twisting around, he glanced from the forest to the lake. Nothing. Even the birds were quiet. Water slapped against the sides of the lake's shore, otherwise there was an eerie stillness. Baboudina waded into the lake to get his net. As he walked through the water, he felt his catch. Three fat fish for dinner.

Returning to his small camp, he found the fire had gone out, leaving only gray ash. After gathering more kindling, he started the fire with two pieces of flint. His feet and toes were now throbbing. The cuts on his hands had started to bleed. Sitting on the forest's dirt floor, he studied the black skin on his knees and toes. As he fell back on dried leaves, he closed his eyes, remembering his family and the good day he had shared with his sons. They had laughed as they told stories while dragging dried wood to the longhouse. His woman had finished making a *chilkat* blanket for his father's *adaox* or animal spirit ceremony. Smiling in his sleep, Baboudina remembered the woven basket hat she wore when they were married. The courting had taken many months of abstinence from eating certain foods to being able to speak to one another. Baboudina was soon to be chosen as chief of his mother's Killer Whale Clan. This would make him a noble, no longer would he be a commoner. Lord of Heaven would surely care for his family.

Suddenly, Baboudina awoke with a start. Rolling over to sit, he removed the cooked fish from the small dying fire. When he had finished picking at the fish bones, he decided to return to the lake with his net. His hunger had not been quenched. There existed a hollowness inside of him, leaving a feeling of extreme cold emptiness. Rubbing soft dirt from the forest floor onto his feet loosened some of the black skin to peel off. Putting his weight on his toes brought a sharp stabbing pain. His knees were no longer red, but now were turning a yellowish color. Shaking his head Baboudina knew soon an infection would set under the dying skin. It was vital to return to the lake for more fish and to wash.

As he neared the lake, he slowly stopped. In disbelief, Baboudina saw the woman. Her brown hair was in long braids, her soft cedar bark skirt was painted with red and yellow pigment and she was swinging one of her bare feet back and forth in the water. In a blink, Baboudina was in the water, over the water, through the water going for her. As his sore feet stood on solid ground, the woman was not there. Slapping his hands hard on his thighs, he growled in frustration. Then he heard her laugh. She was running around the lake, laughing at him. No one traditionally or untraditionally laughs at another person. This goes beyond humiliation. In his village, if someone made fun of someone, they were punished for there was no greater disrespect than that of being laughed at publicly. A red-hot fire burned inside his brain. Rage devoured his soul as he studied her smiling face.

The woman stopped to stare at Baboudina from the opposite side of the lake. His mind worked quickly. Swimming allowed her to run, leaving him feeling stupid and lost. If he chased her on land, she could not swim from him. No longer did he care about food, his goal was to catch this woman. Her laugh brought him back to consciousness. Somehow, she was back on the opposite side of the lake. Now, the air was becoming cold, the water was freezing, but Baboudina didn't think of this as he jumped once again into the water swimming desperately to catch her. Again and again, Baboudina attempted his goal to attack her with his bleeding hands, aching feet and sore knees.

At last exhausted, Baboudina pulled his weak body from the water. Shivering with cold and in severe pain, he glanced at her mocking smile as his large body would no longer hold him upright. He crumbled hard onto the mud. Baboudina heard her high-pitched laugh as he closed his eyes to let *Tu-kina-jek*, his spirit guide take him. His body now numb from the cold, slowly stopped. His limbs stiffened, his skin turned white and his eyes opened to stare at sky vault overhead.

Pointing at him and continuing to laugh, the woman cautiously approached him from around the lake. Her strong hands lifted a heavy tree branch. Laughingly she threw it directly on top of his body. It fell hard to bounce off of his unmoving back. Crouching near Baboudina, the woman pulled a shell from her long skirt to toss at his head. It rolled to the ground after hitting his forehead. Baboudina did not move or flinch. Cautiously, the woman crept behind him to kneel. Taking a sharp knife from her belt, she stabbed at his back to cut the strong muscles open. Her fingers yanked to crack Baboudina's ribs. Using the knife to cut away at his internal organs, she tore Baboudina's heart from his body.

Lifting it over her head, she called out to his spirit, "You haven't any moccasins. You haven't any gloves. The devil clubs and sharp bushes will cut at your way. You have no one to sing songs for you and the wolves and bears will come at you for you haven't a knife!" Laughing, she continued, "How dare you come to attack me? You do not know me, but I soon knew you!"

Suddenly, she became frightened for the heart held in the palms of her uplifted hands began to pulse. Dropping the heart into the lake mud, she stared at it. Baboudina's heart had two eyes and a mouth, it was throbbing as it stared at her through the mud. A voice inside her head whispered softly, "You did not make a feast for me. You laughed at me. You must make amends."

Quickly, she lifted Baboudina's heart from the mud. The eyes stared at her as she wiped the mud from around the beating organ. This woman was now afraid for this was a miracle and she knew the *kayukgwahe'yak* spirits were watching as she carefully washed the heart clean in the lake's water. Slowly, the heart began to pulse louder and glowed an orange red. Baboudina's heart had great powers. A soft wind blew around her head, lifting her hair, whispering, "Baboudina is now *Ant'a'yi-qa*, the man-under the earth. You, you who brought him freedom from his pain, you are *W udzine'xe-yek* or curing spirit. Your path has been chosen."

Baboudina's heart was now enclosed between her two hands. She allowed herself to be spiritually pulled away from the lake, through the forest onto an area at the edge of a small mountain. There, in her mind she spiritually perceived a land where the snow had recently melted. Bodies were strewn all over the desolate landscape. Her eyes filled with tears to see so much death. As her spirit bent over each of the dead bodies, she swung her hands back and forth while holding the pulsating heart of Baboudina now filled with the lake water to drip onto the corpse. Slowly, death fled from the body allowing it to become warm, breathe and come alive. Carefully, patiently, spiritually she hurried back and forth from the lake to the area of bodies, dripping water onto each corpse.

One by one, she brought Baboudina's people back to life, using his heart and the lake water. Most of the revived people were weak, some had broken bones, and the healthier ones helped those who were having more difficulty. Once the people were strong enough, they asked her how she was able to bring about such a miracle. Hiding Baboudina's heart in the folds of her skirt, she gave them a story to believe.

She explained how she had taunted Baboudina, who was in reality the Chief of Mosquitoes. The people were lead to believe the freezing cold water was what had killed him. She related to them, how she had removed his heart and how Baboudina was lying dead beside the lake whose waters had helped heal them. The people asked to be taken to his body. Baboudina's woman, children and family were overcome with grief when they found his body ripped open and bloody. No one knew that his heart was well hidden in the woman's cedar bark skirt. As the people came to the lake, the woman quietly dropped Baboudina's beating heart into the lake. It fell down, down, down, down to disappear into the mud.

As his people knelt beside his body, they carefully placed moccasins on his feet, gloves on his hands and a knife in his belt. A child cried out to point at Baboudina's nose for now there was a large, white crystal. His people were unsure as to what magical quality this crystal had or how it should be prepared. The woman lifted the

Tsimshian the Deluge number 6

clear crystal and tossed it as far as she could into the lake.

A runner was sent to a neighboring longhouse for a shaman. His rattles alerted the people of his arrival. The long bearskin robes covered his sloping shoulders. He wore a leather apron painted with symbols of the sun, moon, and bears. The charms on his ankles and wrists rattled as he placed his tall bear mask on his head. Once he came out of his trance, Shaman told the people it would be best to honor Baboudina since he gave his life in order for them to have life. Building a huge fire pit, the people placed Baboudina's ravaged body upon it and they thanked him. As some of the people blew into the fire to keep it maintained, ashes flew into the air to become the mosquitoes that we have today. The lake still has the power to heal if one truly believes in the miracles of the *Na'guan'yaks*, or the Keeper of the Souls.

Notes:

There are those who believe one cannot heal unless one has felt pain or one has been extremely ill. Tsimshian people lived near the tall mountains covered with snow in the winter and the runoff lakes and rivers of spring and summer. All of these natural sources come with spirits and magic. The Keeper of Souls in the Underworld is kept busy with all of the natural disasters happening in this terrain. Life is fragile and short in a heartbeat. This story reflects the magic of bringing the dead back to life and the magic that still remains. Alfreda Sun Flower told this story to a group of my students at Cochiti Pueblo, during the winter of 1988, in New Mexico. She was eighty three years old and travelled the country, sharing her people's stories.

Glossary:

Ant'a'yi-qa – Man under the EarthVault who helps humans.

Dex-q!aowu'lk – Longhouse made of cedar tree trunks, cedar tree bark and chinked with mud.

Dji'yanasac – Eagle talon charm made from eagle's talon wrapped with a flower.

Chilkat blanket – Woven from softened cedar bark and mountain goat fur.

Hayic'nak' – Old Woman Underneath who guides EarthVault with a frozen beaver leg holds earth. She can shake the earth or hold it still.

Ketl-kiwa – Spiritual place of Torment, trapped between SkyVault and EarthVault.

Kiwa'a – Spiritual place of Happiness in SkyVault place.

Kayukwahe'yak – Spirits who watch and judge those on the EarthVault.

La'aya'k – Milky Way Rainbow, path to SkyVault.

Na'guan'yaks – Keeper of the Souls.

Nas'caki'yel – Supernatural roaming spirits who live in SkyVault.

Nexa'di – All worlds Creator.

Nukw-sati – Evil Witch, must be fed if she visits your home or death follows.

Qatuwu – 'What feels' as in being alive one feels pleasure and pain.

Tack'ku'di-hit – Eagles' nest house used for fasting before the hunt, also as a look out.

Tane'di – Clan emblem of otter.

Tu-kina-jek – A Spirit Guide for you to follow to the SkyVault.

Wasa'tu'wati – 'Kkeep your shadow' as in keep within your body, have a shadow.

Wudzine'ze-yek – Spirit who cures humans in EarthVault.

Yek – Sky Vault World above the earth.

7
SPIRITUAL WISDOM SAVES LIVES

An Angry River Calmed Down
Asian Indian

Long ago, when I was a young child. My father asked me to go with my mother and him to the River Nira to pray. My mother gave my father a look, saying, "She is too young. She will be disrespectful and there will be consequences."

My father smiled, "Don't worry. She is wise for her age and she needs to learn the ways of our village. If she asks, we can explain to her the importance of Mother Nira."

My mother was not convinced, walking ahead of us with her head held humbly, we followed her to the river. As we walked the distance from our small home to the mighty river, my father explained to me, "Pushpa, my cute little girl, your questions are valid. You should feel at ease to ask what you want, but there shouldn't be any disbelief in your heart. You see, every river is a goddess for us." Smiling up at him, while holding his large hand, I nodded. He continued, "What does river mean? River represents the water spirit. So, river is one of the five basic elements. Our lives are dependent on these great elements. We should respect them. Here in our village of Mekhli, water element is in the form of Nira River. She provides water to all of us. We use her water for our lives and for our farms. By watering the farms, we get grains. In this way she feeds us. She is our mother. She is our caretaker. She loves us. That's why we pray to her. While praying, we can feel that Mother Nira is standing near us, in front of us."

As we neared the river, there were other villagers standing in the water with their hands held in prayer. Their eyes were closed in humble prayer as well. My father lowered his voice, "All villagers also pray to Mother Nira just like us. We all ask her for her blessings. We ask for plenty of water for drinking and for irrigating our farms. We ask her to fulfill our wish of plentiful crops. We pray and beg her not to be angry with us in the rainy season."

Stopping, my father pointed to the river bank. "You are old enough now to know the history of our people. See here the shiny running waters of the Nira River are gray in color due to the sculpted stones of the *ghat*. These blackish gray-white colored old temples and the natural abundant shades of greenery give a peaceful, positive and perhaps pious impact on one's mind."

He spoke proudly, "All the villagers are deeply interested in the river and its surroundings. They respect the river because it supports them. Our lives are totally dependent on the river water. Nira River is considered the mother for the villagers, and of course for us. So, people call our river *Niramai* or Mother Nira." Kneeling down to my level, father looked deep into my eyes, his dark brown eyes were sincere as he said, "This is what we ask of her, 'Mother Nira, please be kind to us and do not destroy our village, villagers' homes, livestock and crops.' In this way all of us beg for her love and grace. She should be pleased by our honest prayer."

Mother waited for us near the turn in the path to the river. Pushing back my long bangs, holding my chin up to her face, she explained, "Nira River is able to fulfill our water needs for bathing, washing clothes and drinking water. This is where we get our water to survive. Someday, when you are a grown woman, you will understand how important she is to us." Picking me up in his strong arms, father continued, "The fields of our sugarcane farm, which are on the both sides of the river allows the land to remain lush and green. The river meets our lands' water needs. Our village has many types of trees," He pointed with his hand, "See these *pimpal, kadulimb trees*. Also, see these *vad* trees with their aerial roots maturing into thick trunks. These trees with their many different shades of green foliage shade our village and this graceful *ghat*. This ghat is a flight of sculpted stone steps, leading down to the Nira River. Village people from far away sometimes come to the *ghat*, taking a ritual dip in the river, washing their clothes on the *ghat* and then they go to the nearby *Mahadewa* or Lord Shiva and *Hanuman* temples to worship. It is believed that *Hanuman* is the protector of our village, so everyone goes to this temple for paying obeisance."

Mother said to my father, "Put her down, if she is old enough to come and pray, she is old enough to walk down to the *ghat* with us and into the water. You pamper her too much."

I was set firmly on the ground in front of them. Nodding his head to the other villagers who are wading into the water to pray, he whispered lovingly into my ear, "Do you understand? Are you satisfied now?"

Pulling on my mother's hand, I asked, "*Aai*, are there water snakes in the river water?"

171~

"Hush, my child!" My mother frowned at me, "The water current is fast and the water is holy. Do not ask such questions!"

I held onto my father's hand as we waded into the river to stand next to my mother and the other villagers. Mother glanced at me, then she smiled at my father. Then my father looked at Mother Nira with love in his eyes. My mother's and my eyes followed his gaze. We felt Mother Nira's spirit was just there in front of us. We were standing facing the rising sun. Bowing to the sun, my mother and father cupped their hands to gather water, standing upright they touched the water to their closed eyes.

I watched as their faces filled with virtuousness. Feelings of strong love for my 'mother the river' filled my entire being. Love warmed my body as the river water flowed around my bare ankles. I liked the sandy river bottom. It was soft and warm as it gushed between my toes. Acceptance and respect resided here in the river water, filling my being with love.

Quietly, I whispered to my father, "Oh! Yes! *Baba*, I like your view of the Mother Nira! Now, I understand, I will respect Mother Nira."

Even though I was frightened of behaving inappropriately, for I knew my father expected me to behave correctly, I mirrored their behavior, doing the same.

Lifting river water to my face, closing my eyes tight, tight, I prayed to beautiful Mother Nira. My father's words resonated in my thoughts. Suddenly, a bright light appeared in front of my closed eyes. Rising out of the water, was the image of a woman who was older than me. Lifting slowly up, out of the river with water dripping down her face and long hair, she stared at me. The red *kunku*, or the red spot on her forehead, didn't fall off with the water on her face. Blue bangles were on her arms and the lower half of her body was still under the water.

Large brown eyes blinked at me, startling me to open my eyes. There was nothing there! I glanced at my parents, but their eyes were closed for they were still praying. Quickly, I closed my eyes, again. All I saw was darkness behind my eyelids. Opening and closing my eyes, again and again, I tried to see her, but there was nothing there! Gasping, I became upset and stared at my mother and father who didn't appear to notice my concern.

Finally, my mother and father opened their eyes. Taking my hand, my father led me out of the river water. I skipped ahead of them, trying to hurry them away from the others. Once, we were by ourselves, I tugged on my father's arm, I asked him, "*Baba*, there was a woman who rose out of the water to look at me! She blinked at me! When I opened my eyes to see her better, she disappeared! *Baba*, who was she, why was she in the water, why did she blink at me? Did you see her, too?"

My mother clapped her hands and smiled as she spoke to my father, "You were correct, she is old enough! How wonderful, how blessed we are!"

My father just stood to gaze at me. Then putting his palms together in front of him and shutting his eyes, he turned to bow to Mother Nira. Quietly, he told me, "Pushpa, you are lucky, for do you know who was in your vision?"

Jumping up and down, I answered, "No, that's why I ask you. Who is she? She is older than I am, she was in the water all wet! Who is she?"

Staring at my mother, he lifted me onto his hip, "Mother Nira. Yes, Mother Nira. You saw Mother Nira. This is simply great! You are so lucky!"

My mother Indu looked at me lovingly. "Child, you have been blessed. This is a great honor! How proud we are of you! You are not an ordinary girl, but a special girl to whom Mother Nira gave a glimpse of her divinely self!"

Holding my hands in hers, she added, "Daughter, neither your father nor I have seen Mother Nira. This is a blessing for us and our family for you to have seen her in her beloved river."

All three of us walked quickly to our home. While walking beside my proud parents, I felt as if I was walking on air!

At the bench on the edge of our field, my father lifted me to sit beside him. "Pushpa, we are farmers. See here how our Mekhli village is near the banks of River Nira. Our small Mekhli village holds about four thousand people. Many are farmers. Some are rich because their land is irrigated by the waters of Nira."

Lowering his voice as others walked passed us, he pointed to the west, "River Nira is a tributary of Bhima River and flows through Pune District of Maharashtra in central-western India. Though the Nira River is a tributary, it never dries, not even in summer. Many months of the year, she flows full of water, touching both sides of the banks. See our sugarcane fields? This is our main crop. This is how we make enough money to live and do well."

He broke off a stem of the sugarcane, "Sugarcane requires a lot more water than other crops. The lives of our villagers revolve around farms, crops, bulls, ploughs, and of course water to irrigate our fields. Many times, we hear of people in other nearby places facing hardships with drought, with farmers worried about their farms drying up due to lack of water. Then, we realize how fortunate we are to have the perennial waters of Nira River."

Standing, we followed my mother up the hill to our humble home. Father continued to educate me, "Our family farm is on a higher level than that of the other villagers. Even so, we have a good supply of the river water. These fields here we grow *jowari* (sorghum) and wheat. All in all, our village Mekhli is a happy place with the people occupied with their farm work and blessed by the Nira River."

My mother bowed to the fields, "Our family is a happy family. This is thanks to the River Nira and your hard-working father! Now, you are old enough to help him in the fields and to go with us at dawn to the River Nira to pray. When we enter the house, tell your grandmother of your experience. Be gentle with her for she is old and deserves our respect."

We reached our home. I was anxious to share my new, unique experience with my grandmother. I ran inside our home. Shouting loudly, I said "*Aaji, aaji,* where are you? Come here. I have to tell you about a miracle."

My *aaji* is very old. She has bowed legs and is weak, it isn't easy for her to walk fast. Hearing my uproar, she tried to hurry. When I found her, I ran to hug her for I am so fond of my old *aaji*. Her face is wrinkled and her head is covered with her silvery-white hair.

Being elderly, her eyesight was bad and she could only hear out of one ear. Her few teeth gave her a jagged smile, but even so, her face was fresh and her memory was sharp. We loved her and she didn't just sit, but was always busy helping my mother with the household work.

Still hugging her around her waist, I laughed, telling her this was a blessed day. She put her gnarled fingers on the top of my head, "Pushpa, slow down. Take your time. Let me sit down and listen to you for I cannot hear you. Come, let's sit outside on an empty sack by the warm wall. Come."

Taking her hand, we sat with our backs against the warm wall of our home. Trying to be calm, I told her, "*Baba* and *aai* took me to the River Nira this morning early. I was nervous to go into the water. The village boys warned me about water snakes and bugs, but *aai* said there weren't any and not to be afraid. When I asked *baba* about why we went into the River Nira to pray, he explained it all to me."

"*Aaji,* was I worried I would embarrass my parents. Watching them, I did what they did and, *aaji, aaji* how can I describe to you what happened then? Oh, *aaji*, while my eyes were closed this strange woman rose out of the silvery water! She is older than I am and she was soaking wet. *Aaji*, she had water flowing off of her, down her face, off her hair, and she was dressed in this wet *saree*."

Jumping off, I stood close to *aaji*, "Her *saree* was bluish with water dripping off of her one shoulder. Her long hair looked really black because it was soaking wet, too. Her red dot on her forehead, *aaji*, it didn't fall off! The lower part of her body was stuck in the water, but she didn't look unhappy about it."

Putting my face very close to *aaji*'s eyes, I blinked, "*Aaji*, she blinked at me, like this! Blinked at me! This frightened me for I knew she wasn't real, but she looked real. I opened my eyes and poof! Poof! *Aaji*, she disappeared! She was gone! Even when I closed my eyes again and I really, really tried hard to see her again, she was gone."

Aaji put her arthritic hands on my shoulders, "Pushpa, sit down and listen." I sat down beside her with my excitement. *Aaji* took in a deep breath, "Mother Nira has blessed this family, our fields and our lives coming to you in a vision."

Interrupting her, "But she wasn't a vision, *aaji*! I saw her as alive as I see you right now!"

"Yes, yes, but you see, Pushpa, Mother Nira is a Holy Spirit. She is within the water of the river, she is within all of us, if we respect her and love her with all of our hearts. No one can really touch her for she is holy and she blessed you." *Aaji* wiped tears from her eyes. "Later, when you are in bed, I will tell you what happens if the people do not respect her."

Taking my hand in her rough hand, she pulled me closer to her. Kissing the top of my head, she said softly, "You are a blessing to the whole of our village. You have always been a blessing to this family, but now, you are learning the importance of believing."

"*Aaji*, tell me your story now, please?"

"No, it will be this evening. When you're in bed and your thoughts are clear this story will remain with you. Right now you are excited and filled with energy, tonight the story will mean more to you. Now, go and help your mother for I need to rest and think."

I frowned, sulking I looked down at my feet, "*Aaji*, tonight I might forget what happened this morning."

Aaji, smiled and as she smiled her wrinkles widened. I could see the few teeth in her mouth. She hugged me, touching my face with her skinny rough hand, she said, "Oh my pretty little granddaughter Pushpa,

I will answer all your questions when you are in your bed. I will tell you about a disaster that once happened here in our village. Our prayers worked. Mother Nira saved us from the disaster. I will not tell you now, but will tell you tonight. You need to help your kind mother and I need to meditate. I will tell you this evening after you have helped your mother with her work." Disgruntled, I ran away from her.

True to our family custom, every evening when I went to bed *aaji* would sit at my bedside, brushing my hair with her arthritic fingers. When she stopped, she would kiss me on my forehead. This was the signal for story time. I would nag her to tell me a long story. This was our ritual practice. Above all, she carried on the tradition of being an excellent storyteller.

That night, as usual *aaji* came to me when I was ready for bed. I was anxious to hear about the disaster and about Mother Nira. She smiled as she sat near me, ready to comb my hair with her fingers. Taking her hand, I asked "Please tell me about the disaster that once happened here in our village. How did Mother Nira save us?"

Shaking her head, *aaji* became serious, "You need to be calm or I will not tell you this story. Are you calm?"

Lying down flat on my bed, I nodded to her. She closed her eyes and sighed, "Pushpa, this story is true and this happened long ago when I was about your age." Her face lit up as she opened her eyes, "Believe it or not, I was once young, as young as you are now! I was young and full of energy, believing that I would never grow old."

"*Aaji*, you are still beautiful to me."

"Hush, hush now. Let me tell this story. Pushpa, this was a very long time back. Oh, wait, I was young at that time. I believe I was in my late teens or early twenties. Newly married, I came to live here, in this home, away from my village and my parents. Your grandpa was very handsome and energetic. He was an expert in swimming. He went to swim with his friends in River Nira every day and in all seasons. Many times, he scared me by jumping into River Nira when the water runoff was high and dangerous. He was the expert swimmer! All villagers appreciated his courage and swimming skills.

"At that time, there was no sugarcane farming in our Mekhli village. Villagers were interested in growing *jowar* (or Sorghum) in their farms. Our village was famous for *jowar* crop. I remember, once the *jowar* crop was so abundant. We were all happy. There was a meeting of all villagers. In that meeting they decided that all *jowar* bags would be in bullock carts. Then there would be a grand procession of all the loaded bullock carts. The procession would go to *Hanuman* temple to thank him (Hanuman) for the abundant crop. Because He is a protector of our village."

Clapping her hands, her eyes glowed as she continued, "As per the plan, every farmer loaded his *jowar* bags in bullock carts nicely decorated with garlands. Many bullock carts gathered on the bank of River Nira."

She lifted her index finger on her right hand, "First of all, farmers paid obeisance to Mother Nira. Then the procession started. All the bulls were decorated with ornaments and colorful shawls. Their necks were adorned with garlands of flowers. Oh, Pushpa, it was gloriously beautiful for all the carts were embellished with flowers of all colors. Every farmer on his cart was wearing a new white *dhotar*, a colorful shirt and *pheta* (festive turban) on his head."

Waving her hands over her head, Grandmother demonstrated, "The *phetas* or Marathi traditional turbans of Maharashtra are of red, blue, yellow, and green and some are even in brighter colors. Everyone was in a very joyous mood. Some villagers were playing on *dhol*, a double-headed drum, and on that rhythm many villagers and children were dancing. The scene of decorated bulls, colorful carts, and traditional *phetas* was amazing! A lot of people from nearby villages were also present to watch the grand procession. Pushpa, your grandpa was the leader of that procession."

Recounting the wonderful description of grand procession, grandma became silent. She closed her eyes. She was dreaming sweet memories. she was seeing grandpa with her old weakened eyes. Then I noticed two tears on her wrinkled old cheek. I was at a loss as to how to respond to her. And moreover, I was anxious to hear about the disaster. "But, *aaji*, what happened that was bad?"

Grandma took a long breath. She wiped her eyes. Studying my face, she started to tell the story further. "Pushpa, all was so very well. We were all happy. Every rising sun brought the people countless happy moments. The blessings of the River Nira were plenty and with her blessed water, all the villagers had good crops." Bowing her head, she frowned, "Pushpa, I don't remember the exact year, but I believe two years passed after the grand procession. The rainy season started on time. All villagers were happy. Their farms were well ploughed, ready to sow.

"One morning there was a heavy downpour. The heavy drenching rain continued through the afternoon. We could hear the downpour on the roof through the night. The next morning there was no sun. It seemed that heavy black clouds had swallowed the sun, but there wasn't much rain. The following day there was a storm accompanied by rain and the weather became quite violent. Stormy winds, heavy rainfall and lightning continued. Mother River Nira was rising slowly."

Gasping, Grandmother raised her hands above the height of the bed, "At last River Nira flooded. There had been two days of heavy rain and it wasn't stopping. Everywhere there was water and mud. It was very difficult to go outside as the farms flooded. The animals were in danger for there was too much water! River Nira's water rose higher and higher, soon the river bridge disappeared. Every hour, the floodwater kept rising."

Stroking my arm, she shook her head, "After the sunset, the night was terribly dark. No stars could be seen. Only dark clouds filled the dark sky with rain. The strong winds kept blowing. In the middle of this dark night we could hear the sound of the roaring floodwaters, mixed with the downpour of rain and blustery wind. Trees collapsed into the fast current as the bank of the river collapsed. Every hour, the loud cracking of ripped tree branches came closer and closer. This was terrifying and disheartening. Buffalos and cows were bellowing loudly. Dogs were crying and howling."

Grandmother put her hands over her ears, "Oh, Pushpa, all of us were awake all night just knowing everything could be destroyed by morning! Fear gripped everyone. At last the night passed. In the morning, there was still no sun, but at least there was some daylight."

She shook her head, "In that light villagers saw the destructive muddy, roaring water everywhere. It seemed like Mother Nira was bellowing with rage filled wrath. Terrified villagers ran to be on higher ground. Pushpa, our home is at good elevation so we were relatively safe, but we were still afraid.

"All villagers came together and discussed what to do about this natural disaster. We were worried about the fury of our Mother Nira. People spoke, 'We may have made a serious mistake.' Others said, 'We must have insulted our Mother Nira. So, she is angry.' Many agreed, 'Maybe we have insulted her, but not on purpose. We are her beloved children. She loves us. Believe me, she will not destroy us.' Yet many believed that we might have done something wrong."

Grandmother smiled, "Someone remembered the wise old man at the edge of the village. His name was Ramrao. He was the chief of our village. Ramrao was in his eighties at that time. He had seen many rainy seasons, and experienced Mother Nira's flooding, her storms and other disasters. He was there at the meeting. He was coughing as he listened to the discussion. He spit as he began to talk, yet everyone was eager to hear his words. They were confident that he could show some way out.

"Ramrao looked about to see there that was only the brown colored water roaring swiftly all around us. There were bushes and trees flowing downriver. The broken huts, goats, bulls, cows, and buffalo were being carried away in the flood. Many of the houses were collapsing in front of his eyes. Farms and what had been standing crops had disappeared in the flood. Everywhere there was fear and despair. Death was hovering over us with a feeling of helplessness. Looking upwards, praying to God, everyone was helping each other in whatever way possible, especially children, pregnant women, recently delivered women, and elders."

Grandmother took a deep breath to lower her voice, she continued, "Ramrao began describing to the villagers how they had dealt with the previous major flood. 'People, I have never seen such devastation by Mother Nira in my life. I remember, long before there was a heavy flood, fear and desperation had come to us at that time, also. This time the situation is much worse.

"I remember, my father was the chief of the village and he had advised all villagers to pray to Mother Nira. He asked the *suvasinis,* married women to bring *oti* or the ritual materials to her. At this time it was a green blouse piece, a whole coconut with the dried husk intact, a few whole almonds, a few betel leaves, a few turmeric rhizomes, some *halad* and *kunku* on a copper plate. As per his suggestion and advice, some married women brought *oti* material with them."

Putting her hands together, Grandmother patted her palms, "Then all villagers and married women prayed to Mother Nira with all their being for this was their only hope! The *oti* ritual was performed. First, the married women offered her flowing water some *halad* and *kunku* powder. Carefully, they wrapped the coconut, almonds, betel leaves and turmeric rhizomes in the green blouse piece and offered those to the angry water of Mother Nira."

Bowing her head over me, Grandmother closed her eyes, "The women put together both their palms in front of them and shutting their eyes paid obeisance to Mother Nira. The married women and all the villagers prayed to River Nira to be calm for they loved her. They asked her to withdraw her all destroying flood water. They prayed, 'Please save us. Save our lives, our village, our homes, our farms, our livestock and everything. O Mother Nira, you are so kind. You love us. You give us water. You give us crops. You give us grains. And, you also give us life. We are alive here only because of you. O kind Mother Nira, please calm down. Save us. Save us.'"

"Your grandfather and I were quiet when we heard this story from

An Angry River Calm Down

Ramrao. Every villager was silent, listening intently to the story. They were also watching the rising flood water, acutely aware of imminent further losses. Then as if they understood what he was saying, the people hurried to perform the *oti* ritual.

"Being a married woman, I gathered with the other married women whose husbands were still alive. We went to the houses above the flood water to take quick baths. We put on new *sarees* and prayed to the idols of God in the dry homes. Then, as the married women who were to perform this ritual, we gathered together in a short time at the edge of the fast-flowing river. All of the village people were waiting for us.

"After offering the *halad* and *kunku,* we wrapped the rest of the items in a beautiful green blouse. This we laid on top of the surging, muddy river water of Mother Nira. Immediately, we put our hands together and prayed with all our might to the River Nira. While praying my eyes welled up with tears for this was important and we were responsible for saving our village and our lands."

Sniffing, Grandmother's voice wavered, "While we prayed, 'O our beloved and kind Mother Nira, you have always protected us for you give us life every year, every rainy season. You are so beautiful. Some of us even swim while you are flooded. You have never drowned us. You never took our life. We have never seen you angry. O Mother Nira, we might be wrong, we might have committed some mistakes, we agree. But we haven't done so intentionally. We haven't insulted you on purpose."

Her voice was now a soft whisper, "O mother, do tell us, how a son could insult his mother on purpose? And how a loving mother could ever be angry with her children? How could she take their lives? How could she destroy their homes, farms and livestock? O Mother Nira, if we have committed any mistakes, please do forgive us kindly by your loving heart, big heart. O Mother Nira, we have offered you *oti* to show you respect. Please, put on the green blouse we placed on your flooded roaring waves. Please, put the *halad* and *kunku* on your bright forehead. We have offered fruits in your honor. Please accept our *oti* offerings and bless us. Protect us. Save us. Please! Become your usual calm, soon. O Mother Nira, you are our beloved mother!'"

Wiping her nose on a tissue, Grandmother smiled with all of her wrinkles, "All the villagers and the married women prayed with tears in our eyes."

Clapping her hands suddenly, Grandmother scared me as she said, "Then all of a sudden, there was a sense of calm. We felt that Mother Nira had heard our prayers. We had a firm belief that her flood waters would not increase anymore. There was nothing more that we could do and so we waited and watched. Men took wooden measuring sticks to calculate the water level. The water level didn't seem to be increasing, but it wasn't decreasing either.

"Slowly, slowly the floodwater level started going down... Finally, we were out of danger. What a relief! Everyone was glad. Everyone was happy. Everyone was looking at the decreasing floodwater and praising the kind, beloved Mother Nira. Because of *oti* and our humble prayers, Mother Nira had regained her awareness of our respect and love. She had blessed her children. Now, she had forgiven us, her children. All of us working together, saved our lives. In this way the disaster ended and our Mother Nira, our angry river had calmed down!"

I had been absorbed in listening to my Grandmother's story. I hadn't imagined Mother Nira could ever become such a powerful, destructive force, but then she could be calmed through belief in her motherly love and sincere prayers.

Completing her story, Grandmother asked me, "Pushpa, did you like the story?"

I smiled and said, "Yes, *aaji*, you are an excellent storyteller! But tell me why did I see the beautiful woman with my eyes closed?"

Grandma said, "As your father explained to you, she is Mother Nira. She loves you. She wants you to understand her and know she exists. Now, you need to go every day to her. There you will bathe and pray to her for she will protect you and this village. This is the reason she came to you."

Tucking my sheet around me, she added, "Now sleep, dear, for you must get up early to go to the river and then you have to go school."

I went to sleep thinking of Mother Nira and her love towards us, her villagers, and her children.

Whenever Mother Nira has flooded, villagers of Mekhli pray and the married women or *suvasinis* perform the *oti* ritual. This tradition continues since those bygone days and is done even today. It is believed that if we offer sincere prayers and perform the *oti* ritual, River Nira will never trouble us. The Water Element will be satiated. It will bless you and us, her children.

Notes:

There is a belief that if a married woman performs the ritual of a sacred offering or an oti to a fierce, flooding river, then the raging river is pleased and calms down. Natural elements have unfathomable, boundless and unbridled powers, which man has had to bow down to since the beginning of life on earth. Awed and overwhelmed by these natural enormous powers, humankind has tried to appease them through various rituals. Man has achieved great progress through science, yet still hasn't been able to overcome nature. This realization of his limitations has brought respect for the observance of traditional rituals, which coexist in Eastern Indian society. Traditional Eastern Indians offer coconuts to river flood waters in order to pacify and appease the Water Goddess as they are both of liquid form.

This legend was narrated to me by Smt. Savitri Jag*dal*e. She is a resident of a town called Satara, Maharashtra state. The legend is retold in my own words.

Glossary:

Aai – Mother.
Aaji – Grandmother.

Baba – Father.

Babhul or Babul tree – The gum arabic tree, an acacia (Acacia nilotica) native to India.

Halad and kunku – Turmeric powder.

Kadulimb or Neem – A type of evergreen tree (Azadirachta indica) native to India.

Kunku or kumkuma – A red powder made from turmeric or any other local materials. Women put red colored kunku on their forehead. It looks like a red spot. It has a cultural significance. It represents prosperity. It is also widely used for worshiping the Hindu gods and goddesses. It is a sign of respect in social life.

Pimpal or Peepal or Bodhi tree – Ficus religiosa or sacred fig. It is a species of fig native to the Indian subcontinent.

Suvasini – A married woman whose husband is alive.

Oti – Symbolically, Oti means offering. It is a traditional ritual to honor woman's fertility. Oti literally means the lower abdomen of a woman. This is the part where her uterus is located. To offer Oti is therefore a symbolic expression of one's wish that 'May your womb be filled.' In this ritual, one married woman honors another married woman's fertility by offering a *saree*, blouse piece, rice or wheat grains, coconut, betel nuts, dried dates, and young shoots of turmeric plant, all of which are suggestive of a new creation and in this case, conception. The woman concerned receives the offerings in the folds of her *saree*.

Vad – Banyan tree.

The Story of the Rain Na'wai, Tsia
NATIVE AMERICAN

It is obligatory for all of the young people in the *No-na-ai-te clan* or Cloud Clan to become members of the Rain Society or the *Kat'sina*. Ko'baitya wished to become a member of the *Na'wai* Society, which would lead him through training into the sub-society that best fit his personality. *Na'wai* was the head Medicine Society relegated to those who were highly trained in working with Nature and Healing. It was common for this initiation to take a great deal of time and expense for Ko'baitya would need to provide food for the Elder who trained Ko'baitya in order to belong to the *Na'wai*. Ko'baitya's family had survived a long summer's drought and they did not have enough food to offer for his initiation. He was a tall young man of fifteen, with waist long hair, black and straight that had never been cut as this was traditionally in order to belong to a Medicine Society.

His father had been a member of the Flint Society or the *Hictianyi* and was known to be wise in the way of spiritual healing. Handing his son a long braided strand of multicolored corn, Father told him, "This corn holds great qualities in healing. There is the yellow corn representing the northern spirits of the mountain lion. Blue-green has the healing power of the west, holding the might and strength of bear. South has the embodiment of healing in the spirit energy of the clever badger. White has the brightness of the sun in the east, allowing the wolf to return to their lair and rest. The celestial sphere of the zenith is within the light yellow corn where the sky spirits peer through to watch their people on earth, using the flying eagle. The lowest of our six spheres is the one right underneath your spirit energy. This occurs at a time when you have used all your knowledge and need to pull from the center of Mother Earth. This is the color blue-black, which has all the colors of life intertwined within it. Color personifies intense healing energy brought by the pack rat who can forage for food and find shelter anywhere and with severe deadly force will protect themselves and their young. Go, take this sacred gift to your head medicine man or *Na'wai* Elder and be humble in your being."

Ko'baitya carefully carried the tightly braided corn in both hands as he walked to the door of the *Na'wai* ceremonial chamber. Knocking four times, he waited until an Elder opened it, "What is it you require, my son?"

Lowering his head in modesty, Ko'baitya quietly handed the colored corn to the man, "These are my gifts to the most Elder of the *Na'wai* Society with my humble request to become one of you."

The Elder took the strand of braided corn inside and closed the log door. Ko'baitya stood patiently staring at the width of the logs making up the thick wooden door. Slowly, it opened. "Are you the son of the Flint Healer who lives near the terraced gardening at the edge of the foothills?"

Closing his eyes, nodding gently, he murmured, "Yes, but my request comes from within my soul, not from my father's demands."

Gently laughing, the Elder said, "Come inside, my son. We would not have allowed you in if your father was pushing you to become one with the Society."

Ko'baitya followed the Elder into an inner chamber. This room was specifically placed with the Flint Society room on the northwest side of the Plaza of the Pueblo. The Elders outlined his training, which was intense and took several years to accomplish. Several of the other novices had given their notice and had chosen a different path only after a few months. Ko'baitya stayed firm in his conviction to become a *Na'wai* and after four years he was brought before the Society's council for his final testing. His mother and father had not been allowed involvement in his early training and now they were proud of their son who had endured fasting, purging, testing with solitude and the learning of chants and prayers that were complicated and constantly quizzed even after little sleep. Ko'baitya had grown in maturity and the Elders felt that now he was ready to be tried as a *Na'wai* in the real world.

Ko'baitya was brought before the Society's senior council. He was to sit among them in front of the altar placed against one wall. There were fresh feathers tied to tall poles delicately carved at each end of the altar. Finely ground cornmeal was lying in flat clay bowls at different locations around the slat altar. The floor of the ceremonial chamber was dirt washed in goats' blood to harden and give it a rich red color. In front of the slat altar was the sandpainting. A clay bowl filled with powdered fine cornmeal was given to Ko'baitya as he knelt respectively before the sandpainting. Carefully, he handed the bowl of cornmeal to the Elder of the Flint Society who in turn gave the bowl to the head Elder of the Kapina Society. Again, the bowl was passed to the head of the Snake Society. As the bowl was passed, each Elder took a scoop of the cornmeal to hold in his hand as he shared with the other members of his society who were sitting behind him.

The Elder of the Snake Society opened the leaves of an empty cornhusk. Pouring in the remaining cornmeal into it, he tied four knots in the ends of the cornhusk. Each knot resembled the number of testings Ko'baitya must pass for his training. His mother and father were now given entrance into the ceremonial chamber. Ko'baitya stood, nodding to them as he was escorted out of the chamber. His mother and father had picked three other women and three other men who were to stay with them in the main chamber for four days making important ceremonial items for Ko'baitya transference into becoming a true member.

His mother with the three other women were to make clay fetishes representing what they believed Ko'baitya's purpose was to be. In a separate room, his father with the four other men discussed Ko'baitya's personality, character and their idea of his purpose. Taking a dried piece of cottonwood root, the men carefully carved an 'iariko' or corn-ear 'kat'sina' figure. The curvy piece of root slowly took shape into that of a spirit holder with long black hair, having specific nature symbols relating to Ko'baitya's strengths. The four men passed around this piece of root as each one silently carved or painted a symbol they felt would empower Ko'baitya. The iariko carving was completed with symbols of rain, lightning, and men carrying deer after a successful hunt. The women made their clay fetishes with cornhusk bases. Once they were dried by the altar's fire, they noticed the items were all relative to rain, lightning and the hunt.

After three days, Ko'baitya returned to the main chamber. He wore only his breechcloth. The four women and the four men were kneeling, leaning against the far wall from the slat altar. Ko'baitya chose his Spirit Mother and his Spirit Father who were to guide him in the Fire society. On the fourth day, he was called into the Fire society chamber. Their wooden slat altar was up, a sandpainting was completed on the floor, using the symbols made by his family. His ceremonial mother stood on Ko'baitya's right and Ko'baitya's ceremonial father stood on his left. Four medicine men sang a song and when it ended, the head of the Fire society entered the main room from behind the altar to pick up a basket filled with sticks. These were split twigs of kanyi or juniper.

This medicine man was known as the Na'wai or head medicine healer. Dancing around the sand painting twice, going from west to north to east and finally south, he took the baskets of sticks to the fireplace and ignited them, filling the room with dense gray smoke. As he moved around the sandpainting twice more, the juniper twigs in full flame, he stood with his head high, facing the altar. Removing a small pouch from his belt with his free hand, he tugged on the leather tie to open it. Using his index finger by sticking it into the pouch, he removed some *Hakanyi-wawa* paste to rub on the inside of his mouth. This herb mixture was known to protect the mouth from fire. The flaming sticks continued to burn in the basket. Ko'baitya studied each movement made by the *Na'wai*.

Lifting the wet end of one of the burning sticks from the basket, the *Na'wai* carefully placed the hot fire into his mouth. Quickly, shutting his lips and swallowing, the stick was removed from his mouth as charred wood. The *Na'wai* did this with each of the burning sticks. As he finished with one stick, it was returned into the basket. Once this task was completed, the *Na'wai* knelt beside Ko'baitya. Removing one stick at a time, the charred end of each stick was rubbed over Ko'baitya's body, turning him into a spirit holder. Now, Ko'baitya was to fast until the next day.

On the fifth day of this ceremony, the Elders brought sticks into the ceremonial chamber, placing them into the altar basket. This day was the testing of Ko'baitya's ability to hold magical power. Ko'baitya was brought into the room to stand beside the altar. The *Na'wai* nodded to him. Ko'baitya reached for the basket of sticks. Going to the small fire in front of the altar, he lit each stick carefully placing the wet end of the stick down inside the basket. As he was taught, he walked from the east to the south to the west to the north two times around the sandpainting. The chanters sang as he shuffled to the left side of the altar.

The *Na'wai* handed Ko'baitya the pouch from his waist belt. Ko'baitya opened it as he had been shown the day prior. Swabbing the inside of his mouth carefully, for the basket of flaming sticks was getting hot in his hand, he gave the pouch back to the *Na'wai*. Standing in front of the sandpainting, Ko'baitya lifted a burning stick to place the flames inside his mouth. Gently closing his lips, the fire was extinguished. Ko'baitya did this with each of the flaming sticks. His lips were hot and the palette of his mouth was sore by the time he finished. Handing the basket to his ceremonial mother, he moved to the right side of the altar.

His ceremonial father stood proudly lifting a leather ceremonial bag filled with small sticks sharpened at each end. Taking one of the sticks from the bag, the ceremonial father lifted it into his open mouth with the sharp end down, he swallowed it in one gulp. Handing the bag to Ko'baitya, he nodded. Ko'baitya turned to the Medicine Healer. The *Na'wai* nodded. Ko'baitya studied his ceremonial father's face. There was no sign of emotion. Doing this task was expected, Ko'baitya opened the leather bag wide. Taking one of the smaller sharp sticks from the bag, he closed his eyes as he put the sharp object into this mouth. The end of the stick poked his throat as he maneuvered it with his tongue. Finally, gathering saliva in his mouth, he swallowed. The stick slid down his throat. Ko'baitya completed this testing with the swallowing of all eight of the sharp sticks. As he handed the leather bag back to his ceremonial father, the Na'wai stepped forward to take it from his hand, "Now, you are to be accepted by brother clan members."

Ko'baitya was lead around the sandpainting four times to eventually sit in front of it. This painting was of many different colors, depicting the sacred honawai'aiti animals. These spirit animals represented guides, protectors and wisdom. Illustrated in the sand were all of the predatory animals, including the lion, bear, badger, pack rat, eagle, snake and wolf. Around the outside of the sandpainting were the threatening mocomi or the spiritual enemies of the Tisa Pueblo people.

Ko'baitya was given fire sticks to carry in his medicine bag for these gave him the power to call fire, rain or lightning. The initiation ceremony was done, now it was time for him to complete the Hanykio or summer ceremony. Ko'baitya was taken from the pueblo to be taught by the other Elders. When the sun reached its height in the summer, Ko'baitya entered into the Lake of the Dead where he performed the ceremony for the Dead. At last, he was now a member of the Kwiraina'a society. At the next Pueblo dance, Ko'baitya had become Mokaitc or one who has the spirit of the mountain lion. His face mask was painted yellow with a red design of a hand on the left side of the curved facial mask. Unspun cotton was tied to the top of his mask with eagle and owl feathers tied at the back of his head. There was a horn lifting from the mask's forehead with red lightning designs. He was given a soapweed whip to hold in his righthand and a bow and arrow in his left hand. Ko'baitya was trained to have the power of the mountain lion and the ability and strength to maintain the weather.

Women are allowed to join, but the Tsia prefer men for they are able to leave the Pueblo for long periods of time and they tend to be the most active in the No-na-ai-te clan. The young people are called to belong because of their ability to interrelate with the Cloud People who with the Kat'sina can bring rain and snow. The magical Kat'sina are participants in the Ho'na-ai-te of the Society of Kwiraina'a where they take on the power to stop the rain. Ko'baitya was now considered a Cloud Clan member, or a Ho-na-ai-te known as He-who-stops-rain, and was chosen to accompany the caiyaik or hunting warriors on a seasonal deer hunt.

Cooler winds were blowing down the canyons, bringing northern cranes, honking geese and fat ducks. Large game would begin to travel down from the snowcapped mountains to forge for food. Soon, the Rio Grande would ice over and herds of wild animals would begin to relocate to the southeast, far away from the pueblos. The terraced gardens had been tilled under with wooden hand-held hoes. The last of the berries gathered were preserved in deeply woven baskets, placed in back rooms of thick adobe walled homes. Animal fat used in bread making, treating leather and medicine curing was almost gone. Leather was needed to sew buckskin winter clothes for toddlers born last spring. Meat was needed for the winter meals lasting through seven months of cold. The time had come for hunters to bring in game before the freezing winter months of thick clouds and deep mounds of snow.

The *Caiyeik Nawai* or hunter official went to the political chief or *Tiamunyi* to ask permission for a hunt. This brought a ceremony in the underground kiva. The *Caiyeik* clan or hunting clan discussed the importance and necessity for this hunt with the *Masewi* or war captain. He approved, but first the men chosen must give a prayer feather of *wabanyi* with beads to animal spirit at the altar on top of the Jemez Mountain. Each man was responsible for the taking of the animal's life and the animal's spirit guide must be shown respect. The *Masewi* war chief chose Ko'baitya to go with them for his first initiation. This was a great honor.

Tall black mesas and deep purple gorges accentuated the landscape of crooked flowing canyons and meandering silver river valleys of green turning golden. Men's short breechcloths were wrapped around waist leather belts. Hunters wore buckskin shirts, painted with their own designs to keep them warm in early morning and late evening winds. During the heat of day, the shirts were tied around their waist, allowing the sun to warm their bodies as they ran. Hard soled, soft topped moccasins were tied around ankles. Some men wore leggings for protection against cactus spears and knife grass wounds.

The first day out, the men joked and spoke of family while laughing and sharing stories. Their long hair was tied back in a chongo, or a tight wrap at the nape of their neck, to keep hair away from their faces. Ko'baitya studied the men as he walked beside them. The second day was quieter for the men were moving away from familiar lands. The third day became a concern for the trackers were having difficulty finding any sign of a herd. Ducks and geese were easily brought down with the hunters' arrows for their dinners as they traveled. At night, the men joked about Ko'baitya's ability to transform a herd of deer for them. The lead trackers decided to run ahead, for there was no reason for all of the men to go in a direction if there were no deer. Cool evenings found warm fires. Orange sunsets brought dark shadows while men shared hunting stories. Ko'baitya listened as coals cooled to have the men slowly find burrowing sandy beds for sleep.

By the time the men were gathered in the morning, the trackers had returned to share that they had seen fresh deer tracks going off toward the river, but they weren't worth the effort to follow. Other tracks verged to the higher plains, these were in greater number, but the herd was easily two days ahead of them. It was decided the hunters would stay closer to the tracking team, running full-out to catch the larger herd heading for the flatlands. Ko'baitya kept his water bladder tied against his waist to keep it from banging as he ran.

Hunters tried to nudge him off balance, laughingly calling, "Hey, Medicine Man, where did you get those long legs? Who said you were allowed to keep up with us?"

A short fast runner shoved him to the side, "When are you going to beat your drum, Music Man? Come on, beat that drum and bring the deer to us! I'm tired of running in this heat!"

Shaking his head, Ko'baitya said nothing as he ran ahead of the jokers. His small drum was wrapped in soft leather skin strapped to his back with his father's flute. During the cloudless day, it was hot and bothersome, but in the cold of night the knowledge of its magic kept him warm. Ko'baitya held fast to his purpose.

Traveling east for a three days' time, they arrived at a plateau. Dark sentinel mesas with steep canyon walls were now behind them. Ahead was only a flatland of dry earth, faded brown with scraggly rabbit bush dotting the plains accompanied with stunted juniper trees. The hot sun cooked the land, wilted the bush and baked the runners as they raced behind the trackers. As they traveled to the east, the land split, dividing into two different high ledges with a deep flat gorge separating them. One plateau went due north, the other pointed east.

Dinner was scarce that night for there were no fowl to hunt. Dried jerky was washed down with water from the warm bladder bags. The leaders decided it would be most beneficial if the hunters were to split into two teams. In the morning, one group would go to the north, although why the herds of deer would go north, no one could explain. The other group would run east, hoping to catch the largest herd before it would divide again. This would keep the deep gorge between them, relaying news would have to be done with smoke in the night sky.

Early morning sun, found the original group of hunters detached into two smaller groups. As they migrated, separating further and further apart, they no longer could communicate using whistles. Spirits were high among the hunter warriors for plateau hunting would herd the deer over the cliffs to sudden death. Wounded deer were quickly killed off by dead-aim bow and arrow shooters. Foot holes chiseled into the cliff escarpment allowed hunters to descend, retrieving the game. This meant less danger for hunting out in the open field, which could bring chaos. Animals boxed in would stampede or charge individual men, arrows would fly possibly hitting men as well as deer. Cliff hunts pushed frightened game safely into the spirit world.

Each hunter warrior clan had bundles of sacred cornmeal or *petana* to sprinkle on the heads of the dead deer, asking for forgiveness in prayer from the Great Spirits. Great Spirits provided animals as food to mankind with their divine spirit. Once the animal was killed, thanks was given to the animals' spirits in prayer, allowing the Great Spirit to have the animal reborn again. This maintained the equilibrium of life for animals and mankind.

The two hunting teams traveled for many days. At night, the smoke was kept close to the ground for no new sightings had been found. Their quest for herds of deer appeared endless. The joking was now somber silence. Dark eyes stared into the glowing night fires as bodies rested. Ko'baitya quietly chanted for clouds to show them the way. He had kept pace with the best of them as they trotted across the flat dusty land. They had not seen a single bird, squirrel or jack rabbit. Not even a high flying eagle chose to accompany them. A soft breeze blew the flames of the fire to the east. Ko'baitya took this as a sign that the deer were nearby. One of the men whittled on a piece of wood only to toss it into the fire. Worry of not finding deer had entered into their minds. A hungry winter brought fear, illness and death. Ko'baitya tried to hear the trackers' conversation, but they conversed in soft whispers.

Finally, one morning, they heard the tracker's whistles. Hair was loosened to flow over bare backs. Arrows were pulled from quivers and bows were stretched. Hunters kneeled hunkering close to the earth. Ahead near the edge of a flat cliff was an area of high sweetgrass growing around an indent filled with stagnant rain water. Lead hunters were on all fours creeping through the tall green blades of grass. Feathers tied on the top of their heads, in their hair gave the appearance of birds jumping from bush to bush. Quietly, those behind them fanned out as silent as still air. Deer continued to graze unaware of their foe. One loud whistle cut through the silence. Leaping from their positions, the hunters screamed, catcalled, and raced straight at the confused animals startled by the movement and noise.

In terror the deer fled, jumping over the cliff to the rocks below. As fast they leaped, hunters followed being quick with their deadly arrows to release the spirit of the wounded deer. This hunt was accomplished within minutes. Yucca braided ropes held at the top by stronger men lowered the cliff carvers as they hollowed foot holds down to the lower gorge where the animals were lying dead. Once below, hunters asked the spirits for forgiveness in the killing of the deer. Each of the hunters prayed as they sprinkled sacred cornmeal on the heads of each of the dead deer. Spirits became one with the deer and once the deer were killed, the spirits were released after a sacred prayer of forgiveness. This allowed the spirit of the deceased deer to become another deer once again. This brought the survival of life and the continued strong belief in the spirits for without them man would not flourish.

Sharp knives professionally skinned the deer, sliced meat wrapped tightly into skins. The entrails were placed out in the open to feed migrating birds who carried prayers to the sky. Every part of the deer's body had a purpose and each body part was a sacred gift to man. The head and the backbone of the deer were blessed with beads and red ochre carried by the accompanying war chief. These body parts were placed in shallow troughs of dirt to be lightly covered. It is said that when the hunters leave the kill sight and are far away, the deer rise up as in the circle of life and death and life.

After a day's journey toward the west, the way home, kindling wood was gathered, sharing a good hunt brought the excitement of survival. An evening sky blanketed the earth in dark purple clouds as night fires burned bright. Sentinels called out to tell of smoke on the horizon. The other team had been successful as well. Ko'baitya led the men in a night chant in gratitude to the Great Spirits. The well fed hunters slept peacefully. This winter no one would go hungry. Families would be safely fed, babies would have warm leather clothes and the medicine men would have animal fat for their healings.

In the morning, Ko'baitya helped the men wrap the meat tighter in the deerskins. These meat bundles were attached to collected juniper tree branches and tied with leather strips. Seven branches were heavy with the wrapped freshly cut meat, tied and hanging. The *Caiyaik* were professionals at butchering, wrapping and carrying the fresh kill. Singing and chanting with appreciation to the Spirits, as they had been taught, the men retraced their way west. Ko'baitya now a *Ho-na-ai-te*, or He-who-is-able-to-Stop-Rain, was with the larger group of hunters. Two men carried the thick branch. One end was carried on the shoulder of one man with the other end of the branch on the shoulder of the man behind him.

By evening of the second day, they met the other group of hunters. Laughing and slapping each other on the back, they shared stories of their hunt. The *Tiamunyi* had given them seven days to go out, hunt and return. Therefore, they kept a fast walk until the moon was high in the night's sky. The next morning, they were quick to gather items and set their path home. The distance they had traveled was far from home. Cold mornings gave way to burning hot afternoons with cool winds chilling their bodies as night fell, they kept moving. Clear blue skies, filled with direct sun brought the high mesas into view with colorful canyons pointing the way to their pueblo. Marching, leaden branches behind branches the proud hunters were eager to be home.

Progressing west, the days became cooler, terrain changed to sacred mountains on the horizon. On the sixth day, clouds gathered billowing toward them from the northwest. By mid-afternoon, a soft rain began, the canyon became deep with rain flowing downhill into the gorge. Hunters began to trot, meat packed branches were swinging from side to side, and heavy shoulder bundles of small cuts of meat were hugged to chests as the *Caiyeik* hunters hurried to higher ground. A high wall of water swelled behind them, roaring as rocks and dirt were channeled into its embrace. Men were now racing, carrying the juniper branches tied with the kill high over their heads as they pushed forward.

Suddenly, the water level around them rose higher and higher. Pulsing liquid thundered behind them, wetting their moccasins and then rising to their ankles. Yelling at one another, the two separated groups joined as one. Quickly, tossing the heavy branches from one hunter to another, the meat was transported higher and higher going toward the foothills. Hunters took turns leading, desperate to out race the high wall of water following them. Rain pelted from the sky as they dashed around a steep corner.

Transferring their heavy branches of meat as they slid around a turn, they abruptly stopped. A flash flood roared straight at them, carrying the natural debris of branches, mud and rolling rocks. Where they stood the water was low, but the current under foot was dangerously fast. Frantically calls were passed back from one hunter to another, an emergency message was sent. They needed the *Ho-na-ai-te* Ko'baitya to come forward quickly for soon there would be a convergence of the two flash floods and this would not only completely block their way, but possibly drown them.

Ho-na-ai-te Ko'baitya raced to the front. Older hunters prayed for salvation. *Ho-na-ai-te* Ko'baitya was considered a novice for this was his first hunt and he had remained quiet most of the time. Ko'baitya had just finished his training and his knowledge had not yet been tested. His long legs in fast motion brought him to the oncoming wall of water. The tall flash flood behind the formation had been known to him, what was happening in the front of this procession was a shock.

Ko'baitya studied where they were pointing. Drenching dark clouds were overhead as lightning streaked the dark sky, thunder clapped from the heavens as heavy pelting rain stung their faces. There was no solution for them. Rolling water was coming at them with a deadly flash flood gaining strength behind them. These hunters were completely dependent on Ko'baitya's magical abilities for survival.

One of the hunters quickly pulled the drum free from Ko'baitya's back. Holding the drum's leather handle with two fingers, Ko'baitya studied the spirit flow of the water. Flood water was alive, pulsing higher and higher by the second. It was brown with dirt and debris, the waves fringed in white foam mingled with pieces of wood floating on the surface. Closing his eyes, his body vibrated with the harmonic tone of his lone vocal chant. In his mind, he envisioned the clouds overhead and watching the birds as they flew over the hunters who carried the wrapped meat. Lifting his leather pouch, his eyes still closed, he blindly sprinkled cornmeal patina over the fast-flowing waters as a spiritual offering. Holding the drum in one hand, the fingers of the other hand began to beat the drum skin. His feet pounded the ground in tempo with the pulse of the water. Each time his foot hit the ground, it shook. Lifting his chin to the clouds, his voice grew louder and louder with each drum beat.

"Hen-na-ti he'-ash O'-shats Ta'-wac Mo-kaite ko'hai Tu-o'pi
Ka'kan Ti'a-mi Mai-tu-bo Ma'-a-se-we Yuy-yue'we Sa'mai-hai-a
Shi-no-hai-a Yu-ma-hai-a Ah'-wa-hai-a Pe'ah-hai-a hi-an-ye
Hi-ah-ar-ra hi'-a-mo-ni Hi'shi-ko-ya'sas-pa, sho'pok'ti-a-ma
Sus-sis-tin-na-ko ya'ya ko'-chi-na-ko Mer-ri-na-ko kur-kan-mni-na-ko
Ka'0shi-na-ko quis-ser-ri-na-ko my-nai-na-ko. Hi-an-an-ye Hi'-ah-ar-ra
hi-a-mo-ni.

"White floating clouds like the sun, moon, cougar, bear, badger, wolf, eagle, shrew, elder war here. Name of warriors given, I make a road of cornmeal the ancient road, the ancient road with cornmeal from Yellow Woman creator, Red Woman of the south, White Woman of the east, slightly Yellow Woman of the Zenith, Dark Woman of the nadir. I make an ancient road, the ancient road.

Story of Rain Tsia Pueblo Story Number 7

Water roared, angry and turbulent as Ko'baitya's words grew in strength. Waves pounded in a chaotic spiral, lifting skyward. The earth rumbled with each pound of his feet. Hunters fell to their knees as they watched the swirling waters in front of *Ho-na-ai-te* Ko'baitya magically fly into the air, curling back to lift again and again into two high walls of blocked magical water. This brought a separating pathway of mud. These two walls, twenty feet apart of pulsating water rose up abruptly into the dark sky, held magically by song. Rushing air blew into the men's faces as they watched frenetic water desperately trying to break free.

The first group of hunters screamed a high pitch yell. Two *Caiyeik* hunters lifted their branch tied with meat high over their heads as they raced across the muddy ground to the other side of the flash floods. Quickly, a few other hunters followed. At first, they were cautious with extreme fear in their faces and then suddenly all the hunters bolted across to the opposite side, running to be on elevated dry ground. *Ho-na-ai-te* Ko'baitya beat the drum, his voice strong, his open eyes searched the sky. His deep voice echoed, bouncing off the high walls of water as he walked to be beside the hunters.

The drumming stopped. His chanting stopped. Sound suddenly exploded with a deafening thunderclap as the swirling walls of water slammed down hard. Flash flood waters collided together with an explosive crash as hunters ran, not stopping until they reached the outer lying area of the Pueblo. Rain continued to pelt down as their families welcomed them into the center of the pueblo. As the last hunter entered, the clouds parted, the sun shone down to dry the soaked earth. Lifting his drum skyward and with a soft voice Ko'baitya gave thanks to the Great Spirits for his magic. More cornmeal was poured over the waning flash flood waters.

When he arrived at the pueblo's center, the people were busy dividing the meat. The Cacique or Mayor met him and was followed by the Head of the Cloud Clan. Taking the drum, the Head of the Cloud Clan said, "Ko'baitya, you have saved many. You have learned how to use your powers. Now, you have earned the respect of the people."

The lead *Caiyaik* hunter handed Ko'baitya a large bundle of wrapped meat. No words needed to be said. This testing saved lives. Today, many have learned the ways of the Cloud Clan who guard the Knife Society Altar. Ko'baitya earned his privilege to marry and continued to be a wise man who was known for his magical ways. Such is the way of the Spirits.

Notes:

Mankind is constantly being tested by the spirit world. Flash floods are deadly in many parts of the world, especially in the Southwest even today. Training to appreciate the Spirits, talk to the Spirits and work with the Spirits is specific in the Pueblos of New Mexico. The belief in oneself to be successful in the attempt is also vital. This story relates the traditions and culture of the Pueblo region. Sam Ortiz told me this story when I was a teenager, growing up in San Juan Pueblo, New Mexico. This story was also shared by Alice Marriott.

Glossary:

Caiyeik – Trained hunters.
Cima – Ant.
Ckoyo – Giant Society.
Cocgaina – Door keeper.
Crowi – Snake society.
Diskama – Corn husk.
Do'wahi tcaiyanyi – The only ones who can make things appear magically, usually only in a kiva.
Gac'dyats'tiwa – Rainbow Man.

Ga'otcanyi – Assistants to War Captain.

Hakanyi – Fire Society also means fire.

Hakanyi wawa – Herbal paste used to coat interior of fire eaters' mouths.

Hictianyi – Flint Society, medicine or curing purpose.

Ho-na-ai-te – He Who Stops Rain, secret magical society dealing with nature.

Iariko – Corn ear fetish.

Katsina or Shiwanna – Masked line dancers.

Kat'sina – Part of Rain Society.

Kobict'aiya – Spirit.

Kokoho or Kohaiya – The bear of the Fire Society.

Mokaitc – Kat'sina dancer of Kwiraina Clan, spirit of Mountain Lion.

No-na-ai-te Clan – Cloud clan within Rain Society.

Na'wai – Head Medicine Man.

Petana – Finely ground corn meal used in sacred prayer.

Quer'auna or Kwiraina – Healers.

Tcaiyanyi – Medicine men.

Tiamunyi – Cacique or Census taker sometimes the Mayor.

Wabanyi – Prayer feather bunches.

Wacti – Medicine bowl, sometimes filled with finely ground cornmeal.

Wawa – Medicine.

8
APPEASING SOLITARY GHOSTS

The Legend of the Ghost in Kirtan Wadi Lake
ASIAN INDIAN

The village of Guhagar is a small subdivision in the Ratnagiri district with a population of about fifteen thousand. The village is by the sea. The seashore has soft sand with quiet waves washing ashore. You can hear the deep humming of the waves in the village. The green hills abutting Guhagar are bountiful with thick forests. The pleasant aroma from coconut and betel nut plantations waft on the air. During the monsoon season, the sky appears to be white with rain. Large waterfalls surge down from the surrounding mountains flowing into rivers, filling the underground wells, ponds and lakes. The green fauna and flora all around Guhagar are elating and the serpentine water pathways crisscrossing through the land adds to its beauty. The village dazzles in the sun.

In the daytime, Guhagar is appealing, gorgeous with its natural beauty, having a tranquil peace for there is no hurry, no human noise just a pleasant calm. At night, the small village of Guhagar is closed and quiet. No one goes out after sundown, all are asleep even the animals. Due to the closeness of the coconut and betel nut orchards on one side and the dense forest of thick tree growth with vines climbing from tree to tree on the other, Guhagar is blanketed in complete darkness. The western hills and mountains cause shades of night to befall the village earlier than other places. Once the sun sets, darkness reigns. Night seeps into the village from all sides. It enters all the houses and huts. It swallows the human activity. Inky black fills shadows of the tree cavities and blackens the branches and leaves. Crickets and beetles are the only sounds while all about fireflies are darting.

Kirtan Wadi, was only one of the thirteen *wadis* or a very small residential settlement, near the village of Guhagar, which at night was also draped in pasty black darkness. Even when there was a full moon in the night sky, the dark shadows of the mountains and hills and the huge tree trunks with dense mixed foliage kept the *wadi* from brightening. Shadows rock and swayed with the sea breezes. No light was able to pierce through the blanket of night, leaving Guhagar in the kingdom of darkness.

During the monsoon season, the rains poured down ceaselessly. Everything was drenched in water, even in night's pitch darkness. The rains poured as if a faucet was turned on in the sky, regardless of day or night, water lashed and splashed down on the land, leaving it fully soaked. The mountains, too, became slippery with loose mud. Flowing flash floods raced from outlets in streams that were emanating from the mountain cliffs and crevices. Seeping water collectively gathered high above the town, forming dangerous streams and waterfalls surging from the cliffs to overflow the rivers on both banks and rushed into the sea. The soaked earth allowed the surface runoff to flow through an infinite number of streamlets that traversed the grasslands, farm fields, gorges and craters. Hand-dug crater-ponds were created to catch and deter flash flood water. Irrigation ditches returned the excess overflow back to the sea, saving the village and their vulnerable homes.

Dense woods surrounded these lakes where at times the trees were as motionless as the lakes. Not even a leaf moved. In that wet land, wet forest and the wet darkness, everything became absolutely still. There was no movement, no sound only calm and quiet. The silence felt deafening, similar to the quiet of a graveyard, bringing fear with a mystical eeriness. Kirtan Wadi appears safe during the day, but at night it has an aura of evil. People only left their homes at night in an emergency for a sinister premonition hovered in the air. Only a serious compelling need would bring someone to stare darkness in the eye and step out into it.

Kirtan Wadi Lake had an enclosed forest mixed with thick, dark green trees, also. Fresh greenery intertwined with the trees, were vines and moss, making this forest an impenetrable mesh and virtually black due to the generated dense shadows. The wild, leafy vegetables and tall weedy grasses on the ground near the lake, grew in abundance from the lake's quiet, clear water. Mirrored in the lake were the forest trees as they bent over the water's edge. This deadly combination of the still water, unmoving trees and their green, tranquil reflection together with the scary silence in the atmosphere was chilling. It deepened the mystic aura. At night, the fearful darkness was even more profound and mysterious. That scared people.

There was a distance of about two and a half miles between Kirtan Wadi and the Khalcha Pat Wadi. The lake bisected this distance. If you stood near the lake, you could see the houses in the village. There was a single paved road running along the lake. It was full of potholes and went straight into the village. People only used this road because they were going to the village. No one stopped near the lake. They even avoided looking at it. No one swam or did washing in that lake. Not even in daylight and certainly not at night.

There were two decrepit temples opposite the lake. One of them was in fact, a ruin with crumbling walls. The platform outside of it was cracked and disintegrating. Next to the pathetic temple edifice was a huge, ancient banyan tree with low hanging far reaching branches. And layers of dry leaves form a carpet under the tree. No one went to this haunted temple during the day or night.

The second temple was also in disrepair with the painted colour peeling off the crumbling walls, leaving it in sad condition. The floor was rickety. Lord Ganesha sat in that temple as an anciently sculpted idol. A Brahman came to this little temple every morning, without fail, performing his prayers and the *Puja,* offering fresh flowers to Ganesha. He sang *aarti,* his sacred songs while he lit wicks soaked in purified butter and camphor. Graciously he offered food to the deity. After these humble actions, he would lock what remained of the temple. Throughout the day no one would go there, not even a passerby would stop to pay obeisance to Lord Ganesha. The lake and surrounding area rarely experienced a human being's presence, for few would go or come to the village via the potholed road. Barring this, there would be a complete and total silence there.

Nevertheless, the lake was often the topic of discussion in this village. Everyone had a point of view and a story to go with it regarding the danger of the lake. Grandmothers warned, "No matter what happens, don't go near the lake. Once a woman, who was young, beautiful, and married, jumped into the lake and died."

Another related this, "Once, a man went to the lake to fish. As he waded into the water, he threw in his net. Further and further he slowly walked, until the water was up to his waist. Suddenly, he was pulled under into the sticky silt. Trying desperately to extricate himself, he shouted for help. Some nearby villagers ran to save him. They threw ropes to him, but the more they pulled, the deeper he went until he disappeared completely under the water.

"The men who had attempted to save him were dumbfounded. They were strong men. The rope was thick. The man was strong! How did this not work? Something stronger than they had pulled this man under, drowning him in the muddy silt. This was incomprehensible! Deciding there was still a chance to save him, some of the men ran to the village.

When they returned, there was no sign of the man or his netting. He had completely vanished. Tragically, his family was told. When people returned the next day, they found the poor man's body floating on the surface, bloated and disfigured. It was a horrible, horrible sight!"

In olden days, there was no electricity in the village. Naturally, after dusk it was pitch-black dark all around. A person wouldn't see their own hand if they held it in front of their face. This story was from long ago. It was told that in those days, people saw fire torches dancing on the water while others saw lit earthen-lamps miraculously floating around the lake with no one holding them. Some told of getting a fever if they stood too close to the water. Old ones spoke of the lake water sucking people in, drowning them. The folktales surrounding the lake kept people away from the lake even today with electricity in the village. If a person had to use the paved road running along the lake, they stayed as far away from the water as possible to hurriedly travel away from danger.

The Gawade family, belonging to the *Kunbi* community, and had lived in Kirtan Wadi for four or five generations. Shri Vijay Gawade, the current heir of the family was a simple man who had strange experiences. When he was six or seven years of age in 1973, there was construction work underway at the Community Hall where his family lived. Because of this, Vijay and his family slept outside of the Community Hall under the night sky. There were no lights in Kirtan Wadi at that time, so once the evening fell, complete darkness blanketed the village. Some people used small kerosene lanterns having glass tops, bringing flickering light with a lot of smoke. These burned for only a short time and smelled awful. Once the lanterns went out, it was very dark. The darkness was frightening for strangely shaped silhouettes in the trees added unusual dancing images.

On this one night, all the men in the family were sleeping outside as was usual and women were sleeping inside the home because of fear. The paternal uncle of Vijay Gawade, who was ten years older, needed to answer nature's call. His sleepy eyes studied the landscape. A light appeared. It was on the lake! Fire torches were burning near a floating white cloth. As he watched the lights move, more earthen lamps were lit, reflecting in the lake's water. Terrified, he hurried back to the other sleeping men, shutting his eyes tightly while silently chanting the name of Lord Rama. His father had told him to chant the name of Lord Rama and the ghosts would stay away.

The next night, the same thing happened only this time Uncle saw not just the fire torches and earthen lamps, but he also saw a beautiful woman. Her face was decorated with makeup resembling a fashion model.

The white *saree* billowed around her floating, thin female body, resembling a gorgeous theatrical performer. The uncle was terrified. He could hardly sleep, waiting desperately for the dawn of the next day. When daybreak finally arrived, he related the vision of the night before to his family. They nodded, for they had heard stories of this ghost, but now was the first time someone in their family had seen this phantom. Sharing Uncle's experience with the other villagers, people replied, "There was an actress who lived in this village some time ago. She died young. When a person dies before their time, their desires remain unfulfilled. In such a case, their ghost can take on different forms. Not everyone can see this phantom, only a few can. Perhaps, that is the case here." There are different types of actresses, fat ones, short ones and tall ones, but this vision reached out to him with his concept of beautiful. So, Vijay Gawade's uncle was convinced that the woman was indeed a gorgeous performer after all.

Serious concern spread throughout the village for this phantom woman could be dangerous. Wanting to remove this phantom from the lake, the villagers travelled to a well-known exorcist, a *bhagat*, who was known to give advice in such extraordinary matters.

Uncle's father spoke to the *bhagat*, "My son saw a beautiful woman, floating above the waters of the lake. Fire torches drifted around her with a white cloth floating on the water. This was at night, in the darkness. She terrified him. Can you tell us how to remove her from the lake? We fear for the safety of others and believe her to be evil."

Studying the concern in the villagers' faces, the *bhagat* thought for a moment to say, "There is a solution to this phantom," he replied. "Whenever and whoever sees the beautiful actress again, should immediately call other men to the lake. There, they should stand, facing the floating apparition of the lake. When she faces the men, they are to disrobe quickly. When she sees the naked men, she will disappear out of embarrassment. Believe me, she will not return."

Soon after receiving the *bhagat's* advice, Vijay Gawade's uncle saw the actress once again, floating above the lake in the dark of night. Racing to the village, he called to the men. Rising from their slumber, they quickly followed him to the lake. Floating fire torches circled the lake with earthen lamps gliding around the white cloth in the centre of the clear water. Slowly, the gloriously gorgeous phantom woman lifted from beneath the liquid surface. Droplets glistened in the lanterns' lights as she rose. As she opened her eyes, the men dropped their clothes, revealing their naked bodies to her.

The Legend of the Ghost in Kirtan Wadi Lake

A slight breeze blew across the lake as her hair vaporized, the top of her head vanished. Bright sparks of light glistened around her neck and her *saree* flew into oblivion. White tiny flakes dissipated over the lake that had once been lanterns. The earthen lamps powdered as the white cloth lifted to separate into dust, blowing into the trees. A slight sizzle was heard, leaving the rotten smell of sulphur. The naked men were now alone. Quietly, the men returned to their beds to sleep. Since the naked men night, no one has seen the floating phantom woman. Her apparition appears to have gone.

There is yet another tale to be told. Remember the two ramshackle temples opposite the lake? As recently as four or five years ago Shri Vijay Gawade himself had a strange experience. It was night time and there was an electrical power outage. Darkness engulfed everything. It was somewhat late in the night and there was not a sound anywhere. There was no breeze blowing. The trees did not rustle, leaves did not move and the air was still. A complete silence was all around, barring the crickets and occasionally a frog would croak.

Gawade worked in a neighbouring village. His work had delayed his departure home. Because he was riding a bicycle, he was not worried about going by the lake in the dark of night. The paved road was rough with potholes, cracks and mounds of dirt and this made him bike carefully and cautiously. As he neared the lake, he became worried for there was an eerie presence. Sweating in fear, he began to chant the name of Lord Rama under his breath. Peddling fast for he knew he should not stop, he consciously avoided looking into the lake. When the lake was closer, suddenly his bicycle veered to the left away from the lake. Then his bicycle floated in the air, jerked away from the water toward a farmland. Unable to understand what was happening, Gawade became even more terrified. He tried to control his bicycle, holding the handlebars tightly so as not to fall down. However, the bicycle kept getting dragged on the road to his left. Finally, as if someone had yanked on his bicycle, it swerved wildly and fell into the farmer's field. Gawade hit the ground hard, bruising and scratching his elbows and knees. Blood trickled down his leg as he found he was unable to stand. Quaking in terror, he attempted to shout for help. His throat was dry. He had no voice.

The dark of night surrounded him, he could not see anything and he dared not turn toward the lake. Groping around for his carry bag, he couldn't find it. Again, he attempted to stand, then realized he had lost one of his shoes. The other was torn, barely hanging onto his foot. His hip was sore and his elbow was now bleeding. No matter what had happened, he needed to stand in order to survive. Groaning and grunting, he pushed his body to be on all fours. Straightening his legs, he twisted and stood upright. In the darkness, he blindly reached out to find his bicycle. Holding the handlebars, he tried to lift the bicycle. It was stuck in the earth and would not budge.

Deciding to give up on the bicycle, his hands moved around searching for his carry-bag and broken shoe. All the while, he hadn't stopped chanting the name of Lord Rama. His eyes were of no help, for he was blind in the dark of the night. In spite of being scared, he garnered some courage to throw a furtive glance at the lake. Everything was calm and quiet. There were no lights or movement of any kind. Then he felt a little better. Continuing his chant, he courageously looked at the lake again thinking he might see the gorgeous apparition in the white *saree*. He remembered the *bhagat's* solution of getting naked before her if she was seen. Relaxing, he decided that he would disrobe and stand naked before her if she appeared before him. His hands touched the handlebars of the bicycle again, and with a firm grip, he jerked it upright. Then, holding the handlebars tight and sitting astride, he pe*dal*led hard until he arrived at the village and his house came into sight.

Upon reaching home, he simply dropped his bicycle and ran to the door. Banging loudly, he called out, "Open the door! Open the door!"

Jolted from their sleep, his family hurriedly opened the door, to ask, "What happened?"

Gawade stumbled inside like a drunkard to fall on the floor, chanting the name of Lord Rama. His father smiled, "Ah, Vijay has seen a ghost. Lord Rama protects from ghosts and phantoms. Get him a glass of water."

Slowly, Gawade calmed down enough to relate the entire incident to his family, "I didn't see the woman, nor did I see her white *saree* float. There were no fire torches flying through the air nor earthen lamps on the water, but I was jerked into the air while I was still sitting on my bicycle!" Taking another drink of water, he continued, "A force took hold of my bicycle to lift me up and away from the lake. I landed on the farmland opposite the lake from the road. Then, my bicycle was dragged in the dirt. It was dark, I couldn't see anything at all! It took me awhile to find the bicycle and then it wouldn't lift from the ground. I lost one of my shoes and couldn't find my carry-bag. They are still out there somewhere."

Gulping more water, he sighed, "I don't know what happened. One minute I was pe*dal*ling along and the next minute, I was lying in the dirt on a farmer's field with cuts and bruises, one shoe torn and the other lost."

No one was able to explain his strange experience. In the morning, he found his shoe and his carry-bag. He showed his family the bicycle drag-tracks in the dirt. This was all very unusual and bizarre. This event reiterated to people the importance of avoiding the old paved road by the lake at night. Even today, people stay off the paved road by the lake in the night, especially if they are alone. These stories have become local legends told to protect travellers who dare to pass this way in the dark, in the night, by the lake.

Notes:

Kirtan Wadi Lake has various beliefs among the locals for it has been known to capture a passerby. The narrations of incredible, astonishing experiences by various people, have brought about frightening legends from this area. The land between the Western seacoast of Maharashtra and the 'Sahyadri' mountain ranges is known as 'Konkan'. Pitch-dark nights with scary shapes of rustling trees and eerie, moving shadows in the foliage with oddly shaped branches in the starlight, allow ghost stories to thrive.

There are those who willingly narrate their terrifying personal experiences as these have given birth to blood-curdling ghost stories, death defying happenings and phantasm sightings in this region.

In June 2017, I toured the Chiplun, Guhagar, Palshet areas of the Konkan region in Maharashtra with the objective of compiling legends. The legend "The Ghost in Kirtan Wadi Lake" is based on the actual experience of Vijay Gawade, a local resident of the Kunbi community. Balasaheb Labade, Ph.D. heard the story from him, which later he related to me. I have narrated that experience in my own words.

Glossary:

Pooja or Puja – A prayer ritual performed by Hindus of devotional worship to one or more deities. It is a Sanskrit word. It means reverence, honor, homage, adoration, and worship.

Spirit Woman Ghost, Paiute
NATIVE AMERICAN

The *Aga'idokado* or 'Cutthroat Trout Eaters' and a smaller tribe of Paiute known as *Pakwidokao* or 'Chumb Carp Eaters' along with the Two Northern Paiute tribes called *Kuuidokado* or *Cui-ui*, 'Large Fish Eaters' and the *Tsaiget Tuviwarai* or 'Those Who Live in the Mountains' were pushed together after the *Walker War of 1854*, a war between the Utes and the Mormons. The bands of people were desperate to survive and stay on the land of their ancestors. Mormon settlers infringed on their lands, building cabins closer and closer to the Utes. Along with them came the U.S. Army. The Shoshone to the north felt the squeeze from the outsiders as well. In 1855, a *Friendship Treaty* was signed joining the Paiute with the Shoshone. It was believed there was strength in numbers. Then came the *Pyramid Lake War of 1860*, the natives were outnumbered and lost their lands. The sting of defeat was painful. The Paiute then came to belong to the numerous Shoshonean people and lived in Nevada, southwestern Utah, northwestern Arizona and northwestern and southeastern California. Some had called this particular group of Paiute the *Paviotso*. The name these people used was Pai Utes and became known as the Paiutes of Walker River and Pyramid Lake.

A Spirit Shaman was called to come from the west. He spoke to all of the people, the wounded from war, the elderly, those sick with loss and the orphaned children, "At first the world was all water. The world, this world we now live in was all water everywhere. Then the water began to recede and it went down and down until *Kura'ngwa* or Mount Grant emerged from the disappearing water. This is near the southwest end of Walker Lake. This is a sacred place. Then a fire came to be at the top of *Kura'ngwa* Mount Grant and when the wind blew hard, water flew over the fire and would have put it out, but a sage hen '*hutsi*' flew over the fire, spreading her wings as if nestling her eggs. The heat of the fire scorched her feathers on her breast and today the sage hen has black breast feathers. This is where our people got their first fire from this mountain with the help of Rabbit who is our magical spirit animal. As the water continued to disappear other mountains appeared, until the land is as it is now.

"*Numi 'naa*' our Spirit Father came south from the sacred mountain and with him came *Ibidsii* our Mother and they dressed themselves in skins and lived on deer and mountain sheep meat for there was plenty. They had a family of many and this one family went to Walker Lake and became *Aga'ih-tika'ra* or fish eaters of Walker Lake. Then our family divided. The *Koto'ti'kara* are the buffalo eaters. Now we have come together. *Numi 'naa*' went up into the sky with his wife *Ibidsii* for their families were doing well."

Shaking his head, he continued, "There is a sickness of death coming from the river near the White Eye settlement. It is not good here. There are mountain streams leading into this high lake from the land above where the White Eyes live. I am leaving this camp. It would be wise for all of you to go to the northwest and stay on the plains. This lake holds a demon of death and within the water is a spirit who will take the sacred soul of each one of you. This spirit moves from water place to water place, be careful what water you drink and where you gather it. Leave now before it is too late."

Then the Spirit Shaman departed to the south. The people were tired, wounded and had no energy to pick up camp and move. As the summer progressed the Spirit Shaman's prediction came to the Paiute and Shoshone village. Children began to have terrible head pain, their muscles hurt to move, and body sweats along with hacking dry coughs lasted all night and day. Slowly, the children, old ones and those who had been wounded from the wars were placed in a large *wick-i-up*, all of them lying on their backs with their eyes half open, unable to stand. Some of the women who had given birth in the spring developed internal bleeding as their babies and children became weak and died.

After several months of sickness and death, it was decided, by the Elders as to who were healthy enough to leave should go. The evening before the great migration, the sky turned a dark red with yellow swirls on the horizon. Suddenly as the sun began to bed, a whirlwind moved across the land. The wind lifted *wick-i-up*s, tossed fire flames high into the air, knocked horses down and lifted the dogs and small children to drop them hard onto the ground. People screamed. The sick opened their eyes to see the roof of their *wick-i-up* disappear high into the air. Fear, apprehension and death came that evening. As the night progressed the whirlwind slowly moved to the northeast, to the White Eye Place. Some people scrambled to put out fires on the flatland in the rabbit bush and chamisa. Mothers and fathers gathered up their children who lay wounded on the hard ground. This was a sign.

Two elderly Paiute Shaman stood outside of their camp with their arms wide open to the sky, chanting,

"Ksosi' wumbi'ndoma'
Kosi'wumbi'ndoma'
Kosi'wumbi'ndoma
Kosi'wumbi'ndoma
Kosi'wumbi'ndoma
Kosi'wumbi'ndoma
Ibidsii Kai-va
Numa Do'roni

There is dust from the whirlwind
There is dust from the whirlwind
There is dust from the whirlwind
There is dust from the whirlwind
There is dust from the whirlwind
There is dust from the whirlwind
Mother Mountain
We are rolling."

Early the next morning, Shoshone and Paiute gathered their belongings, leaving behind the ill or wounded who were no longer able to walk with those who refused to abandon the incapacitated. The healthy ones migrated to the base of the mountain by Walker Lake. Everyone worked together to make the central *wick-i-up* in the new location. It was made from a conical form of scraped wooden poles tied together with leather straps. It stood about ten feet high with an opening at the top to allow smoke to rise skyward. Tule rushes of *ho'gap* pulled from the wet area near the lake were woven together over the framework of wooden poles. This kept the *wick-i-up* strong against the *wi'noghan* or 'shaking wind.'

After six days of constructing family *wick-i-ups*, a strange occurrence happened. Four of the Elders went out into the desert to have a vision quest. Each of them returned holding a branch of *Pau"bi* or a sacred willow bundle. Each of them returned with the same vision. Sitting around the central fires of the permanent *wick-i-up* the oldest spoke in the *ba'waa* or circle, "There was an apparition that came to me, showing the Spirits of the Dead arriving to help the Living survive. If we call our Dead Ancestors to our aid while cleansing our own spirits, the Dead Spirits shall end the coming of the White Eye and their sickness."

The next Elder nodded in agreement, "We must remain kind to one another. We must give what we have in excess to those who have nothing. This is the time to reflect on our lives, prepare to reveal our true spirit to the Dead. This will be a time of great magic with humility."

The youngest Elder picked a piece of burning kindling from the fire, "Smoke from this fire shows us its true color. This is our destiny. The Dead perceive our colors. It is time to sweat, cleanse and dance. We live to appreciate life."

Another Elder pointed to the mountain, "We must take our water bladders and fill them with clean water from the lake. Build our sweat lodge and fires to heat the clean water from the lake. The White Eyes call this lake Walker Lake. This water will clean the sweat lodge heated stones and purify our spirits."

The fourth Elder nodded in agreement, "We are the Pa' which is our 'Water' and Pai is our 'True.' We are the *Pai-u-ti* or 'Those Who Truly Come from Water' we must find our harmony and balance in the sweat lodge with water. Let us build and accept the help we need from the Dead Spirits."

Women shook their heads. Men glared at the flames. Their families had dwindled to only a few due to the wars and sickness. Anger and frustration filled their beings. Sadness and despair was evident on many of their faces. The last Elder watched the people, to say, "Pay attention, and heed the Spirit Call. There is evil around us. Lift your spirit from the darkness to behold the goodness within you for our awareness will save all of us. Truth, kindness and awareness must become our way."

The Elder of the largest surviving clan spoke softly, "Take the items you brought here that belonged to the deceased in your family and burn them. Let them go to the other side. Now it is time to help those who live. We must cleanse and allow the spirit world to bring us balance."

Sobbing and crying was heard in many of the *wick-i-up*s that night as the women took their deceased family items outside and burned them in the large central fire. Fathers and sons shook as they placed beautifully colored leather dresses with pigment stained designs on the flames, watching their past loved ones' memories burn away. Children huddled near adopted parents, quiet and forlorn, remembering. The center fire burned all night, at dawn the breeze blew the ashes and gray coals away from the camp. Sorrow blown by Brother Wind, absorbed by Mother Earth allowed room for Hope.

Men had already started on the rounded dome frame of the sweat lodge using willow strips. A small number of young hunters were hunting buffalo on the plains and they returned by end of afternoon with three medium sized buffalo. The older men set to skinning while they women took the sliced meat to hang dry. The larger pieces of meat would be used for the feast to celebrate the end of the sweat in the lodge. The buffalo skins were thrown over the rounded dome frame of the sweat lodge. A fire in the middle, dug into a dirt pit, was started. Boys dragged skins filled with medium sized rocks and large stones to the opening of the lodge. These were placed in and around the central fire. The women brought bladder skins filled with water, hanging them on the outside of the lodge. The buffalo skulls were placed at the doorway of the lodge. All night the men sweated and chanted.

In the morning, Elders drummed as deep purple and soft pink clouds floated from the mountain peaks. Women and men gathered to circle dance with the younger Shoshone and Paiute in front of them. Inside the smallest circle were the youngest of the dancers. Each circle flowed at its own rhythm as drums throbbed with the Earth's heartbeat. Dancers were soaked with perspiration. Long loose hair stuck to their dark, wet skin. No one thought of their sore feet in hot moccasins. Women were bare breasted with sand grass skirts twirling around them. Men with painted bare chests wore their breechcloths tightly tucked into leather thong belts. Naked children hypnotically danced not aware of the heat. Brown eyes were either closed to absorb the earth into their being or watched the fellow spirits dancing on the horizon. Grandfathers circled the dancers picking up pine boughs that may have fallen or to tighten loose moccasins ties. They carried with them bladders of water to give to the younger more fragile dancers.

Slowly, Sun watched this magnificent ceremony. Brother Wind cooled Earth Mother. Ravens flew overhead, carrying sacred prayers skyward. When evening arrived, the people were exhausted, yet each felt cleansed and lighter. A fine feast was shared by all as HOPE for a new life was to begin. Young men hunted with the older surviving hunters. Young girls learned how to catch and contain wild turkeys and sage hens. Mothers found berry bushes and wild herbs to keep cool in earth cellars. Slowly, a life of rhythm returned to the people in their new village.

Summer heat arrived with the awareness of survival. The women gathered and cut sagebrush bark. Retrieving water from the lower river, they soaked the bark until it was pliable. Then they pummeled the soft palpable bark until it became a material they could weave and braid. Breechcloths and moccasins were made. Aprons worn over the women's braided sand grass skirts were formed. In the summer, the women were mostly bare breasted as were the men. New born babies were placed in cradle boards framed with willow boughs, slatted with tree branches and wrapped with pliable bark rope.

Life's awareness of the cold descending from the mountain brought the men to whittle new 'paga' or arrows, cleaned out blowguns to prepare their poisonous darts and poisonous tipped arrowheads. Stone knives were sharpened by the younger men who also used hard quartz to give a double blade to long spears. Rabbit sticks were rubbed flat and digging sticks were pointed. As the summer heat subsided into the cool of fall, the men went to hunt. The younger men taught the boys how to fling rabbit sticks. Young women educated the girls on how to dry edible berries, pick pine nuts free from sap, and dig for roots and stalks and bulbs. The rice grass was harvested as well, all placed in grass baskets woven tight enough to hold water and the smallest of seeds. The cooler winds found Paiute and Shoshone bands doing well with good hearts. Fear remained for everyday runners returned with news of Mormon settlers creeping closer and closer to their camp, hunting their animals, damming their streams and threatening ancestral life.

One fall day, there arrived from the west, a singular man who claimed to be a powerful Shaman. He told the people of his visions. Sitting across from the Elders in the communal teepee, he spoke, "I am here to help you find your way to be free of the White Eye who kill your people, take your land and steal your food. If you believe in me, I shall lead the Paiute and Shoshone to freedom from the White Eye by offering spiritual food to a mountain lake."

Elders stared at this man. The oldest interrupted the Shaman, "We have camped here from spring until fall and we have not found a lake up on a mountain. Where do you believe this lake to be?"

"Ah," said the Shaman, "This one particular lake is beyond the rough terrain to the west. There are steep cliffs to climb, but long ago someone dug foot holds making this not impossible to traverse."

Glancing at one another, the Elders all agreed, "If you choose to go to this mountain lake for your own sacred ceremony, giving spiritual food to remove the White Eye from threatening us, we all agree."

People watched the Shaman pack his back pouch with nuts, roots and fresh flat bread. Lifting his hand, he departed to the west. Shoshone boys followed him until late day to return, telling of seeing a tall mountain on the horizon. Everyone went about their business not giving him a second thought. No one expected the Shaman to return, but he did four days later. His pouch was empty, his bladder of water was half full and his mood was positive.

Joining with the Elders in the communal teepee, he explained, "In four days' time there will be an earthquake and all the white villages, towns, and farms will be swallowed up by the Great Spirit."

The younger Elder asked, "Will this earthquake eat us as well?"

The Shaman shook his head, "Not if you choose to relocate your camp to higher ground. This is my vision." The Shaman unrolled his bedroll to fall into a deep sleep.

People prepared by building temporary *wick-i-up*s above the flatland with layers stones for foundations. Women gathered water, filling tight baskets and large pots. Children and older ones slept outside on elevated ground, waiting for the earth to shake and crack open, saving them from the invaders. Men huddled around night fires, cautious of any sounds. After eight days, the people decided the quaking of the earth was not to happen. Runners appeared with worrisome news of more Mormon wagons led by U.S. Army men gathering by the river. The people questioned the Shaman.

Arranged in the circle with the Elders, the Shaman appeared puzzled by their questioning of him, "My visions tell me of what is to come if what they predicted didn't happen, I am not wrong. The Spirits changed their minds."

Elders studied the man, as one of them asked, "Would you be willing to go back to the mountain lake and ask the Spirits for another vision? Outsiders are coming onto our land eager to kill us and take our animals."

Another Elder shook his head, "Please, ask the Spirits to assist these settlers to migrate somewhere else far away from our camp!"

The Shaman drew in the dirt in front of him, answering, "Yes, it is my purpose to protect you and your people. Tomorrow, I will return to the lake as you requested the Spirits shall be asked for aid."

Again, the Shaman collected food and filled his bladder skins with water and then he disappeared to climb the mountain to the lake. After four days, he returned at evening meal. Cautiously, women brought him food and water. Suspiciously, men observed his mood. Once the meal was completed, he stood to address all of the people in the camp.

Opening his arms as he held his palms skyward, he spoke loudly, "This time there will be a severe shaking of the earth. Fissures and wide mouthed canyons will open and swallow the White Eyes. Some will survive, but they will be on the opposite side of the earth from us. Believe and be of good heart, this will occur."

Men shook their heads at him. A few of the women went back into their regular *wick-i-up*s to care for the children. The Shaman continued, "We will no longer have to fight. We shall be separate and safe from them."

An Elder grumbled, "Perhaps this is more believable, but we are going to stay here in the main camp. If there is a rumble, we can hurry to the higher *wick-i-up*s."

Ten days passed without so much as a thunderstorm. The earth did not tremble nor rumble. There were no fissures or cracking of canyons. Runners returned with warnings of the White Eye felling trees, building square edifices and men with rifles killing the migrating deer. Despair entered the camp. The Elders called warriors together, readying them for war. Many shook their heads, there were not enough of them to fight the U.S. Army. Now, the people were desperate for Spiritual help. No words were spoken in the morning as the Shaman took sacred cornmeal with him to again plod his way up the mountain to sit by the lake and pray. The people impatiently waited for his return and his news. The Shaman did not reappear.

Several of the Elders called for a council. It was decided two young runners were told to go to the mountain lake and request his return. The runners left early at dawn to come down by late afternoon to relate, "There is no one there. He has vanished. He is gone. His sacred cornmeal pouch is by the lake and a small circle of ash from a fire, but he is not there. The Creator took him."

This was not good. This Shaman was a man the people respected and knew even if the Spirits kept changing the outcome. The Elders considered another man who was trained in spiritual knowledge to visit the mountainous lake. One of the Elders told him, "Take Coyote Tea with you. Perhaps if you drink the tea, purge and fast by this lake the Spirits will give you a vision."

The chosen young man disappeared toward the west with the runners beside him until he came to the steep cliff face. He was observed as he climbed the footholds to the top, then the runners turned back to the camp. Four days passed, his family became worried. Silence from the mountain concerned the Elders. Again, they called runners to find him.

They returned saying, "There is no one there. He is gone. The Creator took him." The family tore their hair, put char on their faces and mourned their loss for they were without a body to send to the Place of the Dead. This was not good.

Another young man volunteered for he was known for his wisdom in the ways of Spirits. Standing in the center of the camp, he told everyone, "I will remain on the mountain by the lake for only four days. If I do not return, then the Spirits were against the people." He hurried away to the mountain lake.

Everyone watched for him as now there was a westward path from the camp to the mountain. Five days passed. News arrived of U.S. Army soldiers traveling closer with the Mormon pioneers. The Paiute and Shoshone village no longer had the quantity of men to fight nor did they want any more of their people to die. The sounds of hammering echoed across the flatland to their camp in the night. During the day, the people heard guns being fired at their game. Two of their young men had disappeared to the mountain lake. These were men who were important for they were hunters, fighters and had families. The Elders were worried for this was not a good sign. Deciding to try and find these men, they sent the runners to find information, any information as to where these men might have gone.

Runners reappeared with the reoccurring message, "There is no one there. They're gone. The Creator must have taken them."

Families mourned. Elders shared thoughts, deciding these men were no longer alive. The sound of nearby rifle shots grew louder. Sentinels spoke of trees being felled in the next valley for square houses. Cattle herds were found in the valley not far from the river where the U.S. Army soldiers were guarding. Shoshone and Paiute women hurriedly rolled household items in leather bundles. Sentinels cantered to the top of ridges to observe the encroaching foreigners. All the while, people were concerned about the mountain lake and the disappearing men. Families were in turmoil not knowing if it was wise to migrate or stay in case the men were to return. Another vision quest was called by the Elders. The same vision occurred to all of them.

Putting his hands out to quiet the people around the main campfire, the Elder's face appeared solemn, "We have chosen a younger man to take the path to the mountain lake. This time he needs to mark his way with raven feathers. Once at the top, where he camps, raven feather are to be placed in a circle around his body. This will mark his presence. When he leaves, it will be necessary for him to remove the feathers to replace them inside his pouch."

Another Elder nodded in agreement, "This young man will speak with the Water Spirits and ask for aid. No more tricks or games. Our people are in serious danger. The Spirits should guide us to a better life than this."

This young man was called Waugh'se'waw'brah. His deceased father had been a leader of the Paiute for many years. Waugh'se'waw'brah was considered to be a strong young man with his father's wisdom. Tied to his leather belt was a large woven pouch filled with white tipped, black raven feathers. Tying feathers to each bush as he ascended the mountain, Waugh'se'waw'brah arrived at the edge of a silver lake. Before he sat to meditate, he wrapped feather ties around the bushes beside the lake. Praying and meditating each day, a black feather was tied to a willow stick stuck in the wet bank of the lake. Birds flitted around him, pulling worms from the moist earth. Beetles and ants quickly redirected their path around him. Night stars studied this solitary youth who was deep in Spiritual thought. Brother Wind tasseled his hair in the evening as Sky Father floated fat white clouds over him during the day.

On the fourth evening as the sun settled into the horizon, Waugh'se'waw'brah prepared to collect the black feathers around him. A glowing yellow orb glided toward him underneath the lake water. As the yellow orb neared, a vision of a woman lifted from the water, dripping and hovering above the sparkling water. Her sparkling beauty was blinding in the dark dusk. Water droplets glistened, as they fell from her ankle length dark hair. Fluorescent brilliance reflected from her sweet grass skirt. Gleaming feathers shining with moisture floated around her body. Her bare feet appeared to walk on air. Loving brown eyes pierced through the darkness of night into Waugh'se'waw'brah's soul. Slender sensual arms extended with open hands, reaching for him. Breathing with desire, Waugh'se'waw'brah lifted from the ground. Fearfully, Waugh'se'waw'brah tilted his head to watch the ground disappear beneath him as the tied raven's black feathers trembled, breaking the spirit woman's visual hold on him.

Shutting his eyes, he shouted, "No, I cannot go with you! I have family and must return to them!"

Suddenly, Waugh'se'waw'brah's body hit the ground. Lifting on one elbow, he turned his vision away from the lake to wait for the sparkling lights to retreat. Slowly, squinting at the water, he realized all was quiet. When his eyes focused in the dark, Waugh'se'waw'brah felt the night's blanket of tranquility. Grappling with the feather ties, he untied them to descend the cliff. Stumbling in the moonless night, he arrived bruised and bleeding to find his family camped at the edge of the village. Everyone was relieved at his return.

In the morning, Waugh'se'waw'brah counseled with the Elders to explain the spirit woman in the lake. As he spoke, dark clouds hovered over the land. Ravens screamed overhead as eagles perched nearby. Elders separated him from the others while Waugh'se'waw'brah related his experiences. Waugh'se'waw'brah was quizzed as to what this woman wore, why she was able to float, how she lifted from the water and her transition from a glowing orb to a spirit person. A feeling of joy had entered into him as she had sensually pulled him toward her with her long arms. His elation for her was unexplainable.

One Elder spoke in his deep voice, "This may be a spirit from the white people's camp who is taking our men away from us."

Thunder roared out overhead as another Elder whispered, "She may be the Creator who needs our young men for her own protection."

Rain pounded the ground, lightning flared in the night sky. Another Elder shook his head, "This woman is not a woman, but a Spirit. She knows how to have our young men enter into the water to appease her desires for she is trapped between two worlds. She must be freed."

The oldest of the Elders shook his head, "This is a Water Woman Spirit. She is one of the strongest spirits. Women garner their strength from the darkness of night and the power of water. Something has been done to upset her. We shall have to do a testing, allowing her the freedom from being earth bound."

A fellow Elder, smiled, "Yes, we remember the old stories. We must please her. This will not be easy and we will need other strong men to go along with Waugh'se'waw'brah in order for this to be successful."

A doubting Elder frowned, "Why can't we go up there and tell her to leave our young men alone? She is stripping us of our men! What can we offer her that she has not already taken?"

Older Elder laughed, "No. She wants to be pleased not argued with or told what to do. She is a Spirit. A woman spirit that needs to be pleased and then she will leave us alone. Perhaps she may even help us. We need the water from the lake. We need our men within our tribe. She is a woman who needs to be pleased. Listen to my plan."

The following night, Elders chanted. Waugh'se'waw'brah dreamt of the Woman Spirit calling him. Guards surrounded Waugh'se'waw'brah's *wick-i-up* to contain him if he tried to leave. In the morning, the Elders collected four of their best hunters. These were strong men with muscular bodies. Their women were asked to wash these men in animal fat, giving their bodies a glistening appearance. Yucca root pulp was used to shampoo the men's hair, allowing it to blow loose and shine. Plain headbands were tightly tied. Sun bleached breechcloths were wrapped between the men's legs tied with a simple leather strap. No sweet grass apron was placed over the front of the breechcloths. No weapons were allowed, their weapon was part of their bodies.

The oldest Elder, spoke softly, "This Woman Spirit is alone on the mountain with no one to please her or do for her. She has taken the Shaman who will inform her of our people and of our ways. The two other men have joined her to satisfy her needs, also, assist with food and protection. Her awareness of these strong men has not brought her satisfactory pleasure."

Standing next to one of the hunters, he pulled on the breechcloth waist band. He continued, "This has a braid around the center. When pulled loose, the breechcloth will fall. You are strong men with patience and endurance, having the ability to resist temptation. Remember to stare at the ground, do not raise your eyes to the water! Tonight, you are to follow Waugh'se'waw'brah for he desperately wants to go back to the lake."

Dusk light brought a peaceful hue to the land. Waugh'se'waw'brah impatiently yanked the bark door covering aside. There were no guards. His emotions soared as he studied the village, there was no one within sight. Slipping his moccasins on, he crouched around the wicki-ups to race through the rabbit brush, prickly pear cactus and sweet grasses of the flatland to the base of the mountain. Fingers felt alongside the cliff face to the footholds. Silent as the hare in the night, he ascended the escarpment, letting the slight sliver of moon guide him. Waugh'se'waw'brah was not aware of the four strong hunters who quietly tracked him from a distance. Waugh'se'waw'brah patiently perched at the edge of the lake where he had his previous encounter with her. Soundlessly, the four other men quietly knelt in a half circle an arms' length behind him.

As the moon sliver disappeared over the horizon and the night became flat black, there was a gurgling noise that rippled across the mountain lake's water. Sleeping ducks beat their wings to take flight. Slithering water snakes surged slipping onto the muddy embankment. Waugh'se'waw'brah's breathing quickened as he stared without blinking at the water. Underneath the dark surface of the lake, a glowing yellow orb surged straight for him. Water rippled, slapping against the shore as the golden orb ascended closer and brighter to the surface. Four hunters

stiffly rose to stare at the ground near their feet as they had been ordered. Harsh words had been given to not even think about observing this Spirit Woman. Spirit Woman flew into the air, hovering over the men. Water flickered, sparkling all around, imposing on the hunters' stoic stance.

Spirit Woman extended her hands, lustful fingers spread wide zealously eager to grab Waugh'se'waw'brah's body. Slowly, he bent forward as his feet started to rise from the ground. Hovering with desire, Waugh'se'waw'brah began to soar, floating gracefully toward her. Quickly, hands grabbed him. Two on each side seized his wrists while the other two pushed down on his shoulders. Waugh'se'waw'brah was trapped, held firmly grounded. An animalistic scream emerged from his open mouth. As informed, the four hunters pulled their braided belts with their free hands, allowing their woven breechcloths to descend, falling to their moccasined feet. Sternly, each disrobed naked man kept their chins to their chests, eyes closed as chaos ensued all around them.

First, there was an ear-piercing scream slicing through the quiet night's air. Then the nasty odor of hot sulfur as something splattered on the lake's water. A whirling tornado of hot air was punctuated with popping and crackling lights. The bright orb exploded to disappear into splinters of flame ricocheting off of the lake's edge. A nasty smell hung heavy as the air became still. The four men felt Waugh'se'waw'brah tumble to the ground. Turning their backs to the lake, the four men retrieved their breechcloths, tying them firmly in place.

One of the men laughed, "We must have given her extreme pleasure for she exploded!"

Another shushed him, "Do we know if she is gone? Perhaps we should show her our manliness one more time?"

Whispering, the tallest man held his nose, "She may have been beautiful, but she did stink!"

The fourth man peeked over his shoulder at the lake, "She has gone. There is no sign of her. Come, we must get Waugh'se'waw'brah down the mountain just in case she gets interested again."

Quickly, the four strong hunters knelt to assist Waugh'waw'brah. Gasping for air, he rolled onto his back. His arms were covered with small burns. "Why? Why didn't you let me go with her? Ahhhh!"

The sound of splashing water, brought their attention once again to the lake. Wading onto solid ground came the Shaman. Surging behind him came the other two men. The hunters caught each of them as they fell onto dry land. Hushed breaking waves noted the absence of spirit energy. The stillness of Spirit Woman's disappearance brought Waugh'se'waw'brah to release an agonizing yell, "No, I wanted to go with her! No!"

Waugh'se'waw'brah wrenched his arms free from the men as he tried to plunge himself into the cold water. Floundering in his search for the Spirit Woman, he almost drown. Two of the hunters dragged him ashore while he sobbed uncontrollably. "She held the answers! You have sent her to the Land of the Dead! We needed her wisdom! I wanted to go with her! She was not a *nadowe*, not a spirit taker!" His body was racked with emotional pain.

Dawn brought all of the men to the village. Elders drilled the Shaman and the others about Spirit Woman. Waugh'se'waw'brah refused to speak as his woman tended to his burns. His children and his father attempted to calm him, but Waugh'se'waw'brah was inconsolable. The Elders congratulated the strong hunters, asking them all kinds of questions. Hunters shook their heads for their only concepts were of the sickening smell of sulfur and the piercing scream. Once the Shaman had explained his dark existence under the lake, he gathered his bedroll to leave, following the path to the east. His vision while in the lake told him to live by the Mississippi River.

Waugh'se'waw'brah continued to dream of the Woman Spirit, but no one ever saw her again. Settlers continued to infringe on their land with an endless supply of cattle, horses and weapons. Finally, the U.S. Government corralled the Native People to the government reservation at Walker Lake. This all happened a very long time ago.

Notes:

The term Paiute has been given to the Shoshone tribes of west Utah, northern Arizona, southern Idaho, eastern Oregon, Nevada, eastern and southern California. The Paiute in this story are relative to Utah. The magic of water in a place where water is scarce, can be disconcerting for sometimes the spirit in the water is friendly and at osther times deadly. This story holds a concept of water as the feminine, alone and lonely. There are times when one must use magic to overcome magic, as found in this story. While collecting stories for my book White Wolf Woman, I met a Shoshone man at the Indian Cultural Center who was visiting his family. He was sitting next to my family later when we were at the Pow-wow and he told this story with a Paiute friend who was bragging about how good looking the Paiute men still are today.

Glossary:

Aga'ih-tika'ra – Fish Eaters.
Aga'idokado – Cut Throat Trout Eaters.
Ba'waa – Going around a circle, ceremonial council or meeting.
Cui-ui – Large Fish Eaters.
Friendship Treaty 1855 – Some Paiute joined with Shshone to survive.
Ho'gap – Tule Rushes found neat Cat Tails in wet soil.
Hutsi – Sage hen.
Ibidsii – Spirit Mother (Creator).
Koto'ti'kara – Buffalo Eaters.
Kura'ngwa – Mount Grant also high peak southwest of Lake Walker, Nevada.
Kuuidokado – Large fish eaters.
Nadowe – Beheader, Spirit taker.
Numi'naa' – Spirit Father (Creator).
Pakwidokao – Chumb Carp Eaters.
Pa – Water.
Pai' – True.
P'agu'nava – Fog, lake fog.
Pai-u-ti – What the Paiute call themselves, 'Those who come from Water.'
Pau"bi – Sacred Willow bundle.
Pyramid Lake War 1860 – Paiute were defeated and more joined the

Shoshone against outsiders
Takwau'kwij – lightning
Tsiaget Tuvi'warai – Those who lived in the mountains
Ya'natatu' – I am still sitting.
Walker War 1854 – Utes versus the Mormons and U.S. Army.
Wick-i-up – frame hut covered with matting of bark and brush with oval base.
Temporary shelter easy to take down, move and put up.
Wi'noghan – Shaking wind.

9
THE WEEPING OF EARTH MOTHER

The Story of the New Mother Well, Red Water Well
ASIAN INDIAN

This story tells of a mighty Muslim Sultan who with his murdering hordes took over the villages and lands in the state now known as Maharashtra. Five hundred years ago, this strong and ferocious Muslim Sultan who became ruler of the land around Solapur, enslaved the farming people. The Bahmani kingdom was founded around the year 1346. The chief economic activity in the Bahmani kingdom was agriculture and the main revenue of the state was produced in the form of agricultural products. The Bahmani kingdom flourished in architectural monuments. It is said that the Solapur *bhuikot* was built in the 14th century under the rule of Bahmani Dynasty in the memory of Hutatma Bagh. Since then it has been conquered by many rulers.

In 1357, the land belonging to the Muslim Sultan was to have built on it a huge fort with tall, diametrically shaped turrets. Once it was decided that the *bhuikot* should be built at Solapur, this huge task needed to be carried out responsibly. The preparations began with a well-planned design. An appropriate location with elevated land was found. There was ample water for mixing the chink to use, holding the large cut stones in place as they were building the walls and bastions. Wells were already there, dug by the Hindu farmers for irrigation and drinking water. These wells had never dried out. Therefore, there was no lack of water for drinking and usage.

Once the land was finalized, the building began in earnest. There were some policy decisions with respect to the construction of the fort. It was decided that the fort would have two protective walls for security. The total land area inside the external wall was planned to contain twenty-four acres. Four bastions were to be built in the four corners of the land and a second protective wall was planned on the inside of the external wall. Bastions were also to be built within the inside wall. A number of other details about the inner construction work of the fort were agreed to by the architect and the Muslim Sultan.

The first task was to dig the land for the laying of the foundation. This required deep trenching for the first layers of stones to be rolled, cut and formed fitting the foundations as these had to be specially shaped and fit. These stones needed to be level, placed in a deeply dug solid ground for the next layer of stones to be layered. Trenches were at least six to eight feet deep, dug into the rich earth's soil to sustain the weight of the walls and bastions. Again, stones were rolled, cut and formed, placed and chinked, rising higher and higher for fortification.

The construction work of the Solapur *bhuikot* was thus underway at a rapid pace. Wage slaves were doing hard labour, even women and young children were ordered to the task. The work force toiled to the point of collapsing. The scorching sun made them faint, yet the building didn't stop. In fact, it went on day and night. Strong, healthy bull oxen were brought to turn the grinding stones, milling the lime powder to put into the chinking mud. Lime stones were ground twenty-four hours a day. Even the strong oxen were exhausted for they were not allowed to rest while walking round and round, grinding lime stones in horizontal mills. The output of lime powder was stored in hundreds of large open tanks.

Whips lashed out constantly as overseers pushed the labourers to work harder, faster and into the night. The yokes on their necks rubbed their skin raw, the whips cut deeply bleeding their bare backs. Hundreds of elephants were employed to drag large stones to the construction site and have them arranged as required. The same elephants were used over and over again to hoist the heavy timber, haul immense boulders only to be whipped repeatedly.

Women and children transported medium to small stones, stacking them at the edge of the deep trenches where they were lifted, hand over hand to the stone masons deep inside. There was no time to rest for the Sultan wanted his fort to be built quickly! The endless toil drove the workers to a breaking point, many died, others collapsed, but the Sultan wanted the fort to be constructed fast, so he himself oversaw the progress. The Sultan was carried in his litter, or king carrier, to the site. There, he would dismount from his seat of soft silk pillows protected from the sun with an elaborately embroidered cloth roof to speak with the overseer of the area. Sweepers cleared the ground in front of him to keep stones and debris from hurting his feet dressed in silk slippers. Once his approval was noted, he was decadently returned to his luxurious palace. As a result, the concerned overseers and officials were extra conscientious in fervently performing their duty to accelerate slaves and beasts in their drudgery.

The foundation tunnelling for the inner protective wall was completed. The wall's lengthy excavation was packed with specifically cut stones when work on the first bastion began. At the same time, the diagonally opposite bastion in the NorthEast corner started. Deeper trenches, diagonally excavated radiated from the ten-foot-deep hole, forming a solid foundation. This area needed to be firm, strong with an open room in the base for storing goods or weapons in case of war. First the stone stairs were built, allowing for the ease in transferring stones to the masons. A narrow area was left open for those who were laying the stone work. Each stone mason stood within a hole, placed in a precariously tight space, allowing short quick movements to lay the heavy stone, chink it with hot mud laced with limestone powder. Fingers bled as the limestone powder ate away at their skin.

The first bastion rose quickly, however, the work of the second bastion languished. When the filling of the bastions' foundations were completed and the construction of the upper portions rose to about six to eight feet, barely reaching halfway to normal height, the girth of the bastions were fine. The Sultan came, inspected it and was pleased. He expressed satisfaction about the pace of work in progress.

Four days later, the height of the second bastion was a work in progress. The bastion tilted, inclining slightly. Days passed with the bastion noticeably drooping, before the workers were able to file out of the narrow space tunnelled beside it, there was a thunderous crash. The land shook. The bastion crumbled to the ground, maiming workers, ripping limbs from brick layers! Others were buried in the manmade tomb of deadly rock debris. A calamitous cloud choked the air as the fine dust ascended into the sky. The deafening sound caused the elephants to go berserk. As they ran amok in fear, they crushed the people in their path. Chaos, confusion and loss of control erupted at the construction site.

The Sultan's voice roared, "What? What has happened now? You workers, are to build not destroy!! You should all be whipped! Fix This! This is not to happen again!"

Officials knelt before the short Sultan with his jewelled slippers. The Sultan's golden sword was sheathed in its hilt, hanging on his woven gold belt. His closely trimmed beard trembled as did his rage, "Are you idiots? We are building a fort not piles of stone!"

Men in charge were threatened with death if the work was not resumed promptly. Officials ran to the fallen bastion. Whips in hand, faces red with anger, they questioned overseers. Slaves lashed, crazed elephants captured, women and children frantically retrenched, removed, and hollowed the trench. How did this happen? What went wrong? Whose mistake was it? An inquiry was conducted and the stone masons were blamed for the disaster. They were given severe punishments. Injured workers were tossed out of the way. Mothers and wives wailed searching for their mutilated or dead children and husbands. Children were crying for their parents. Officials cracked whips to keep order, the building was to begin, again. The bastion was to be rebuilt promptly!

More experienced and skilled stone masons were relocated here, brought in to lay the deep stonework in the bastion's trenching at the Northeast corner. The work was carefully done, inspected and continued. The construction rose to only a few feet before the stones in the angled walls began to tilt to one side. Hurriedly, elephant guards were ordered to drag in strong wooden posts made from wide rounded trees. Loggers pounded these in place with heavily weighted wooden sledge hammers. Ropes girdled the stone structure to hold the bastion upright and tightly in place. Slowly, the thick posts cracked, creaked, and fractured, gradually crumbling stone by stone to slide into a cave-in within hours.

"What?" Roared the Sultan, his face red with anger, "What! This cannot happen again! We are building this fort!"

Perched in finery on his throne, this time he chose blame, "You two on the end, you are to be whipped forty times! You three, take them away! This bastion is killing workers, they are hard to find! Get this bastion built! No more excuses! Go!"

New officials were given instructions and orders. An epidemic of fear rippled throughout the compound. Four times the number of slave workers were retrieved from neighbouring counties. Each day, they trembled at the thought of being down in that subterranean trench to be maimed or killed under the heavy rock. Whips were cracked constantly over bare flesh. Guards were placed to be stringently aware of each worker, making sure no one was purposely causing destruction. Each stone was officiated by the architect, the chink mud mixture with limestone was carefully inspected. This bastion was costing the Sultan time and labour.

In one full morning's worth of labour, the bastion only reached five feet in height, which was still not even close to being level with the land around it. Bloody hands of the masons collected only certain stones to carefully chink mud mixed with lime powder, checking to maintain a level balance. Wooden buckets filled with mud were brought, mixers coughed up thick phlegm as the lime powder was inhaled. Aching bent backs of the women and children who continuously carried building stone and rock flowed to the site. The bastion crept taller with careful inspection, rising a few feet every hour. Then cracks appeared. A creaking and groaning started at the base of the bastion.

Officials yelled, "Workers, get over here. Hold this up! All of you push, push up against this! The mud and lime are deficient, the rocks are too heavy, push with all of your strength! Push with might, keep this bastion upright!"

Whips cut through bleeding bare skin. Elephants leaned against the tall posts placed to hold the bastion's walls straight. A deep rumbling shook inside the earth as trembling stones splintered into pieces. The bastion shivered and sighed as it crumbled to crush the workers. Exhausted overseers watched in disbelief.

"No! No!" Officials fell to their knees, staring down at the piles of stone and mud. Wounded workers crawled out with raw backs and broken bones, swearing never to return. Tied elephants trumpeted as they stamped their feet, quaking the earth. This same mishap repeated a third time!

Who would tell the Sultan? Dropping their whips, conversing with each other, the officials knew some of them would have to pay for this tragedy. The sound of men arriving turned their attention to the Sultan's litter arriving. Red faced carriers gently placed it on the ground. The Sultan leapt from his cushioned chair.

Directly storming to the officials, his jewelled fingers were clenched in fists of rage, "Again! Again, this bastion falls!" Stomping to the lead official, he bellowed, "Did you do this? Was this your idea of success? Are you a complete idiot?"

Kneeling before the great Sultan, the official meekly answered, "No, The Great Sultan. The bastion shook from the base, from the ground. The stones, the mud, the lime, the stone placement was all done to specifications. The falling of the bastion appears to have come from deep inside the earth, Sir."

Shoving a stone aside with his small foot in a jewelled slipper, the Sultan wiped his hand on his white pleated pantaloons with gold trim. "Call the architects! Call the counsellors! It is time for a discussion!"

Rubbing his ring finger across his short moustache, he raised his trimmed eyebrows. "It is time for a discussion on matters of building and supernatural interference!" He got into his litter and orded his slaves to hurry and get back to his palace.

It was decided by the conferring architects that the stone masons had done excellent work. The stone, the mud, the lime powder and the workers were all professionals. The Sultan was not convinced, "What if the angles of the walls continually collapse again and again? We cannot waste time building and rebuilding! If there is no logical reason for the falling of the bastion's foundation wall, then it must be spiritual! This must be resolved or more will die!"

After consulting with his architects who failed to explain the phenomenon, it was decided an astrologer should be consulted. The Sultan sat on his pillowed chair with a peacock fan waved over his head by a slave, "Who would be the best to consult? Who knows of the problems with earth and building?"

A high caste official bowed to him, "Perhaps an astrologer who has knowledge of this land and of these people. Perhaps a Hindu astrologer who lives on the hill above the fort? Perhaps, he would be able to suggest a solution." This was agreed upon unanimously.

On the Muslim Sultan's order this Hindu Brahman astrologer was brought to him. A thin man, in his later years, perplexedly arrived. His white hair was long and plaited to form a crest on the top of his head, his long white beard flowed to his belly and a long red mark was painted on his forehead. This humble man wore a simple white cloth wrapped around his thin waist. This skinny, tanned astrologer with his sturdy bare feet, stood cautiously eyeing the mighty ruler. The heavy, well dressed Sultan sat cross-legged on his silk pillows with trays of decadent food surrounding him, studying the thin man. Finally, the Sultan explained the frustrating situation.

The Hindu Brahman explained, "This predicament asks for the preparation of a horoscope for this fort. To do this, one must check the positions of the various planets."

The Sultan's voice roared, "Do it and do it quickly!"

The Brahman shook his head, "In order for the measurements to be precise, I must visit the site of the bastion and speak with the people there."

Grabbing a handful of nuts, the Sultan waved his hand at him, "Then go! Go! When shall you have an answer?"

The skinny man put his index finger to his lips, "Ah, if I am not hurried and am given time to meditate clearly, possibly late tomorrow." Bowing, the Hindu Brahman exited the palace to find his way to the actual site of the bastion. Soon one of the Sultan's guards met with him, ordering the officials and overseers to share their views leading to the events of the bastion's doom. Contemplating the situation, the thin Hindu Brahman slowly ambled his way home to bathe, think and sit in meditation. Contemplating the bastion enigma, he focused all his mental energy on the construction site, the sighing of the earth and the specific spot where the bastion was being built.

Invoking the Land Goddess and receiving supernatural gyrations, he channelled into a divinely inspired communication, 'This specific area of land needs a sacrifice, a human sacrifice. The bastion would stand with the Land Goddesses' support if she received a sacrifice. The resident Supreme Being must receive the sacrifice of a new mother, pregnant with child to be given to her alive. This will appease the Supreme Being. Only then will she allow the bastion to stand tall.' The astrologer understood the spiritual communication. The planets had given him the solution.

The next day, the Hindu Brahman astrologer bathed, performed *puja*, or time of worship and tended to his domestic deities. After deep meditation, he decided to bestow the message to the Sultan. As he neared the palace, guards approached him, escorting the little man directly to the high throne of the mighty Muslim Sultan.

Sitting, the Sultan welcomed him, asking, "O wise Brahman, you are the authority on this subject. You hold the knowledge of the past, the present and the future. You know how to communicate with the spiritual powers, tell me what they say? What do your planets of science say about this? What's the solution? Will the bastion hold at all? Shall we rebuild?"

Testing the Sultan's patience, the Hindu Brahman silently focused his mind into a trance-like state to speak in a monotone, "O Sultan, the planetary position in your horoscope is good. Your success in this work is positive. There is no doubt in my mind that the fort will be completed and shall stand for hundreds of years. The land area is good. All is suitable and favourable."

Hearing the Brahman, the Sultan gave a sigh of relief, however, this was not a solution to the immediate problem. The Sultan shook his head, barking at the Hindu astrologer in a booming voice, "O Brahman, I am relieved to hear your assuring words. The immediate problem is not yet solved by your prediction. Why does the bastion keep crashing? It has happened three times. Is there any specific reason behind this? Can you please suggest a solution to this issue?"

The Hindu Brahman softly spoke in a sad tone, "O Sultan, there is a solution to this problem. If you do what I tell you to do, the bastion will be built and will be strong."

The thin man shook his head, "The problem lies in the land's demands. Listen, the land under the bastion needs a sacrifice. A human sacrifice! This sacrifice must be a pregnant woman who is close to giving birth to her child!" Saying this, the astrologer stopped.

A stunned silence fell over the Sultan's court. Sighing, the Sultan frowned, "The land demands a pregnant woman and her unborn child? What or how does she demand this to happen?"

Placing his palms together in front of his bare chest, the Brahman closed his eyes to say, "She must be buried alive under the bastion foundation for her and her unborn infant must be gifts to the Land Goddess. Although, this new mother must volunteer. She cannot be pressured or harassed to do this or your bastion will not be completed."

Clapping his hands, the Sultan ordered the Hindu Brahman astrologer to be paid handsomely for his vision. The Brahman graciously took the Sultan's leave and pleasantly returned to his home. This harsh prophecy left the Sultan to ponder how this would be brought to happen. Quickly, the Sultan called for the ministers' court who were told of the Brahman astrologer's vision. These courtiers appreciated the wisdom and power of this astrologer. The decision was to garner all the pregnant women to volunteer, but they needed someone who knew the people and their families.

The responsibility of finding an appropriate pregnant woman was soon entrusted to the *patil* or the chief of the town. He was easily noticed for his wrapped white turban and thick moustache. Reviewing the public announcement, *patil* chose words appropriate for the people of the whole town, including the workers, officials and warriors. *Patil* made the necessary arrangements as to when and who would announce this serious public request.

Early one morning, the town crier beat his drum in Solapur, "Listen! Listen! Listen! All of you subjects! Listen! Listen! Listen! God's representative for the great Sultan has ordered this fort to be built in your town. He has ordered for the bastions to be built and wants them to be built quickly."

Beckoning the people to him with his hands, he continued, "Listen all, come forward! Listen carefully. The great Sultan wants this fort to be strong and sturdy. The Northeast bastion of this fort requires a human sacrifice. It asks for a pregnant woman to come forth, sacrificing herself and her unborn child for the good of the fort and its people. The bastion will continue to fall, killing the workers until a pregnant woman comes to offer herself. Therefore, the fort is not being completed."

Taking a deep breath, he shouted, "Listen, all subjects! Listen! Listen! Listen! The bastion of the fort must have a live sacrifice. The Spiritual Being wants a pregnant woman in order for the Northeast bastion to hold strong. It is asking for a mother-to-be who is still pregnant with her baby. Every day workers are killed, please, come forward."

Putting his hands out to quiet the masses standing around him, he continued to call out, "Listen, all! The mother-to-be who comes forward shall be given a handsome reward for her family's loss. Come forward, pregnant women, come quickly!"

People were listening to him anxiously and fearfully. They were curious about what more was going to be in his announcement.

Again, he put his hands out to get their attention, "Listen! Listen! Listen! The great Sultan is anxious to have the Northeast bastion completed. Please, all pregnant women come forward quickly! Offer yourself and your child to save others!" Announcing the Sultan's proclamation, he beat his drum. "Many will die, a pregnant mother must come forward or more will die!"

Hearing the announcement, the townspeople became terrified. Pregnant women hid, covering their extended abdomens. Husbands told their expectant wives to stay inside, to avoid the Sultan's men who were searching the streets for pregnant women. Many of the workers stopped going to work for fear their family would be whipped or beaten because they would not comply. No one wanted to sacrifice their unborn baby or themselves. This decree filled the town with a quiet terror, fearful of everyone and anyone who might tell the Sultan's men. An undercurrent of extreme tension permeated every home, every work place and every person. Everyone was scared.

The town's chief known as the Patil was also a well-respected Hindu *Lingayat vani* or the grocer of the town. The Sultan favored this Patil, buying all his supplies for the palace, for the guards and his officials from him. This favoritism to Patil brought him great wealth and prestige. Patil's elaborate home included all of his extended and immediate family as tradition would have it. There were his adult children and everyone's in-laws. The whole family enjoyed Patil's success for he was a rich man. His family was well aware of the bastion collapsing for this had been discussed many times over dinner.

When Patil's family heard of the public announcement, they grew anxious. They thought, "Will pregnant women come forward willingly for sacrifice? Who would be the brave woman?"

At that time, there was a good news in the Patil's home. His daughter-in-law was pregnant. Patil and family members were delighted. They were eager to welcome this new child for this one would have the importance of being part of this well-off family, a continuation of *patils*.

Her pregnancy was in its advanced stage. Clothes, plans and ceremonies were already set for this new-born who would be spoiled and loved by the whole family. Her husband, Patil's son was excited and pleased. Patil grew each day in his importance in becoming a grandfather, once again. Patil's wife, the soon-to-be grandmother talked incessantly about her daughter-in-law and the baby. Overall, the family felt safe, content and happy.

Patil, who arranged for the public announcement, was worried and uncertain. During the day while out in public, he became grim, curt and pale while losing interest in his businesses. Days passed, his short temper became more noticeable. Padmavati or sacred lotus, his pregnant daughter-in-law had very strong rigid ethics. This young woman spoke her mind and her views were realistic. She was balanced and resolute and had the uncanny knack of reading other people's minds. Padmavati knew her mother-in-law loved and cared for her, wanting to keep her healthy and well. During the day, her mother-in-law patted Padmavati's abdomen, rubbing it to feel the baby move. These two discussed baby names and had chosen all the baby clothes and needs for the new born. The experienced and knowledgeable *suyin*, midwife was ready when the time came. *patil* constantly asked about her health. The young wife Padmavati was happy with all this care and love.

Patil's pale face and nervous tendencies became obvious to her. She noticed his preoccupation and constant worry. He wasn't eating and this was most unusual. When she spoke to him, he avoided looking into her eyes. Days would pass and now, he wouldn't ask about her health or how she was feeling. Keeping quiet, Padmavati pondered on how to relieve her father-in-law's preoccupation. Questioning her actions in relation to him, she asked the house deities to guide her in this situation. She prayed to Lord Shiva and Goddess Parvati for peace of mind while, also, seeking blessings for her family. Feeling her baby move in her womb, helped reassure her.

Weeks had passed after the announcement and no one had come forward. The work was stopped at the bastion, but the Sultan's patience was waning. Workers hastily continued at the rest of the fort, making good progress. Soon something had to be done or more would die at the bastion that was not appeased. Women spoke in hushed voices during the day and behind locked doors in the night. Children were cautioned of saying anything about their mothers, aunts or older sisters. Solapur became a town filled with apprehension and dread. Certainly, someone would break a promise to tell the Sultan's men of a pregnant woman regardless of unity.

This one typical night when darkness fell and stars dotted the sky, the town went to sleep as did *patil*'s home. Padmavati snuggled close to her husband, studying his happy, carefree face. Then she tightly closed her eyes. Her husband noticed the strain in her face. Wrinkle lines appeared across her forehead. He wondered why his beautiful wife worried. Watching her sleep, he thought, "Why is she tense? What does she worry about when I give her everything? Maybe she is hiding something from me. What is she not telling me?" Lovingly, he put his hand on her arm, patting her, kissing her, he whispered, "My beloved Padmavati, what is the matter? Why are you restless? Are you hiding something from me?"

She opened her eyes, but said nothing.

He whispered, "My Padmavati, we love each other. We share everything with one another, what has happened to make you worried? Please tell me your thoughts, what is on your mind?"

Padmavati lifted on her bent elbow to focus on his brown eyes filled with love. She spoke softly, "Our family is very prestigious, yes? Everyone respects us. Even the great Sultan honours our family. Your beloved father, my successful father-in-law has respect from all the town's people of Solapur. Now, he has a serious responsibility. There is a desperate need for a pregnant woman to save Solapur, the fort and all the people who work within it. Your father will suffer if no one comes forward. Again, this is his responsibility."

Searching for the correct words, she reached for his hand, "One pregnant woman is the salvation of the many. Your father is terrified no one will volunteer. Remember this woman must offer herself, she must choose this role or the bastion will not hold. Someone needs to come forward." She paused, noticing the worry in her husband's face.

Interrupting her, he squeezed her hand, "Padmavati, what can I do? I can't help him? Father should be satisfied for our great Sultan understands why the bastion falls. The Fort must be built as soon as possible for the people's security, for the Kingdom's safety. What woman would honestly give their life to this cause? Who would sacrifice their unborn child for this cause? Where do we find a woman, who is pregnant and wants to do this?"

Padmavati heard his words. She fell back on the bed to a deep breath, "Listen, carefully, I believe our family should take responsibility to solve this problem."

Nervously, her husband asked, "But how? How could we help? How can we take responsibility for this? How would we convince a pregnant woman to sacrifice herself and her unborn child? How would this be possible? Tell me?"

Padmavati closed her eyes. Once more, she took hold of his hand, "I love you. I love all of our family. I love my unborn child who is waiting to enter this world. I am eager to see his innocent face, but at the same time, I love all of our people."

Sitting up, staring at her, he gasped, "What? What are you proposing?"

Warmly studying his eyes, she went on, "Our Great Sultan is erecting a fort for our people's security and also for our kingdom to remain safe. I keep thinking of the Great Sultan. I am sure, no pregnant woman will come forward to help."

Quietly, she stopped. Her husband stared at her with disbelieving eyes. Gasping, he asked her, "What? What are you talking about? Are you mad? What do you mean by 'help?' What?"

Padmavati nodded her head, 'yes.'

Angrily, he shouted, "No. No. No! It is not possible! I love you, you are my beloved wife! I love my son, our child! No! I will find a pregnant woman who will gladly give her life and her child to save the fort and the workers. We can pay a woman, or her whole family or someone from another village to come forward. No! You are not going to do this, No! I will not allow this! No!"

Tension filled the room. Both were standing, facing the other at the foot of the bed. Neither of them spoke. The only sound was of a cricket, chirping.

After a few moments, Padmavati pushed her long hair from her face to whisper, "Yes, it is true that I will die with our baby, but look at this positively. If I do this, the bastion will hold. The fort will be built and the Great Sultan will be pleased. The people will be safe. Our kingdom will be secure. And another thing, your prestige will grow. Our family's prestige will grow. Our family will be remembered, forever. As it is, everyone has to die someday. I could die in childbirth. No one is immortal. Who remembers those who die doing nothing? Many live and die and aren't remembered for anything at all. Isn't it better to die and be remembered for something important?"

Frantically, he shook his head, yet she continued, "Everyone's life is valuable. Death should have a purpose as well. There should be significance in dying. If I die to better the welfare of others, then I am happy to do this. Soldiers die to protect life. I will die, but the bastion shall hold and the kingdom will be safe, our people will be live."

Her husband turned away from her, trying to get her to stop. Padmavati hurried to face him, adding, "Also, this would be for our family's prestige. I will die, but many will be saved." Her face was shining because of her patriotism and confidence. Again, it was quiet, one could hear a pin drop. Not even the cricket chirped now. No one spoke.

Her husband put his hands on her shoulders, "Do you love me? Do you care about my feelings?"

Glancing at his bare feet, she whispered, "You know I do."

Pulling her down to kneel with him, he asked, "This child within you is mine as well as yours." His hand rested on her abdomen, "You may carry this child, but I am responsible for him. I will fight for his life even if you choose to give your life away."

Quickly shoving his chest away, she gasped, "You would fight me on this? Really? You are ready to go against me and all the gods of this household?" Leaning on the side of the bed, her face was red with anger. "Yes, this decision was not made lightly! I didn't just wake up and decide to do this, oh, no, I prayed and asked for guidance as we have all been taught!"

Her husband's hand rubbed his forehead, "You mean you have prayed about this without discussing this huge decision with me?"

Taking hold of his wrist, she lifted his chin, "What would you have said then that you aren't saying now? Don't you know me? Of course, I love you. I love this baby, but the gods have a higher purpose designed for me and the baby. How could I discuss this with you rationally? This isn't something I could talk about to anyone, but I could pray and ask for guidance."

Not knowing how to continue this conversation, her husband helped her into the bed. Grabbing his day clothes off of a peg, he answered her, "If you have found your answer from prayer, it must be so, but I cannot stay here tonight. I need to walk and think and pray."

Padmavati loudly whispered, "Please, please, allow me to do this. Even though I will die doing this, my heart will still be with you. Our child will always be in your memory. Please, this is important."

Padmavati's husband knew his wife was dedicated to this for she was patriotic and loyal to her people. Lifting his hand, he rubbed her abdomen, feeling the unborn infant move inside of her. Tears fell from his eyes as he left the room. Padmavati's husband was stunned! He was completely at a loss for words. Going outside of the home, studying the stars, his brain stopped working. After leaning against the side of the house for a time, knowing she would want his company, he returned to the bedroom. Pulling her close, he held her tightly. He was overwhelmed by his wife's dedication to her religious beliefs as well as her consideration for others. Humbly, he would support her, mutely. A long time passed where they just lay there silently in each other's embrace. The cool breeze of the early morning, found them sleeping.

As the sky began to brighten, Padmavati awoke. She was calm now and cheerful. She bowed before Lord Shiva and Goddess Parvati and asked them to give her the strength to carry out this important life decision. She bathed and then went to the household shrine to apply *vibhuti*, holy ash on her forehead. Once again, she performed the *puja* ritual to Lord Shiva, seeking the Lord's blessings and courage, praying for the family idol to care for the family after she was gone. Then she called all of her family together, including her in-laws to gather around her. Everyone was interested to know why she called for them so early in the morning.

Padmavati remained silent as she knelt to touch the feet of her in-laws and her husband. Rising, she studied each face to speak in a resolute voice, "*Mananji* father-in-law, the fort of our Great Sultan needs to be completed. In order for the bastion to hold something should be done or more of our people will die. This town is our way of life and must be protected. The Sultan has a lot of honor for you and you respect him. I have noticed your worry because of his impatience. Especially since the public announcement about the sacrifice, I see this has disturbed you, though you have done arrangements for the announcement you are constantly lost in thought. You're not eating or sleeping and for the past couple of days, you didn't remember to even inquire about my well-being!"

"No, my child," *patil* said nervously, "nothing of what you say is happening. You're being too sensitive. Pregnant women have a way of reading too much into things."

"I know what all of you are thinking," Padmavati continued. "As a responsible authority and the chief of the town, you, are worried about the fort, about the bastion. You are thinking which pregnant woman would willingly sacrifice herself and her baby? Aren't you? You are anxious about who would help the Great Sultan? You think it's your responsibility to find an answer. So, please don't worry. Don't trouble yourself so much."

Quietly, she stopped to notice her family's response, especially her husband's. They studied her as she seriously said with conviction, "Well, I'm a pregnant woman myself." Touching her protruding abdomen, she continued, "I have our eight-month old baby inside my womb. I fit the requirements of the task. No more people should die! If I give my life and my baby's life to the bastion many others will live."

Struggling with the words and trying not to cry, Padmavati continued, "Our kingdom's security and the people's safety is more important than my life or the life of our baby. I am a responsible daughter-in-law with a responsible father-in-law. Our lives have been dedicated to the people and the Great Sultan's kingdom."

Noticing the worry in her family's faces, Padmavati lowered her voice, "Please allow me to do this. I have prayed and prayed, waiting for an answer. Lord Shiva and Goddess Parvati have given me the courage. Please. Last night, I spoke with my honourable husband," nodding to her in-laws, "Your son was asked and I requested his permission to do this. I convinced him."

Her husband wiped a tear from his cheek as she spoke, "My loving husband has allowed me to do this. Understand, there is a great sadness in his heart." Studying her hands, she said, "Now, I am requesting you, my *mamanji* and *sasubai*, father-in-law and my mother-in-law, to please give your permission in my saving our people and to have a strong fort built. Let me save the dying people. Please allow me to do this, please! Please! Please!"

Forcefully, she added, "Inform the Great Sultan right away that I am ready. What are you thinking? Let's plan for this today!"

Padmavati let her words be absorbed. Some just stared at her in disbelief. Others shook their heads to mumble. The women were quietly crying. Her family was too startled to speak. They were in shock. Nervous energy filled Padmavati until the mother-in-law sobbing uncontrollably went to her daughter-in-law and hugged her.

In a wavering voice, Padmavati's mother-in-law asked, "My dear daughter, who told you to do this? Why are you doing this? Why this deadly thought?" Being beside Padmavati, the mother-in-law was not able to say more. She caressed and patted her, trying to understand.

Padmavati's father-in-law was a courageous rational man, but when he heard of her decision, he quickly dismissed her, "You are a silly girl, and I wasn't worried about that. Never, never did I want you to give your life or the life of my grandchild to the bastion! Never!" Standing tall, he added, "Pregnant women have irrational thoughts. I certainly did not need for you to even consider doing such a thing. We need you here with us! We want our grandchild. Abandon this stupid thought at once!"

The family discussion became heated and continued for some time, but in the end, Padmavati was firm in her conviction. She repeated the words, "It's true that I will die with my baby, but look at the positive aspect. If I do this, the bastion will hold, and the Great Sultan's fort will be completed! No more people will die! No more people will be whipped, killed, wounded or hurt! If we wait, people suffer!"

Padmavati placed her hands in her lap, "This fort must come into existence! Your prestige will grow and you will be rewarded. Our family will be remembered forever for saving lives!"

Her husband stood behind her as she continued, "As it is, everyone has to die someday. No one's immortal. Do you remember those who have died doing nothing worthwhile? Certainly, everyone is vital to their family and their community, but I am willing to die so others shall live. This bastion shall kill many more unless someone does something and that someone is me. The bastion of the fort will hold and so will our family's memory. So, please allow me."

Everyone fell silent as the father-in-law Patil grumbled his way out of the family home to have a meeting at the Sultan's palace. Bowing before the great Sultan, *patil*'s voice was hesitant, "My daughter-in-law Padmavati is pregnant. In order to allay your anxiety, in order to have the fort built to protect the town and in order to have the bastion completed, she willingly offers to be sacrificed with her unborn baby. We are ready. Kindly give your permission to proceed."

The great Sultan stared at *patil*'s blunt honesty. Smiling as he stroked his moustache, the great Sultan nodded, "Good, now the work can continue. Once your daughter-in-law has performed her duty, your family shall be rewarded greatly for this sacrifice. She is to be honored."

The next morning, Padmavati awoke early. She showered, went to the household shrine and applied the *vibhuti* on her forehead to perform the *puja* ritual to Lord Shiva as usual. Afterward, she draped herself in a new green *saree* and rolled green bangles on her forearms. Along with all of her gold facial jewellery, she laced a red *kunku* onto her forehead. Bowing, she made obeisance to her elders for their blessings. They blessed her with sad hearts. Her mother-in-law gave her a cup of milk. Then put some yogurt on her palm. Her mother-in-law applied *halad* and *kunku* on her forehead and placed a garland of flowers around her neck.

The path from her house to the construction site of the fort's bastion was already sprayed with a mixture of water, *halad* and *kunku*. The villagers and workers had laid cloth strips on the road as a carpet. Strongly scented flowers were scattered on these cloth strips for this honorable woman to walk upon as she passed through town. Everyone for miles around had gathered to accompany her as she courageously marched from her home to the site. *Sanai*-chaughda played music. Lining the road was a grateful crowd of all religions, castes, and faiths, who had come especially to behold this brave woman. Many of them joined in her procession. Her path was overflowing with a gracious public, tossing *halad* and *kunku* out of respect. Children showered her with flowers, placing blossoms before her. Overwhelmed by her courage and generosity, many workers knelt to her or reached out to touch her feet. Her name was chanted as people called out her glory.

The sun was high in the sky when the sacrificial ritual began. As the procession reached her destination, she became serene. After touching the feet of her father-in-law and her mother-in-law, she gazed into the pained eyes of her husband. Stoically, her fingers gently rubbed his feet for the final time. Chin high, eyes forward, she gracefully descended the stone stairs into the underground room at the base of the bastion. A stunned silence fell all around. Padmavati had requested for the cold underground room to be prepared. Food and water were in hampers. Some of her clothes were neatly folded. Someone had brought in a cradle for the baby. Padmavati was calm. Noticing the sun fade as stones were layered to lock her inside, she remembered Lord Shiva and Parvati.

Masons continued laying stone over stone above her solitary room. The bastion rose taller and higher. Once the solid stone foundation was complete over Padmavati, the crowd erupted chanting her name. Stones handed to masons, placed, chinked and done again brought the voices of the people to be louder and louder.

Finally, the bastion was completed. The strong walls held this time even though the stone structure had swallowed Padmavati and her unborn child! A messenger was sent to the Sultan, informing him of the bastion's completion. There was no mishap this time. The Sultan was elated on hearing the news. Remembering that the construction of the bastion was made possible because of young Padmavati's supreme sacrifice, he declared that henceforth the bastion be called the 'Padmavati Buruj'. The Sultan also bequeathed the post of 'Patil of the Fort' or 'Durg-o-Patil' to Padmavati's father-in-law. Since then, he came to be known as the 'Durgo Patil' and his family as the 'Durgo Patil Family'. Before that his post was 'Town Patil.'

Now, Patil was the chief of town as well as the chief of the fort. The Sultan blessed the family with rich rewards and gifted them several villages as a token of his gratitude. Nearby the bastion, where Padmavati had been sacrificed, was a drinking well. The water was sweet, clean and bluish-green in colour. This well was important to the fort for it never ceased to replenish the people with naturally fresh water. The waterwheel on the well was used to draw water, which was also used for the construction of the fort. Besides, this sweet water quenched the thirst of one and all.

In order to supply this sweet water to Padmavati, under the bastion, an earthen pipeline was installed from the well to her underground room and also a drainage line was installed to an outside area. The idea was to provide enough water for Padmavati to bathe, use and drink, also, allowing for waste to be cleanly removed.

The Story of the New Mother well - Red Water Well

Days passed, when a baby's cries were heard coming from the underground sacrificial room. Padmavati had delivered the baby by herself, alone under the bastion, in the earth. The land received what was asked for and now the sacrifice was complete.

Padmavati was tired due to the effort of childbirth. She needed to clean the baby and wanted to bathe herself as well, but she was weak. Finally, after fainting, she rose to gather water from the pipe and in the cold water bathed them both. The sweet water felt good. Sitting against the cool wall of the room, she nursed her baby. People noticed red, bloody water running out of the drainage pipe, mixing with the well water. The original bluish-green water had acquired a reddish tint. After this, the well became popular as the New Mother Well or Red Water Well. This name allows us to remember the new mother Padmavati. It is important for her supreme sacrifice to not be forgotten.

Some people insist they see the red in the water, others don't notice the color difference. Others argue the red can only be seen on the night of a full moon or no moon nights, many refute this theory saying the reddish tint is only seen now and again and perhaps it is from natural minerals.

Notes:

This legend is related to the earthen fort of Solapur, in the state of Maharashtra. The fort was built a few centuries ago and in it is a well known as *Jajagi Bawadi* or *Balantin Vihir,* meaning the Well of a New Mother. This interesting and dramatic legend attempts to explain why this well is known as the New Mother well and why its water is red. Since the fort at Solapur is a part of the architectural history, this legend is based on historical events that took place about five hundred years ago. References to the bastion collapsing repeatedly, and with a pregnant woman being sacrificed in order to prevent deaths and to protect her people, are found in chapter fourteen, pages 500-501 of the *Gazetteer, Bombay Presidency, Solapur,* published by the British Government in August, 1884.

History is validated by historical edifices, objects and documents. However, when there is a dramatic incident attached to an edifice, the incident soon takes the form of a legend and folk mind being fond of dramatic and miraculous events, gives birth to a legend by mixing history with a concerned dramatic event. Such historical legends keep getting told and retold in an interesting manner from generations to generations. This historical legend is the example for such type of legends.

I visited Solapur in June 2017 with the object of seeing the fort. I was accompanied by Dr. Umakant Walvekar, a gynecologist and a resident of Solapur. We went to the well, where we found it covered with bushes and wild growth and could not see the water. I was told the water is a normal color. However, Dr. Walvekar affirmed that as a child, he had seen the water to be reddish. I met with Mr. Bhimanna Durgo Patil, who is a descendent of the woman sacrificed, and he told me the details of this event of long ago. I met with Mr. Nitin Anavekar, who has published the book '*Bhuikot Solapurcha*' *(The Earthen Fort of Solapur)* in the Marathi language. Harish Dasare, a Junior Conservation Officer from the Department of Archaeology of the Solapur Fort, as well as Nilesh Jamadar, an employee of the Department of Archaeology, both told me the legend.

The sixty years old security guard of the fort, a Mr. Pritam Chhotu

Birla, also related how a year and a half ago, Shri Pritam Chhotu Birla heard an infant crying and was being patted for about four minutes at two in the morning near the bastion. In my videotaped interview, Mr. Pritam Chhotu Birla gave a detailed account of this and how the four other security guards on duty with him were petrified. The legend is narrated in my own words.

Glossary:

Bhuikot – Bhui means land and Kot means fort. So, Bhuyikot is a fort that is built on flat land rather than on a mountain.

Halad – Turmeric powder.

Kunku or kumkuma – A red powder made from turmeric or any other local materials. Women put red colored kunku on their forehead. It looks like a red spot. It has a cultural significance. It represents prosperity. It is also widely used for worshiping the Hindu gods and goddesses. It is a sign of respect in social life.

Patil – As the collector of revenue and as the head of police and justice, the headman of an Asian Indian village. Patil is also an Indian last name in the states of Maharashtra and Karnataka, and it indicates the social status and duties.

Padmavati – 'Padma' means lotus and 'vati' means to possess. One who has a sacred lotus flower is Padmavati. This is the literary meaning. This female name is used in Indian mythology with a special reference. Padmavati means Goddess Laxmi – The wife of the Lord Vishnu. *Goddess Laxmi* sits on the lotus and holds two lotuses in her two hands. So, she is Padmavati.

Pooja or puja ritual – A prayer ritual performed by Hindus of devotional worship to one or more deities. It is a Sanskrit word. It means reverence, honor, homage, adoration, and worship.

Sanai-chaughda – These two are different types of musical instruments. Both of them are played at festive events or special occasions. *Sanai* or *shehnai* is a musical instrument similar to the oboe and the chaughda or the nagara is a membranophone instrument that is considered to be the lead instrument in ceremonies and weddings.

Chief's Burial, Chickasaw
Native American

In the 1700s, the Iroquois decided to invade Chickasaw country. The Chickasaw referred to themselves as the Chicka'sha. The different *iksa* or clans of the Chickasaw banded together to battle the Iroquois off their lands. There were two bands of Chickasaw living in the area of the Tennessee River valley and along the Ohio River. Each of these had their own religion and their own government function. The *Imosakatca* or the "Hickory Chopping Band" were tall and superior in war and in the hunt. They preferred to live on the flatlands near the forested river areas. The other was the *Intcukwalipa*, also known as 'Those who are Worn Out.' The *Intcukwalipa* lived in the forested areas under trees, secretly relocating to retain their invisibility.

This area became known as Chickasaw Old Fields on the north bank of the Tennessee River, which today would be Madison County, Arkansas. The Chickasaw separated from a larger clan of people all of whom were moving east from the far west. As they migrated the Chickasaw carried with them a *Kohta* or sacred pole that each night was placed in the ground. At dawn the pole was found to be bending east and so the Chickasaw followed the direction of the *Kohta* until the pole stood straight and no longer would bend. This became the *Sakti la'fa* or boundary bank, otherwise known as the 'center of the earth,' the place to settle.

The Chickasaw arrived at this final destination on horseback with serious weapons. The Creek who lived in this area at the time, had no choice but to concede this land to the Chickasaw. Although at one time, the Creek sided with the Osage in an attempt at retrieving their land. The story goes that the Osage or *Wacaci* were put under a spell by the Chickasaw dogs. The *Wacaci* fell to the ground as if in a deep sleep as the Chickasaw won the battle. These two dogs were invisible to the Chickasaw, but not to the enemy. The ferocious dogs would knock the enemy down, allowing the Chickasaw to have the upper hand in battle.

The *sho-wa* or Chickasaw chief and his men would float down *Sakti-la-fa'okena* or the Mississippi River in their bark canoes to trade goods at *Balbancha*, the old name for New Orleans. The items won in war were usually traded for items the Chickasaw needed to survive. Their shaman would tell them when to fight and when to trade for he followed the wisdom of their prophet who traveled the *Ofit'oxube ihinna* or the Milky Way to become a supernatural wise one. When the full group of Chickasaw was called to assemble, each had their own location to sit within a specific square area defined by a line running north and south. These areas were respected and defined each group.

At this time there was a *sho-wa* or head chief of the *Imosakatca iksa*, his name was Choollishke. This *sho-wa* or head chief Choollishke was not an arrogant man for as tradition dictated he never bragged or gloated about himself or his family. His wife Koyoke had born him two fine sons. The eldest son was an excellent hunter belonging to those of the *Inkobuk'ca* or 'those with the hump.' The younger son belonged to the *Hataaqan'an* or the 'fish persons.' Both were trained to be warriors, as was the custom. The men shaved the sides of their heads bald, leaving a mane of hair flowing from the top center of the head down to their waist. In times of war, they wore porcupine roaches going from the front center of the forehead to the nape of the neck, giving them the appearance of an animal forging through the bush when crouched down, tracking the enemy.

Choollishke was known as a quiet man, he led his warriors well and cared for the land and his people of the Raccoon Clan or the *Cawi'iksa*. This clan was noted for being cunning and clever with spiritual guidance from a Conjurer or *Ap'oloma*. Choolishke and his *iksa* or clan were far away from the village fighting in heavy battle against the Iroquois. It was at this time, when strangers from the north crept down the sloping brown mountains surrounding the village to steal women and children in the night only to disappear across the flowing Tennessee River into the darkness. Young boys limited in number attempted to fight the night stealers. Grandparents flung hatchets and spears, but these fast moving thieves were unfazed. The village was desperately losing people as the enemy raiding parties grew in size.

Upon return from the warring party, Choollishke was met with worried villagers. Hearing their concerns, he was led to several of the *Daub house*s with exterior damage. *Daub house*s were circularly formed, using willow boughs to design the frame with rivercane, interwoven with small branches to form sturdy walls chinked with mud, which were sealed air tight. The houses had elevated thatched roofs of grasses and shingled bark packed with river mud. The smoke hole was centered in the highest point of each thatched roof. *Daub* houses were constructed upon a two to three foot elevated stone foundation, raising the interior floors in case of flashfloods or overflowing rivers. Hollowed log canoes were being inverted on wooden cross structures to dry.

A stooped grandfather pointed to the reinforced walls surrounding this village. This palisade consisted of fat tree trunks stacked horizontally with smaller logs pounded vertically, bracing the protective fortification. "The night raiders pulled the top logs from the wall to have their horses jump into our village! They did this while we slept. This made us vulnerable to them."

Choollishke nodded in agreement as he observed men replacing the logs onto the palisade. "This is being repaired now. Did you see any of these horsemen? Did they have distinguishing marks?"

The grandfather sighed, "The village fires were low and by the time we raced outside, they were gone and with them our women and children. Some entered on foot to steal into the houses. One woman who escaped spoke of them holding a knife to her throat while they pulled her by her hair. When her sons raced to her rescue, two more men grabbed them. She bit her abductor on the thigh after he held her while on his horse. They were swift, quiet and deadly. My elderly sister cut one of them with my old hatchet, he ripped her open with his sharp knife." The grandfather shook his head in despair.

Choollishke studied his active village. Wild turkeys were tended by young women and small children. Women sat outside the *Daub* houses, weaving tight baskets for holding water or for gathering seeds, berries, nuts and herbs. Wild plums bordered the rivers. Plotted terraced vegetable gardens of corn, beans, squash, sunflowers and wild berry bushes were irrigated from river trenches. Wild sassafras plants were cultivated from the perimeter of the terraced gardens in that sassafras was used in teas for healing and in ceremony.

Hunters were skinning their latest catch of deer, rabbits, squirrels, porcupines and raccoons. Fishermen sharpened spears as arrows were whittled, bows were stretched and nets were repaired. This summer diet was of fish and fresh vegetables, fruits, nuts and berries. This fall, hunters would go after larger game to provide dried meat for the winter months and animal skins for warmth and clothing. Softened animal skins were worn for women's wraparound skirts and thin leather poncho-like blouses embroidered with beads. Men wore leather *breechcloth*s going over the waist belt in the back, between the legs and then up and over the waist belt in the front. Front leather aprons were folded in front over the belts as well to protect their upper thighs. Leather leggings were wrapped and tied around men's legs to protect their skin while in sticker bushes and for protection from knife grass cuts. Everyone wore low moccasins with beaded work on the top to individualize.

Choollishke noticed grandmothers and mothers working the thicker animal skins with fur to be capes for women and men while the heavy poncho-like shirts clothed children in frigid temperatures. Hunters threw larger and thicker animal skins over tree branch structures for cleaning, later they would be used for warm sleeping palettes on colder nights. Busy women pulled their hair up away from their faces to tie with beaded leather strips. Cradle boards, tightly tied, enveloped sleeping infants.

Choollishke called for a meeting of his *Co-ish-to* or second chief, *Ous-peh-ne* or third in command and his *Mim-ne* or fourth officer. The *Hus-con-na* or his ark carrier came bringing the sacred items needed for this special conference. *Hopa-ye* or his personal shaman arrived with his seer's tools. *Icta-holo* or his Wizard and his *Alektci* or Spirit Doctor were already there with his *Ap'oloma* or Conjurer who sat next to him in the communal *Daub house*.

Nodding to his officials, Choollishke spoke solemnly, "*Chokma* or greetings. Who do you believe is raiding our village and taking our women and children?"

Ap'oloma the Conjuror spoke first, "There are the *Lo'fa* who live in the woods and have the appearance of men. They are as tall as the Cyprus trees, at least ten feet in height. Using their long arms, they are able to grab our people."

Icta holo the Wizard smiled, "Ah, but they have small heads and do not think clearly." Chuckling softly, the others agreed.

Apoloma the Conjuror shook his finger at *Icta holo* Wizard, "*Lo'fa* are known to carry off women. Sometimes they have killed and flayed men and this is why we call them the *Lo'fa* or those 'who skin.'"

Aledktci the Spirit Doctor, raised his hand to speak, "There are the *Iyaganasha* the little people only about three-feet tall who follow us and haunt us. Perhaps they want to train our women to become wiser and help us win the wars?" Mumbling to one another, the men disagreed.

Ous-peh-ne or Third in Command let the silence return before he spoke, "If it is the *Iyaganasha*, we should certainly move from here for they are tricksters none of us wish to confront." The circle of men agreed.

Co-ish-to or Second Chief frowned to add, "There are the *Tiboli* who are the size of a man. Their one arm is shaped like a club. They pound on trees before they attack. Has anyone heard them approach?"

Choollishke answered him, "These *Tiboli* creatures only attack in the winter. They come with the horned snake *sint-holo* our sacred snake who live along creeks or in caves. It is too warm for the *sint-holo* and the *Tiboli* to come here. No, these raiders who are our enemy ride on horseback. We must find them and stop them."

Icta holo Wizard thought for a time to say, "There are the *Ik'sca*. They wander from place to place and don't own anything. They are lazy, begging for food, refusing to work and if they are in a group, possibly they would steal the women and children to do their work."

Choollishke became angry, "No! We cannot make excuses for these raiders by allowing them to become those who we fear. If your woman was stolen, you would not be here avoiding the fight. If my woman Koyoke was taken from me, I would make war on the nearest tribe regardless of their name! Spirits don't need horses nor do they need our women and our children."

Taking some powdery fine cornmeal from the clay bowl in front of him, Choollishke sprinkled it over the palm of his left hand. "We need to either catch or kill these horseback raiders. This raiding must be stopped if we are to survive." The powdered cornmeal bowl was passed around the circle with each sprinkling some into their left palm. Finally it came to *Alektci* the Spirit Doctor.

Alektci Spirit Doctor blew the finely ground cornmeal out of the bowl and into the room, "Let us join with the *Ko-in-chush iksa* or the Wildcat Clan. They sleep during the day to become ruthless in the night. Let us ask them for they see and feel the night better than most during the day." The official ceremony ended with each of the men, nodding to the other, saying, "*Ayali.*"

It was decided. Runners were sent with a message to the *Ko-in-chush iksa* Wildcat Clan chief who returned with a positive response. *Ko-in-chush iksa* Wildcat Clan would arrive in the night since they would not do anything during the day. Choollishke and his *Cawi iksa* Raccoon Clan warriors guarded the village. Many nights went by with no action, they waited.

Choollishke chose the *Na-coba iksa* Wolf Clan to go with his warriors to the north to aid in the battles against the Iroquois. First a war party ceremony was in order. The women were informed of the plans to ally with the *Na-coba iksa* Wolf Clan. The extra population coming demanded an excess of food supplies to feed everyone, including the four surrounding villages near Choollishke's village. When the feast day was decided a group of warriors arrived from the west. The *Tcuka falaha iksa* or Flatland Clan *sho-wa* or Chief spoke with Choolishke for his warriors were ready to join in the confrontation with the Iroquois as their lands were in jeopardy, as well. The *Tcuka falaha iksa* women stacked their food baskets alongside the *Imosaktca* women's in the cooking area. This would be a true feast of flavors.

Women gathered their large black cooking pots to scrub with dirt. Youths were sent to bring back kindling wood. Girls harvested beans, squash, corn, berries, sunflowers and acorn nuts. A millet was made from pounded grasses and root tubers. Baskets of berries and acorn nuts were piled one on top of the other inside the storage houses. The *Icta holo* Wizard visited each of the warriors' homes to bless and comfort the warriors' families.

Na-coba iksa Wolf Clan warriors arrived ready to join in the purging, cold river water cleansing with the Raccoon Clan. Ceremoniously the warriors then cleaned and prepared their weaponry of spears, bows and arrows, tomahawks and lances. While awaiting for the feast day, the warriors' relatives and friends observed a strict fast and engaged in solemn and supplicating prayers to their one supreme being whom they call *Ababinili* or the One Who Sits Above or Dwelling Above.

Hopa'ye Shaman with his spiritual wisdom explained to the people their warring purpose and how families could support their warriors by remaining pure and good. *Hopa'ye* Shaman reminded them of the four beloved beings, "Clouds, Sun, Clear Sky and He who Lives in the Clear Sky are our guides. *Loak-ishto-hoolo-Aba* our Great Holy Above Fire resides above the clouds and also on earth, but only benefits the unpolluted people or "Those who have Not Killed." *Icta holo* Wizard and *Alektci* Spirit Doctor employ the wisdom of *Loak-ishto-hoolo-Aba* when assisting the people. The flames of our fires relate wisdom, healing our sick. Remember during these troubling times, it is taboo to put any of our fires out with water for water will wash away the wisdom of the flames and the remaining knowledge of the ash."

In a deep rolling voice *Hopa'ye* Shaman held his arms straight out in front of his chest with his hands flat, lecturing to his people, "Creator *Ababinili* Sitting Above is in smoke and in the clouds. He towers above the sky and is the magical element within the holy annual fire. *Ishtohoollo Aba Eloa* is the Big Holy One Above of our Beloved Thunder Chieftain, who when he wishes to bring us his sacred rain as he shakes the sky with his thunder. This pleasure of his is done out of respect for *Ababinili* Creator Sitting Above. *Ishtohoollo Aba Eloa* Thunder Chieftain dwells far above the clouds and blesses the unpolluted holy fires of the long nights and days of cold winter, bringing rain and snow to the unpolluted holy fires. These spirits we pray to for warriors' successes against our enemies and for their safe return." Silently, the people nodded in agreement.

Several nights prior to the feast the Wolf Clan and Raccoon Clan warriors danced through the night, dressed in their warpath regalia. Cooking fires filled the air with delicious odors of roasted nuts, roasting meats, baked fish stuffed with squash, roasting corn, stews, and baked millet and honey breads. Finally, the food was ready and it was time for the feast. The enormous food preparations were done. Women oversaw the young men preparing the *Daub* communal floors with sun bleached bearskin rugs and carved wooden platters, plates and bowls. As the young men readied the Daub longhouse, an old chief who was a noted old warrior was chosen to speak before the warriors of his past actions and wisdom learned.

In the warriors' longhouse, known as the *Wattle house*, sat the elderly warrior with warriors and officials circled around him. Holding the war pipe in his hand, he delivered a speech to the Wolf Clan and Raccoon Clan. He illustrated his exploits, not out of arrogance, but as lessons to remember. He encouraged them to go with manly courage, have a strong heart, be watchful and see beyond the obvious, keeping ready to flee if need be for their survival was of utmost importance.

His voice crackled as he related to be attentive in listening and have unfailing endurance, to be cunning as the wolf and clever as the raccoon, and agile as the panther. "Do not be too eager, for caution and wisdom dictates to flee as swiftly as the antelope. Lives are of utmost worth to the clan and every life is necessary and should not be sacrificed for it will bring sorrow to all of the hearts of their people and to Earth Herself."

Then he filled his war pipe with prepared sumac leaves and tobacco. Putting flame to the pipe's bowl, he lit it to draw a few whiffs and then passed it to the war chief leader of the outgoing war party, who also drew a few puffs and from him it went the rounds of the entire war party. There were over one hundred warriors and each warrior retained complete silence, drawing a whiff or two and then passing it to the next in turn. Each of the chiefs restocked the sacred pipe. After this ceremony, the men eagerly attended to the delicious foods waiting for their appreciation in the Daub longhouse. Set on the bearskin rugs on the floor were the platters and bowls of their prepared feast. Fresh baked cornbread was dipped in meat and fish stews. Animal fat fried fish rolled in wild herbs with sliced baked tubers were on flatwood trays. Freshly washed berries and ripe purple plums glistened in baskets ready for the plucking. Juicy roasted turkeys stuffed with herbs and nuts were quickly devoured. Little girls, hugging their cornhusk dolls, passed around honey bowls as they licked their fingers. Young boys, with tight headbands, went from man to man with a clay pitcher of fermented plum and herb drink. After all the warriors had eaten their fill, they retired outside where the war post was painted red and buried upright.

A screaming war cry shrieked out in the still night air, as the *Co-ish-to* Second in Command Chief, used all his strength to rush forward striking the war pole with his tomahawk as if it were the enemy. His warriors repeated this in regular order, each doing the same. Each *ik'sa* had their own red pole to attack. At the end of the pole attack, warriors laughed, slapping one another on the back at their successful kill of the red war post! Retrieving their personal tomahawks, they gloated at the strength and sharpness or dullness of the weapon's edge. *Co-ish-to* Second in Command Chief called the men to silence for now it was time for the final war ceremony.

Gathering their weapons, warriors pounded the earth as they twirled, catcalled and howled performing the last of the ceremonial war dances. Wooden bowls of powdered pigment mixed with animal grease were prepared in the main '*asi*' house or *Daub* house. It was time for Chickasaw warriors to paint their faces with stripes across the forehead and up and down marks on the cheekbones. This was called *imo'saktc* and done to give their faces expressions of fierceness and terror. Sharp stone knives shaved the sides of the warriors' heads bald to apply porcupine quill roaches onto their center manes of hair. As dawn approached, fearsome warriors slipped away to do battle.

In the village, Choollishke with a few of his Raccoon Clan warriors slept during the day to night guard. Sentinels hid in hillside brush above the village while the main number of warriors were scattered throughout the area. No one attacked and no one was taken. Men became impatient for they were eager to fight the Iroquois not sit in the dark while listening to the gurgling of the Tennessee River. Some warriors who were guarding near the small streams and tributaries, fished in the moonless night.

Then one night came the pounding of horse hooves, racing through the river water. Sentinels whistled warnings of unwanted horseback riders. Darkness and brush hid Choollishke and his men as they flowed over the palisade, racing around the fires as horsemen galloped straight into the village. Screaming women raced out of houses, waving their arms to frighten the horses. Yelling children jumped from under canoes with torches lit, flinging the flames at the horses' heads. Whinnying equines reared to canter away into the dark. Painted faces of unknown men scurried frantically disappearing. No one was taken that night.

The following night found the Raccoon Clan crouching in the dark ready to kill. Sharp knives held between teeth, bows steady with arrows at the ready. The horsemen returned. Chickasaw warrors leapt upon the intruders as throats were cut and wide eyed horses were reined to the ground. Quietly and quickly, death came to these raiding men. Choollishke and his few men had taken no prisoners. The dark skinned invaders with yellow striped faces were unknown to them. Horses taken from the intruders were fat and small with yellow handprints on their rumps. Several raids followed, again, Choollishke Chief and his men protected the people. It was on the fourth raid when trouble began. Before dawn's light, the bodies of the intruders were placed in a pile at the far edge of the river by a round of trees. As the sun topped the mountain peaks, the bodies disappeared.

Somehow the numbers of the raiding tribe had increased. Galloping horsemen shrieked as they flew over the protecting walls of the village at sundown. People were not prepared for they were milling around the night fires, getting ready to collect water baskets for early cooking in the morning. This sudden intrusion of raiders caught the women around the waist, flinging them over the horses' withers to be quickly struck unconscious or tied with grass braided ropes. Children were grabbed by the hair. Chaos was everywhere. Women screamed, children cried, desperate to escape being taken as slaves or worse.

Choollishke Chief and his men raced down the hillside. They shot flaming arrows, threw their tomahawks, but hit only a few of the raiders for the crazed village people were in their way, running and screaming. Some women were hurt as they had fallen from the galloping horses. Children who had been hit by the horses had broken bones and gaping open wounds. This had not been good. Devastation was everywhere. Choollishke's woman Koyoke had been grabbed, but she had escaped after stabbing the raiding mount in the leg to fall under his horse. Limping, she helped the wounded and calmed those who had lost family.

Choollishke Chief devised a plan. Men were to dress as women, act as women and stay with the women while they were doing chores at dusk and dawn. The next morning, as people gathered for the first meal, raiders galloped in at a dead run invading the village. As they reached to grab women, they were met with strong hands welding hunting knives, cutting their throats. Most of the women had chosen to stay inside while the men learned women's work. This was a success. Once again, the dead intruders were placed in a pile on the far side of the river. No one recognized these men or their facial symbols. In the morning, the dead had disappeared.

Four days of quiet brought on more vicious raids. This time it was in the middle of the day, while children played in the cool water of the Tennessee River and streams, horsemen snatched them. The raiders chose not to enter the village, but galloped to return the way they had come. Choollishke and his men changed their tactics to be ready near the river, but then the raids stopped. Night sentinels were sent out to scout for the camps of these intruders. At dawn the sentinels returned after not finding anything, not even smoke from a cooking fire.

One moonless night, the raiders crept stealthily close to the village from the above the forested foothills. Choollishke and his men quietly watched their people below not knowing of the raiding horsemen above who were quietly descending behind them. The intruders had wrapped their horses' hooves in leather booties. The raiders soundlessly shot their arrows into the bush and behind rocks. Silently, dismounting, they scooped dirt to toss into the brush, stabbing deadly long knives into surprised Chickasaw. Choollishke and his few warriors of the *Cawi iksa* or Raccoon Clan were ruthlessly butchered along with most of the *Ko-in-chush iksa* or Wildcat Clan. Unknowing of this, their courageous women in the village heroically battled off most of the invading raiders until dawn.

Weary and wounded the children and exhausted women were heartsick when hearing news of Choollishke and his men who were found dead. Runners were sent to inform the villagers of the *Ko-in-chush iksa* Wildcat Clan people of their men's deaths. It was important for the families to claim the bodies immediately.

Now the village was without protection. Choollishke's woman Koyoke called two young men runners, explaining to them, "You are to fly as fast as the eagle can fly and ride the wind to the north. Find the Wolf Clan warriors and our brother Raccoon Clan warriors. Tell them what has happened here."

The war between the Iroquois and the Chickasaw had come to a stalemate. News of Choollishke's death brought blood boiling anger to the *Cawi iksa* Raccoon Clan warriors and Nacoba *iksa* Wolf Clan warriors. Intense outrage developed and desperate energy produced a powerful surge within the Chickasaw warriors who promptly defeated the northern

Iroquois enemies. Reverently, the wounded and dead were collected to return home. The exhausted Raccoon Clan and Wolf Clan warriors rejoined their grieving Chickasaw families, bringing sadness mixed with a relief to find some families alive and whole. Many of the physically wounded were taken to the *Alektci* Spirit Doctor who had women Shaman healers to assist.

Spiritually debilitated clan warriors went immediately to a cleansing ceremony with *icta holo* Wizard and *Hopa-ye* Shaman. These two repaired, purified and purged the war anguish from the warriors' spirit. Returning warriors' war sickness was dangerous for if let unattended a man could die from perpetual despair or reoccurring hopelessness festering in his soul. This cleansing took four days for some, others needed a lifetime of healing work. These men were kept separate from others for it was believed death had enveloped their souls and needed to be released in order for them to become whole once again for their families.

Death platform stages were erected for the dead on the hillside above the village. Each corpse was placed upon it, blanketed with a bearskin cover. Warriors' platform stages had poles painted with vermilion red and bear oil. Children who had died in the raids were placed on platforms with stakes set crossways. Family members grieved on the hillside praying for the souls of the dead. The pain and agony of loss was screamed skyward day after day, as family members reminded the *Inki-Abu* Above Boss of their grief. Those who were alone in their mourning, howled and screamed day and night until they collapsed from exhaustion. Kindly, a neighbor or a friend would return them to their village home and take their place grieving at the platform stages.

Dead bodies lying on staked platforms kept the enemy raids away. No one wanted to cross paths with those who were on their final journey. The raiding enemy moved east, leaving this devastated village to mourn in their ceremony for the dead.

Finally, a young boy appeared, guiding an elderly Shaman *Hopa-ye* who was a follower of the Milky Way. Wisdom was held in each wrinkle of the Shaman's face. *Hopa-ye* Shaman stood tall in the center of the village. His head was shaved on both sides with his mane of gray hair pulled into a long wrap behind his head, flowing to his waist. Stamping his cane forcefully upon the ground, he called the village people to him. His gruff voice spoke fiercely, "It is time."

Dutifully scurrying, the villagers gathered firewood, placing it in a heap near the death staked hill. Larger logs were placed in the center of a fire pit as flint lit the kindling. The young boy held the elderly Shaman's free arm as the Shaman used his cane to balance, arriving at a flat space near the staked platforms. Brushing the ground of weeds and stone, the young boy assisted the elderly Shaman to sit, facing the newly burning fire in the pit. Water baskets filled with fresh Tennessee River water were brought to the Shaman. After dipping his fingers in one of the water baskets, he dragged red hot ash from the burning fire pit. Rubbing the cooling gray ash between his palms, he rubbed it on his face and the bald sides of his head. Using a cooled char branch from the fire, he drew four long black lines from his forehead to his chin. Kneeling, the young boy placed a rolled leather bundle beside the elderly Shaman.

The bleached deerskin bundle, was unwrapped to lift a headdress of many feathers. The elderly Shaman placed it onto his own head. A dried leather rattle with a colorful wooden handle was removed as well from the same deerskin wrap, this was put in the elderly Shaman's lap. As the flames reached high into the early day's sky, one of the bodies was brought to him. The elderly Shaman's thumb, forefinger and middle fingers had long sharp fingernails. These tore and ripped at the dried flesh of the dead body. The flesh was thrown into the flames, sending the smoke of the body to the Clear Sky Spirit.

Chanting, the Shaman called to the sky, "Creator, take this one into your care. Let this one be as your own child. Creator, take this one into your own care. This one is your child."

Once the skin was removed, the elderly Shaman tore and pulled the muscle, meat, ligaments and tendons from around the bones of the dead. Again, these body parts were thrown into the flames to crackle and burn. Sacred cornmeal was tossed into the fire by the young boy, changing the smoke from gray to different colors. All of this was very magical.

The elderly Shaman's voice continued to call to the Clear Sky Spirit, "This is your child who you birthed and gave to us. This one is your child born from you. This is your child. This is your child born from you."

Soon the naked bones were revealed. Chanting stopped. Gently gathering the bones, they were carefully placed with the untouched person's severed head. Once the bones and the deceased warrior's severed head were placed together, then the vermilion red pigment was painted on the cheeks and the chin of the deaceased's face. The vermilion red paint had been prepared ahead of time from grinding cinnabar found near the basalt rock cliffs. The deceased children's body parts were separated and placed in a different location from the warriors' bones and severed heads.

At last, the Elder called for Choollishke the Chief's body. Choollishke's platform stage was the highest, closest to the sky. White deerskin robes covered Choollishke's body with skinned raccoons by his head and feet. He was the Chief of *Cawi Iksa* Raccoon Clan of the Chickasaw. On his platform a large bearskin was tightly stretched, tied from one pole to the other as a large shield facing the sun. His warriors had placed his bow, finely whittled arrows, and his musical flute around his body. At the top of each of the poles was wrapped a single white swan feather, representing his honorable soul.

Four warriors shimmied up each of the platform poles to gently lower Choollishke's stiff body to the other warriors standing on the ground. Choollishke's woman Koyoke and other family women dipped their fingers in vermilion red pigment to completely paint his whole face. All of the village, wailed as Choollishke was placed before the elderly Shaman. Taking the rattle from his lap, the Elder began to shake it over Choollishke's full body. A kneeling warrior with a sharp stone knife severed Choollishke's head from his body at the neck. Koyoke and the other women circled his body, tearing at their hair and faces in mournful agony. Surviving warriors let their sorrow be heard as their feet pounded the ground while hammering spear poles on the earth, to echo their grief. Lamenting villagers knelt beside the funeral fire.

Sharp long nails pulled, tore and ripped skin from the Choollishke's body to be tossed into flames. Muscle and tendons, once strong, now joined the flames of death, smoke lifting to the Creator. As Choollishke's bones were set aside, his head was placed on top of his skeletal remains. Sacred cornmeal was sprinkled over them.

Chanting continued from the Elder, "Take your child. This child born from you. Take your child, our leader, born from you."

The younger men who had been sent to collect the wooden chests of death, returned. Families took the bones and heads of their departed to place them gingerly in the large chests. Each of the matrilineal funereal chests held their deceased family's remains. A special chest had been carved specifically for Choollishke. The Chief's war weapons were set in the bottom of this chest, first with his moccasins, ceremonial flute, ceremonial clothes and headdress gear. Slowly, with reverence each bone was placed within the chest. Lastly, his head coated in vermilion, was settled on top of his war feathers. Once the chest was shut, his family completely coated the wooden chest in vermilion as they prayed for him to have a peaceful journey to the Creator.

These ceremonial chests were then carried to the hillside of the Dead into which a cave for the dead had been dug and established as a housing. This cave was referred to as the 'bone-house' for the walls, roof and flooring were all of ancient hickory tree wood, carved and painted vermilion red. Each chest was carefully placed on the matrilineal shelves inside the cave with a prayer for peaceful transference to *Aba'Binn'I'li* or He Who is Sitting or Dwelling Above.

Chief Choollishke's chest was settled in a separate internal singular shelf, carved alone into the side of the cave. The hickory tree wood shelves surrounding the Chief's area had been sanded, bleached in the sun and painted vermilion red as well. His loft-shelf was six-feet away, separated from the other chests in the main 'bone-house.' A door of thin wooden logs, wrapped with leather, was shut tightly, closing the main 'bone-house.'

A separate door of thicker logs closed tightly the entrance of Chief Choollishke's 'bone-house' cave. Standing outside the firmly closed doors, the elderly Shaman called for those within to be carried to *Aba'Binn'I'li* in peace, "May all within find harmony in the life beyond."

Warriors stood outside of the cave area to relate stories of their friends and Choollishke's great warring styles. They remembered his ability to lead and his trust and fondness for his men. This was done with great honor and respect. When the conversing went quiet, his warriors lifted each a corner of the Chief's bearskin death rug. Walking into the village, they moved around his home three times, holding the bearskin tightly as a shield. Once they returned to the area where they had started, they would stop to call out, "Yah!" This was done out of respect. Everyone following them would echo the same. At the end of the third time, his warriors carried the bearskin rug to his 'bone-house' to drape it over the shut door.

A great sadness entered the village with this loss. Raccoon Clan *Cawi Iksa* warriors were ready to seek revenge for the death of their Choollishke. *Hopa'ye* Shaman held a council, telling the warriors, "Respect our Chief and those who have gone to the Creator. Too many lives have already been lost. It is time to let the dead find their way."

He required the warriors to celebrate life by going through an extreme cleansing in order to leave death alone. Those who felt they had relinquished their spirit to emptiness, *Icta Holo* called together, "This village is in need of repair. Men gather for the hunt. There are families who have lost their men and will be without food or clothing against the cold. It is time for a council to help those children who are to be trained in wrestling, hunting, basket weaving and have no parents. We are as one. We must work as one. There is no separation. We are as one if we are to survive."

Fires burned through the night as councils met in *Daub houses*. Trees were chopped to rebuild the heavy wood fence around the villages. Large logs were dragged into the longhouses to teach the young men how to hollow canoes. Young girls were shown where the best grasses and willow boughs were found to weave. Older boys taught the younger how to swim in the ice cold tributaries and rivers of floating ice. Girls and boys were taught wrestling, use of bows and arrows, woodcarving, net weaving, use of flaming arrows, and how to play *Toli* or the stick ball game.

Chickasaw burial mourning number 9

Boys ready to become young men hunted for their porcupine roaches while girls learned women's crafts of pottery, mulberry bark textiles, beading and bread making. Squash, corn, beans, sunflowers and sassafras were harvested, allowing for the terraced gardens to be dug and earth flipped to prepare for the far away spring. Shaman's chants echoed through the night, healing those whose hearts were burdened in darkness. Women wore paths to and from the hillside of the Dead, mourning relentlessly in their love for lost family.

Heavy winter rains returned hope to the small thriving village. Children were heard laughing again. Women became busy stripping fur from fresh skins brought to them by hunters. Mysteriously, the old ones found stacks of firewood placed around their small homes by an adopted family. Singing was heard as winter plans were made for ceremonies in the main *Daub* longhouse. Cut meat dried and smoked was hanging from long horizontal poles. No one would be hungry this cold season. Spirits blessed these sorrowful people into the lightness of life.

One morning, a small boy ran into the village yelling. Men and woman hurried to his side, anxious and concerned. Leading his grandfather by the hand, the small boy guided him to the Hillside of the Dead. People clicked their tongues in despair for death was still fresh in their hurt. The small boy pointed at something to his grandfather. The older man lifted his hand, turning he spoke, "It is time for only the men to approach. A sacred duty is to be done."

Women huddled together, watching the older men confer with the grandfather. Then the younger men followed. One of the recovering wounded warriors fell to his knees, lifting his hands skyward. Other men joined him, chanting, "Creator has found his child and has blessed this earth!"

Koyoke screamed, running up the hill. There oozing out from under the Choollishke Chief's 'bone-house' was a vermilion red liquid. Each day, more and more bubbling of this red water gushed downhill until it became a small stream flowing beside the village. Wrapped feathers and blessed ceremonial skins decorated the muddy outflow of this red water in honor of the Choollishke Chief. Everyone believed Earth Mother mourned the loss of her great Chief.

It was later, when the Chickasaw were pushed from their villages to live on reservations that this happening was almost forgotten. Colonists infringed on the village, noticing the red stained earth as it flowed from the cave. The Chickasaw were relocated again and again. Some still tell of the time when Earth Mother mourned the loss of the Choollishke Chief. No longer do we live in river cane framed *Daub houses,* wrapped with vines, coated with mud. Our thatched roofs are no longer shingled bark. We have become civilized. We pray the spirits will continue to bless us.

Notes:

The Chickasaw people are part of the Muskhogean Tribe of the southeastern Woodlands of Mississippi, Alabama and Tennessee. They were hunters and fighters who were extremely orderly in their duties, believing to keep everything they might need close at hand. The Chickasaw were extremely religious and superstitious with the importance of being 'honorable.' It was important to be remembered for your good qualities and avoid bad ones. The Chickasaw people were dissolved under the Dawes Act of 1887, when the U.S. federal government divided up the Indian land into individual parcelled allotments rather than having the people live in a communal setting. While teaching American History at the University of New Mexico, Valencia Campus, a visiting anthropologist told this story to my class. Historical data and magical superstition can be interchangeable.

Glossary:

Aba'Binili – He Who Sits Above/ Great Spirit Father.

Aleckci – Spirit Doctor, works on healing emotions and spirit.

Ap'oloma – Conjurer, Calls for Spiritual Help and Guidance.

Asi House – Communal longhouse.

Ayali – Goodbye greeting.

Balbancha – Old Name for New Orleans.

Breechloth – A type of loin cloth, passed between thighs, held up in back and in front by a belt or string. Many men wear an apron of leather over this in front.

Cawi'iksa – Raccoon clan.

Chokma – Greeting.

Co-ish-to – Second Chief or Assistant to Chief.

Daub House – Circular building of willow and river cane frame with interwoven branches chinked with mud. Have elevated thatched roofs of grass and shingled bark with mud. Elevated on stone foundations to remain dry during river floods.

Hataaqan'an – Fish People.

Hataganan – Fish Persons.

Hiloha – Lightning or Thunder Spirit.

Hopa-ye – Personal Shaman, Seer.

Hus-con-na – Ark carrier of Clan's sacred items

Icta-holo – Wizard, works magic

Iksa – Clan

Ik'sca – Lazy Spirits who steal people to do their work for them.

Imo'saktc – Painting of war symbols on warriors' face before battle

Imosakatca – Hickory Chopping Band of people

Inki Abu – Above Boss, lives abouve clouds and creator of warmth, light and all life.

Inkobukee – Hunters of Large Game

Inkobuk'ca – Those with Hump Band of people

Intcukwalipa – Those who are worn out Band of people

Istohoola Aba Eloa – Big Holy One Above/ Thunder Chief

Iyaganasha – Three foot tall spirit people who are tricksters and dangerous

Kohta – Sacred Pole

Kohta Fa-lala – Long Sacred Pole

Ko-in-chush – Wild Cat

Loak-ishto-hoola-Aba – Great Holy above Fire

Lo'fa – "Who Skin," ten foot tall spirit men with long arms who steal people

Min-ne – Fourth Chief or Assistant to Chief

Minko – War Chief or military or political leader

Na-coba Iksa – Wolf Clan

Nde'indaai – Enemy People

Ous-peh-ne – Third Chief or Assistant to Chief

Sakti lal'fa – Boundary bank or Center of Earth Place

Sakti la fa'okena – Mississippi River

Sho-wa – Head Chief

Sint-holo – Sacred Horned Snake

Tcuka Falaha Iksa – Flatland Clan

Tcukilissa – Peaceful Forest

Tiboli – Spirit men with one club arm. They pound trees before attacking.

Toli – Stick game played by children

Wacaci – Osage People

Wattle House – Warriors' Longhouse can hold over one hundred persons, made of wet soil, clay, sand, animal dung and dried grasses.

10
FERTILE BLESSINGS

Blessings of Bhivai Devi
ASIAN INDIAN

It was not long ago, nor was it recently, when this happened. In the late nineteenth century, the people in the state of Maharashtra in the country of India, had a strange and beautiful blessing occur in their small unique village. Usually the villages in India are developed along the riverbanks, but this one was not situated near a water source. The village was not in a jungle, not on a mountain nor near any lake or pond. It was situated on dry plain ground. Why was it situated on such dry land?

No one knows. But the village had about a hundred or less small homes. The homes were built of mud and wood from *babhul* or *kadulimb* trees; the wood from these trees is tough and resistant to pests. The timber was cut, shaped and formed to support the roof, doors and windows. Because rainfall was poor throughout the year, these houses maintained a cooler temperature inside and a strong exterior against the arid heat outside.

Most of villagers had small farms. Others were carpenters, blacksmiths, cobblers, masons, and barbers who complimented the farmers' lives. The average rainfall for the area was low. There were some wells, but they were deep and even then, they didn't have much water. Many of these wells dried-up in the heat of summer. Water was a luxury for villagers. It was a very difficult life in summer. There were families in other villages where well water was abundant. These distant relatives had plenty of well water, but it was impolite to stay with these relatives every summer for this would be inappropriate and ungracious. Some villagers from the dry well area managed to stay with generous relatives who were aware of the hardship and kindly invited them to stay the summers of drought in their homes.

In the 'dry village,' a women's life was trying for they had to carry water in earthen pots over long distances. Traditionally men were responsible for the family. They were to earn money and maintain the family's needs. Men had to do their regular businesses to support their family financially. This was not the case with women for they were in charge of the kitchen, doing the house work, taking care of the children and extended family, helping their husbands on the farm and also taking great effort in the carrying of the home's water supply.

In this village lived the Kisan and Rukmini Kadam family. Kisan was a farmer who was muscular, short in height with bright brown eyes, who was a hard worker with a kind heart. Kisan was a smart farmer who knew how to work and respect the land. He wore a *dhotar* or Indian-style folded pants, a plain shirt and a *pheta,* which is a traditional turban of Maharashtra, on his head.

Rukmini was his wife. She in turn was smart, fair in beauty and was extremely religious. Her main concern was in cooking and housework, although she worked diligently beside her husband. These two fine people birthed a son who was named Sopan and whose appearance reflected and complemented the typical Indian style and appearance of his father.

Sopan was pleased with this similarity to his father, since he respected his father and was proud of his father's knowledge. Sopan didn't have schooling except for the education he received from working hard on their farm, which had a well with excellent water year-round. Kisan pleasantly shared his well water with those in need. His generosity saved many of his neighbors. This brought the family great respect. They were not rich nor were they poor. All three members of this family lived their lives in pleasantly as they maintained keeping busy on their farm all day long leading a productive, content life with neighborly kindness.

After a time, a new person joined their blessed family. This was Sumal, a charismatic young woman who became Sopan's charming wife. She was fair, with black hair to her waist, dreamy eyes of black brown and on one cheek a mole to praise her beauty. Green tattoo spots on her forehead and chin contrasted with her fair skin. She was all the more attractive when she dressed in her colorful *sarees.* The red *kumku* spot on her forehead complimented her sparkling eyes with her hair coiled into a soft bun at the nape of her neck. Her wrists jingled with colorful bangles. Sumal's captivating radiance mesmerized Sopan to win his love and respect.

Many times, he stared into her dreamy eyes to admit, "You are beautiful, and how I love you. Your dark intense eyes reflect the mystery that exists within the new moon's absence in the night."

Hearing her husband's words Sumal would wink and smile. Sopan further added, "Our son will be like you. His eyes will be like your eyes." The couple shared their dreams of having a child. Sumal was also deeply in love with her husband Sopan. They were a joyous couple.

The days flew quickly like butterflies. Three years passed filled with a life of work, cheer and love. Life was like a sweet dream. Sopan and Sumal enjoyed their married life. Sopan's parents Kisan and Rukmini were pleased knowing their son enjoyed a good marriage. They loved Sumal as their daughter-in-law for she was smart, expert in cooking, eager to share with any work and took care of all the family. Everything in their lives was satisfactory, although she was not yet blessed with a child. Many relatives and friends questioned her as to why she had not gotten pregnant. They were anxious to see a baby in this hardworking pleasant family. Her husband Sopan and her mother-in-law Rukmini worried for they were eager to hear a crying baby and to see a crawling baby, a grandchild in their home. Day after day their pressure on Sopan to become a father only increased Sumal's depression and confusion at her inability to conceive.

After many discussions, the family gave their support for them to visit a *vaidya*, a traditional Ayurvedic Indian doctor who was well-known in helping with infertility and practiced in a nearby town. There were many questions that needed answers for instance why did they have no child after three years of trying? Were there problems with their bodies? Would Sumal ever be able to conceive? If and what treatment should they do?

The *vaidya* examined Sumal, to relate, "Don't worry, Sumal. You, can be a mother." Sopan was called into the examining room.

The *vaidya* called them into his office to relate his findings, "There are no physical problems with either of you. I recommend that you wait for a few months or a year before trying again. Sumal's body needs to rest."

Noticing their questioning faces, he continued, "You shall have a child, there is no problem and as for treatment, there is no need for you both are extremely healthy. Try to be calm and relax. Your urgency and tenseness are preventing you from conceiving."

Deep in thought, Sopan and Sumal returned home to inform the family of the good news. Patiently, they waited. After a year, Sumal did not become pregnant. Slowly, another year passed with no results. Sopan worked harder in the fields to burn off his frustration and with hope his good crops would bless them with a child. Sumal knew he was as anxious and restless, their relationship reverberated with tension. Sopan's parents were also concerned. Four years had passed with no sign of a baby.

One day, Sopan's mother Rukmini took them aside, explaining, "You were examined by the *vaidya*. He is a well-known *vaidya*, yet he did not help now you need to find a different solution. Our family's religion has helped us."

Tears fell from Sumal's eyes as she listened to her mother-in-law, "Many people from the nearby towns have related stories of how they were able to address their problems after praying to the shrine with the stone gods." Wiping the tears from her daughter-in-laws face, she smiled, "Perhaps, if you visit this village shrine and pray to the gods, they will help you."

Sopan held out his hand to his wife, "Let's pray to the stone gods. The pain you feel is destroying us. I don't wish for you to be so sad and depressed. We are healthy and this may be our answer?"

Nodding her head, Sumal whispered, "All right. What more can we do? Let's go together and the gods may listen to our prayers."

Sopan and Sumal respectfully took their mother's advice to pray at the village shrine, taking with them the vermilion mixture. Following the directions described, the three of them arrived at the shrine where there were three large pebbles coated with vermilion by previous followers. Villagers believed these were not normal stones, but held the spirits of their gods who were the protectors of the village and the people. These village gods who dwelt within the stones had helped those who had faith in them.

Sopan's mother Rukmini who had accompanied them, showed them how to use their bare hands to delicately coat each stone. They begged for spiritual assistance in conceiving a child. Pouring all of their love and energy into their actions, Sopan and Sumal prayed to these stone gods. Sopan and Sumal prostrated themselves on the ground, beseeching with strong faith to these deities. Rukmini knelt as she prayed, reflecting on the goodness of Sopan and Sumal. These three Rukmini, Sopan and Sumal implored with all their might for the blessings of the gods.

Months passed as their married life entered its fifth year. There was no sign of a pregnancy. Rukmini's heart yearned for them and their fruitless endeavor in having a child in their home. Sumal's calm face turned pale and gaunt. Nervously, she busied herself around the house, easily frustrated to cry and become despondent. Losing interest in festivals and enjoyments, she retreated into herself, hiding from life. Each day when she awoke, this was another day of disappointment.

One fine evening Kamal, who was a childhood friend of Sumal, arrived for a visit. Kamal lived in Kambleshwar a village not far from their home. Kamal was smart like Sumal and was a happy person who had a husband. She visited Sumal bringing along her adorable new born son. Sumal welcomed her friend Kamal by preparing a special dinner of traditional Indian sweet *besan ladoo* for her. Both enjoyed sharing news and chitchatting before going to bed.

Kamal noticed Sumal's longing towards her son and her sadness. As the visit continued, Kamal further noticed Sumal's anxiety and her eagerness to have a baby.

The next day, Sumal and Kamal ate lunch, sharing stories about their childhood. Kamal decided to take this opportunity, "Sumal, you know very well that our Kambleshwar is a small village situated on the bank of beautiful Nira River. Fortunately, the Nira River never dries up and we have plenty of water throughout the year. People from Kambleshwar and many nearby towns enjoy the Nira River's sweet water. Most of the agricultural land is irrigated by the Nira River. We refer to our river as *Niramai* or Mother Nira."

Sumal smiled, "Yes, it is beautiful and peaceful. Nira River flows gracefully."

Kamal continued, "Our people think Nira is kind for she shares her sweet drinking water with us, the animals, birds, and nurtures our crops. People harvest excellent food, grain and grasses with the help from our Nira River. They endear their survival to her and this is why we worship *Niramai*. She is our mother. She is our goddess."

Smiling, Sumal said, "Yes, I know of *Niramai*."

Kamal caressed her baby boy's face, "Sumal, your family shares your well water with others. You have a connection to water. Our Nira River helps with land fertility, perhaps *Niramai* helps women with their fertility, also! Think about this, there were couples who weren't blessed with a baby who went to worship and pray in her flowing waters. Their strong faith in the Nira River brought them the blessings of having a child."

Tears fell from Sumal's eyes, rolling down her cheeks to fall in her lap. Kamal spoke kindly to her friend, "Sumal, if any childless woman performs the ritual of offering *oti* to the Nira River, the river will bless this woman. This is true!"

Shaking her head, Sumal explained to Kamal of all their attempts and how they had tried different prayers and a doctor. Nothing had worked! Kamal hugged her baby son to her. She spoke convincingly, "Many women have trouble becoming pregnant. This is not unusual, but these women performed the ritual of offering *oti* to *Niramai*, our Mother Nira River and they were blessed with children."

Kamal watched Sumal sigh, lost in thought. Studying her face, Kamal wasn't giving up on her friend, "Though people worship *Niramai* there isn't really a temple or small shrine on the riverbank. People take sacred gifts to her when they go to *Niramai*, and directly worship the River *Niramai*. Do you know, *Niramai* is also known as *Bhivai Devi*? But there is no idol for *Bhivai Devi* neither is there a temple, nor a shrine."

Looking deeply into the sad eyes of Sumal, Kamal said, "My friend, please believe me and come with me to our village Kambleshwar for a day or two. We will go to the Nira River, to our *Niramai* for *oti* ritual. Please?"

Hearing Kamal's kind words, Sumal was deeply impressed. Keeping with tradition, Sumal waited to get approval from elders and her husband to travel out of their village.

Sumal spoke with Sopan about going with Kamal to Kambleshwar. She asked him, "Do you believe this will work? We have tried and tried."

Sumal closed her eyes as he held her and whispered in her ear, "Somehow, I believe this will bring the answer to our prayers. Kamal is your close friend and if she has witnessed this miracle from the river, then we have to believe."

Sopan combed his fingers through her hair, as Sumal softly said, "Kamal has heard from others of the river's miracles. Oh, Sopan, if this doesn't work…"

Embracing her to his chest, he responded, "Positive, we must be positive! Please, put away all your negative thoughts. It is time for you to love yourself and believe and trust the river. Yes, you have my permission! You know I cannot go with you because of the crops. Please, let your dreams be known to the Nira River."

Sumal touched her husband's cheek, "Yes, I shall let her know of our dreams and prayers. In the morning, I will request this trip from the elders." They held onto each other until dawn when Sopan slipped away to his work in the fields.

The elders knew of Sumal and Sopan and their troubles. Her request to go was answered, "Yes, this will be good. Go with Kamal for she is wise in *oti* and able to explain what you will need to take with you. We shall pray for your safe return."

After her visit with the Elders, Sumal met with Kamal and Kamal's baby boy. Hugging Kamal's baby and dancing around the room, Sumal said, "Yes, I want to go with you to the fertile waters of *Niramai* who will bless me. Please, help me prepare for this trip! We can gather everything we need before we leave and you know what I should offer to the river. Can you stay with us for a couple of days? Then we will go to Kambleshwar and you can show me your lovely home and your fine husband."

Clapping her hands, Kamal agreed. The two women stayed busy packing necessary items, taking care of Kamal's baby and praying to the House Gods for a safe trip.

Early one morning, Sumal and Kamal with the small infant boy traveled by bullock cart to Kambleshwar. Kamal's family greeted her warmly and were anxious to assist her. Sumal was energized and excited with all of these positive people around her. Everyone she met assured her that the Nira River would help her achieve her pregnancy.

On the planned morning at Kamal's home in Kambleshwar, Sumal showered, put on her green *saree* and green bangles and applied the red *kunku* dot to her forehead. Following Kamal's guidance, Sumal had prepared the river's gifts the night prior. The two women collected the sacred ritual items, which were a fresh coconut, a rolled package of wheat grains, areca or betel nuts, almonds, and a new blouse piece. *Halad* and red *kunku* powder were carefully packaged separately. There were small lamps formed from wheat dough. They carefully placed all of the collected items on a copper plate and covered those with a piece of cloth. Proudly, Sumal wrapped the food offerings that she and Kamal had cooked for the river goddess. This was *puran poli* which is an Indian sweet flatbread mixed with some delicious yogurt rice. Once at the river, Sumal would graciously offer all these sacred items of worship to the river.

Sumal and Kamal solemnly arrived at *Bhivai Devi* also known as the Nira River or *Niramai*. Peacefully, they absorbed the energy of the calm, clean flow of the quiet *Niramai*, the Mother River. Sweet water gurgled passed them. The river had a width spanning more than a quarter mile and in the center a depth of twenty feet or more. There were many *kadulimb, babhul* and *vad* trees on both sides of the river. Combinations of colors were reflected in the water. Peace surrounded them. Sumal became emotionally overwhelmed at the sight of the river's shining calm water with reflective trees. Profoundly, she knew this ritual was the answer to their prayers. Sumal waded into the river, her palm resting on the flow of the water. Closing her eyes with river water pushing through her fingers, she pleaded, *"Bhivai Devi*, oh, Narmada River remove the sorrow from my heart!"

Kamal stood on the banks of Nira River. As Sumal waded deeper into the water, she smiled at its refreshing coolness. She formed a cup from her palms to hold water. She bent down and filled the cup formed with her palms with the river water. She closed her eyes. Her mind was filled with affection, dedication, and devotion. The fluid floating around Sumal's body dissolved her frustration and anxiousness, allowing her to meditate.

Joyful warmth and relief flooded into her being. Sumal lost all awareness of her surroundings for she felt only the pulse of the river *Niramai*. Sumal visualized the silver cascading liquid pouring around her, between and within her. *Niramai* washed Sumal's spirit, assuring her of motherhood. This surge of feeling gave Sumal pleasure and confidence as she prayed to the river with all of her heart, asking her for a baby.

Sumal's closed eyes, hands folded in prayer palm to palm, she cried with earnest emotion, begging, "*Niramai*, I am your childless daughter, eager for motherhood. You are the only one who can fulfill my desire. I have prayed for a child of my own for five years. Now, I have hope. *Niramai*, please give me your blessings, please, so I can be a mother. I have faith in you and you have given your faith back to me. Please, will you will fulfill my dream?"

Sumal's green *saree* floated around her. Dutifully, Sumal remembered Kamal, who was waiting on the riverbank. Returning to shore, Sumal retrieved from Kamal's hands the copper plate heavy with her offerings. Once again, wading into deep river water, balancing the plate on her hand, Sumal began her *oti* ritual. Shaking the *halad* and *kunku* powder from a small bag, she softly prayed, "*Niramai*, I am offering you *oti* with *halad kunku*. Please, put these on your forehead."

Carefully, removing the green blouse piece from the side of the plate with one hand, she spoke to the river, "I am offering you a green blouse piece. Please, accept this offering and put it on your sweet and holy flow." Then she put the blouse piece on the river water. The blouse piece floated downstream.

Sumal had to reposition her hand under the plate as her fingers grasped the almonds, sprinkling them over the flowing water, she prayed, "I am offering you almonds, Mother Nira, for almond seeds have a hard shell and like the almond, I expect to have a fertile family seed within my womb. Please, be kind and bless me."

The copper plate with the remaining offerings was gently tilted, relieving her offerings into the river's current. Sumal tucked the plate under one arm, lifting her hands in prayer she whispered, "I am performing this *oti* ritual especially for you, oh, sacred Nira River. Please, accept my *oti*, please."

When she watched the sun reflect on the flowing *Niramai* and all of her *oti* material was accepted, Sumal's eyes overflowed with tears. The sacred *oti* items were gone. As she fell into a trance, her whole being was pulsating with hope and an indescribable feeling. After some time, she waded to the shore. Handing the empty copper plate to Kamal, Sumal folded her hands together in gratitude.

Kamal stood watching her to say, "Don't worry, Sumal, certainly *Niramai* will bless you. Once you are large with child, come again to offer *oti* in honor of *Niramai*." Sumal accepted her suggestion with a positive mind. Kamal and Sumal slowly ambled to Kamal's home, speaking of hope for the future.

That night, she slept peacefully for her mind was calm for the first time in a long time. Dreaming, she envisioned a world in blue light with a cool breeze, birds chirped sweetly as she glowed standing in *Niramai*'s holy water. In this dream, she prayed to *Niramai* who was a radiant woman with ankle length flowing hair. She was floating upright through the drifting river. The woman magically came to her wearing a white *saree* with golden ornaments. The red dot on her forehead was the first thing she noticed in her dream, until this mystical woman rose above the water, carrying a newborn baby in her arms. Lovingly, the woman placed the baby into Sumal's waiting arms and then the spiritual woman disappeared.

Sumal quickly awoke, realizing she was alone in her bed. Anxious about this dream, she wasn't able to fall asleep again. She revisited her dream again and again as she caressed her abdomen. In the morning, she

Blessings of Bhivai Devi

told no one of her dream. She chose to stay with Kamal, in Kambleshwar, for the next three days. Then, she hurriedly returned to her home.

All of her family noticed her pleasant mood and her refreshed appearance. They were curious to know about her experiences in Kambleshwar and her ceremony at the Nira River. Joyfully, Sumal shared with them about Kamal's family, her help, the sweet water of *Niramai* and the pleasant environment and calm surroundings. Quietly, Sumal described the warmth and extraordinary feeling that overcame her when she first arrived at *Niramai* and how confident she was about the river's blessings.

That night, alone with her husband in their bedroom, she explained her strange new emotions, "After praying to *Niramai,* I had a feeling of good fortune."

Sopan smiled at her happiness, "All right, tell me all. What brought about this joy inside of you?"

Sumal related, "Oh, Sopan, I had the most magnificent dream. There was a magical woman who was dressed in a white *saree* embroidered with golden thread. This glorious woman rose from the water to hand me a baby, a newborn baby!"

Sopan laughed, "Was this the river goddess or was this my mother?"

Smacking him, she frowned, "Sopan, I am serious! We are going to have a child. The river showed me! We are going to have our own child. I no longer have any doubts. This home shall have a new guest, a tiny little person shall come into our lives."

Sopan listened as he studied her excited eyes filled with new confidence. Sopan folded his hands together palm to palm as he gazed toward the ceiling, praying for *Niramai*'s blessings.

Three months passed in quiet expectation. One sunny morning, Sumal fell ill. After their early breakfast, Sumal excused herself to lose her food. Her mother-in-law Rukmini had followed her. Lifting her daughter-in-law's hair from her face, Rukmini clapped her hands in joy. Sumal stared at her only to throw up again and again. Once Sumal had recovered, she asked her mother-in-law why she was so pleased. As Rukmini tenderly washed Sumal's face, she gingerly said, "It is obvious to me, my dear one, that you are with child for you have morning sickness!"

Staring at her in disbelief, Sumal shook her head, "No, I am sick. My belly hurts, I'm hot and truly I am sick. I feel awful."

Rukmini felt Sumal's forehead, "Lovely Sumal, you are suffering from morning sickness. It will pass, but not without patience. Being pregnant is only for women! Men could never endure our agony, believe me! Come, we must tell Sopan!"

The family was overjoyed. Rukmini warned Sopan to be thoughtful to his wife for there would be times of short temper, loss of gratitude and eagerness for him to leave her alone. Sopan's father explained to him the duties of fatherhood and how to care for Sumal, "This will be a time of patience. You must wait nine months for your child to be born. During this time, you will find a deep love for your woman. She has brought your seed to life, a seed passed from grandfather to father to you, my son. This is truly a miracle, cherish your woman with all of your being. Also, be glad there are other women around to help her. It is traditional for the men to leave the women to care for her. Come, let us thank the gods while we work the fields."

The family busied with sewing clothes, finding needs for a newborn. As the months slowly passed, a very pregnant Sumal and her proud husband Sopan visited Kamal and her family. Early one morning, Sumal took Sopan's hand as they waded into the Nira River to release gifts and appreciative prayers.

Months dragged by before their dreams were realized. Every waking moment of her day, Sumal visualized *Niramai* and how the sacred waters had surged around her body. Sopan listened again and again as Sumal retold him of her dream relating the glorious woman who brought her a newborn from the river. No longer did Sopan work far from home, but stayed nearby with eager anticipation. Sumal waddled carefully doing her chores, resting every afternoon. Finally, Sopan was called to his home for Sumal's contractions had begun. She had an easy labour, giving birth to a healthy baby boy.

Their home filled with joy. Generous Sopan gave *pedhas,* sweets to all his relatives and friends while everyone congratulated Sopan and Sumal on their beautiful, strong newborn son. As the family enjoyed best wishes, they thought of *Bhivai Devi* and the Nira River mother *Niramai.* Her blessings had given them their dream child. How blessed their lives were now, thanks to *Bhivai Devi*'s blessings.

Notes:

This legend combines a woman's eagerness for motherhood, a belief in a kind river spirit, and how a traditional ritual performed with strong faith helps one to become a mother. This incident took place in the village of Kambleshwar in the Maharashtra state. On the bank of the River Nira is Kambleshwar village. The people hold a sacred respect for this river in that it represents their mother. Their life is dependent on the river and the holy water within it. If a childless woman prays and worships to the river, and performs the *oti* ritual, the River Nira blesses and fulfills the wish of her becoming a mother. This is the local belief.

Becoming a mother is a natural thing. But if there is a problem, the couple may turn to traditional medicine or doctor. If that doesn't help, at some point they lose patience. Holding on to hope, they search for some other way. Considering other's experiences and having the influence of tradition, some might turn to traditional beliefs, faiths, and submit to natural elements and the holder of supernatural powers. This legend is the example of such human behaviors.

This legend was made available to me by Smt. Savitri Jag*dale*. The myth was told to her by Ashatai Nalawade of Wadange in Kolhapur district. I have retold the legend in my own words.

Glossary:

Babhul or Babul tree – The gum arabic tree, an acacia (Acacia nilotica) native to India.

Halad – Turmeric powder.

Kunku or kumkuma – A red powder made from turmeric or any other local materials. Women put red colored kunku on their forehead. It looks like a red spot. It has a cultural significance. It represents prosperity. It is also widely used for worshiping the Hindu gods and goddesses. It is a sign of respect in social life.

Kadulimb or Neem – A type of evergreen tree (Azadirachta indica) native to India.

Oti – Symbolically, Oti means offering. It is a traditional ritual to honor woman's fertility. Oti literally means the lower abdomen of a woman. This is the part where her uterus is located. To offer Oti is therefore a symbolic expression of one's wish that 'May your womb be filled.' In this ritual, one married woman honors another married woman's fertility by offering a *saree*, blouse piece, rice or wheat grains, coconut, betel nuts, dried dates, and young shoots of turmeric plant, all of which are suggestive of a new creation and in this case, conception. The woman concerned receives the offerings in the folds of her *saree*.

Vad – Banyan tree.

Goddess Laxmibai – A village-local female deity.

Pooja or puja ritual – A prayer ritual performed by Hindus of devotional worship to one or more deities. It is a Sanskrit word. It means reverence, honor, homage, adoration, and worship.

Sanai-chaughda – These two are different types of musical instruments. Both of them are played at festive events or special occasions. *Sanai* or *shehnai* is a musical instrument similar to oboe and chaughda or nagara is a membranophone instrument that is considered to be the lead instrument in ceremonies and weddings.

Water Blessing, Yurok
NATIVE AMERICAN

Long ago, soon after the Oriental influence arrived from the East onto the northeast coast of the America's with modern ideas of metal and copper, there was a small village of *Yurok* people who lived near the Klamath River and they used such metal and copper when fishing and hunting. This village was referred to as *Pulikla* or Down River, within walking distance of the Pacific Ocean. There was a fisherman named *Pa'ah Chi'ish*, who was known as Water Dog for he caught more salmon in one morning than any other. He could dive for *smelt fish* with great success. His twenty foot long *harpoon* was tied with a whale bone barb, his shot was expertise and his reward was plenty. Salmon was the main staple of the *Yurok* people and to be the best fisherman was considered a great honor. Many other young men tried to outdo nineteen year old Pa'ah Chi'ish, but none could compare.

One late morning, Chi'ish's father hurried to keep step with his son, "What is it? Why are you here away from the others?" *Hliul'tl* studied his son's solemn face. "You are the greatest of fishermen in our village and yet you are here on dry land!"

Pa'ah Chi'ish twisted a green twig from a tall redwood tree beside him, "Father, how can I fish when my hands are clenched in pain."

Hliul'tl lifted his son's hand to examine his fingers. "Your fingers are hot, but they bend and are still strong. Why would your hands be clenched in pain?"

Pa'ah Chi'ish shrugged to shake his head, his deep dark eyes distantly stared into the thick forest of redwood trees, "There are times when my spirit is good and then there are times when my spirit is filled with such sadness that my hands won't function."

"Then it's time for us to go see the woman at the end of the village.

She's a strong Shaman and knows of herbs. Her power is great. Let's go and find out what your problem is from her." *Hliul'tl* nodded his head toward the village.

"Father, this is serious. It wouldn't be wise for you to give her your shells, she'll tell you that I'm hopeless." *Pa'ah Chi'ish* turned away from his father.

"You're not hopeless. Sometimes you make me frustrated, but your mother and I have shells we can spare. Let's go and speak to the Shaman right now. It will soon be time to bring in the *Smelt Fish* and you're our finest fisherman." *Hliul'tl* nudged *Pah'ah Chi'ish* on the shoulder. "Come, let's go, now."

The two men, father and son walked through the village. People stared at them for *Pah'ah Chi'ish* was usually out fishing in his redwood canoe by early morning and it was now midday. Slowly, he moved for he was tall and lanky and his movements were flowing and fluid. *Hliul'tl* greeted the other men, "*Oyuukwi,*" an acknowledgement of friendship.

At the edge of the village sat one lone redwood paneled house. It was a squat building with a small oval door typically found in the eastern corner. *Hliul'tl* called a greeting and waited. An older woman with white hair flowing around her shoulders carefully crawled from her circular doorway. Stooping as she raised, she nodded to the men with the jingling of the denalium shells woven into her knee length skirt for that was all she wore.

Hliul'tl asked about her health and her supply of fish. She nodded as she spoke, "Many bring me fish and as of today, I am well. What is your purpose for your visit?"

Pa'ah Chi'ish stepped back as his father spoke, "My son *Pa'ah Chi'ish* has fingers that will not work for there is a pain within him. He doesn't know why he hurts. Your services are needed to help him understand."

The elderly Shaman woman laughed, "Oh, so you are a water dog? Isn't this what your name means?"

Pa'ah Chi'ish answered in a soft voice, "Yes." In the soft breeze, his long hair floated across his face to settle across his shoulders.

The Shaman woman put her hand out, "You're a big strong man. Let me see your hands. For someone so tall and muscular, you have a very soft voice." Taking his hand in hers, she turned it palm-up to examine. Tracing the lines of his palm with her index finger, her eyes lifted to his. Then she stroked his wrist and felt the strong muscles in his arm. Putting her fingers on his chin, she turned his head this way and that, noticing his eyes, his lips and his nose. Placing her index and middle finger on the pulse on his neck, she clicked her tongue.

Suddenly, her eyes became fixed as if she was peering at something behind *Pa'ah Chi'ish*. "There's no mystery here. Your son is in love. He has an affection for a young woman and he's afraid you will not approve."

Pa'ah Chi'ish stared down at the braided sandals on his feet. *Hliul'tl* cleared his throat, "Son, is this true? Is there someone you wish to marry?"

"Father, she doesn't belong to our village and she lives upstream. She is a *Karok* an Up River woman. Her father doesn't have much and we only met by chance."

"Son, this doesn't matter. If this woman is someone who you wish to spend your life with then you must have her invite us to her parents' home." *Hliul'tl* turned to the elderly Shaman woman. She was patting her grass skirt, again, noticing the shells as they jingled. The Shaman woman wore no blouse or top, as was traditional. The three line tattoos on her chin had faded. *Hliul'tl* bowed his head to her, "How many *dentalium shells* are needed for your wisdom?"

Laughing, the elderly woman put her hand up, "There will be no cost. Probably his mother already knows about this woman. You're the one who has no knowledge of her. Your son prefers to hide his feelings. This isn't good, especially if he is a fisherman for he must be honest with the water and the sea to receive the blessings of water. There is no cost. I'm delighted to know people still fall in love."

Bending over onto all fours, she rubbed her calloused kneels as she crawled back into her redwood cabin. *Hliul'tl* patted his son on the back, "I'd prefer if you were to tell me these things. It isn't good for me to appear stupid in front of others. Come, let's speak with your mother."

At their paneled cabin of redwood, the naked men bent down on all fours to enter through the small circular door in the corner. The cabin had upright redwood panels, four walls joined a short post at each of the four corners. The slanted roof was planked as well, allowing the rain runoff to flow away from the cabin. Inside, the cabin was a dugout cellar five feet deep and twelve feet wide by fifteen feet long. Every person in *Hliul'tl*'s family lived within this cabin. There were fourteen people who slept on a high earthen embankment shelf around the dugout cellar within the cabin's walls. The dugout cellar was for cooking, eating, and family discussions. The four foot earth wide inside embankment shelf around the dugout cellar, next to the interior cabin walls, was for sleeping at night, resting if ill and also the cooking utensils were placed on part of this ledge.

Hliul'tl's woman *Ta'anep* was kneeling in the center of the cellar area. The cooking fire was stoked. A wide mouthed pot, black from many cooking fires hung from metal ceiling hooks. Liquid boiled in the black pot as *Ta'anep* added spices to mix with fish and herbs. Delicious odors filled the cabin. Dried fish was cut and placed in conical baskets hanging from metal hooks in the ceiling. Willow boughs and redwood twigs were stacked near the door to be used in the weaving of baskets. Herbs wrapped in braided grass strings were draped from roughly hewn redwood planking.

Ta'anep wore a woven skull cap on her head to keep her hair out of her face while cooking. The black and white geometric designs in her cap represented her clan, her family's wealth and the number of children she had born. Quickly turning as they entered, she asked, "What are you doing here? You're to be out fishing? Why am I preparing herbs for fish stew when you have not brought more fish?"

Pa'ah Chi'ish quickly lifted a woven fishnet from the cabin wall. Not waiting, he disappeared through the crawl hole. *Hliul'tl* stood above his woman, "Are you aware of our son's infatuation with a woman of the *Karok* people?"

Ta'anep lifted her dripping wooden spoon, "Certainly. He told me about her ages ago. Why don't you listen to him when he tries to speak with you? It feels as if you're always too busy to listen to our children. You and the other old men are always talking about the olden times. You should listen to the younger people, they know about life, too." Stirring the liquid in the boiling black pot, she added. "Now, go and get me some fish. There are many mouths to feed tonight! Go!"

Hliul'tl trudged along the path to the ocean's beach, deciding to be with men his own age, those who understood him. His wife's deep conical basket woven on a fir frame intertwined with willow and vines was slung over his bare shoulder. The older men were roaming the beach, searching for a beached whale. His people did not hunt whales for they were sacred, but if a whale chose to wash ashore, already dead and offer itself to his people, then they would eat whale meat. Whale flesh was a sacred gift from the Pacific Ocean. As *Hliul'tl* noticed the men ahead of him, he reflected on the fact that the path to the beach was long and was halfway between the *Yurok* or Down River People and the *Karok* or Up River People. Thirty-foot long canoes went up and down the Klamath River to the different villages trading goods, sharing knowledge and having ceremonies together. It was strange for them to be differentiated as the Up River or the Down River people.

Soon, *Hliul'tl* joined the group of older men ambling along on the sandy beach. Some of the men had thinly rolled deerskins flung over their shoulders while others carried deep conical basket for collecting whale meat. All of them were nude as was tradition. Fish oil covered their naked bodies to keep their dark skin from burning in the midday sun. It was a clear day, the ocean breeze was cool and the clouds dotting the sky kept the sun from burning the sand. Calling out to the men, they stopped and waited for him. There were several men his age that he did not know. His friends greeted him with the usual "*Aiyuquo.*"

His oldest friend, who had helped with the tattoos on his shoulders, introduced him to a man known as *NrtMry* who burst into a big smile once he knew his name. "*Hliul'tl* is your name? Well, I know this name well. My daughter talks of you and your woman all the time, but mostly she speaks of your son *Pa'ah Chi'ish.*"

Hliul'tl stared out at the ocean, "Oh, how nice for your daughter to know my son. What is your daughter's name?"

NrtMry laughed out loud, "He hasn't told you? How strange! My daughter's name is *Ch'uch'ish Ko'm* or Bird who Hears. Are you sure you haven't heard of her?"

Now, *Hliul'tl* smiled, "Oh, yes! *Pa'ah Chi'ish* is most fond of your daughter. He was just telling me of her this morning. How bizarre that you haven't invited us to dinner at your cabin?" *Hliul'tl* noticed the single tattoo stripe on *NrtMry*'s shoulders denoting he didn't own much land or *dentalium shells*, therefore he wasn't wealthy. Not like *Hliul'tl* who had three stripes on each of his shoulders and owned land from the center of the village to the clearing near the redwood forest.

NrtMry's smile quickly turned to a frown, "Oh, is this the way the *Pulikla* or Down River people do things? Your son is the one who should invite us to his home for dinner after all he is the great fisherman! He is the one who is to pay the dowry, am I right? I'm a mere whale hunter, like yourself. I have only one daughter *Ch'uch'ish Ko'm*. She may be beautiful, but she's no fisherman."

The two men strode quietly along the beach with the group. As they turned a bend on the coastal shore, there on the beach was a stranded, dead whale of enormous proportions. The whale's odor was fresh, his meat would still be good. The group joined together in a thankful chant. Taking knives from their pouches tied around their naked waists to cut the meat from the whale's bones, several men unwrapped deerskins, where the fresh meat was placed in bulk. *Hliul'tl* and *NrtMry* had deep conical baskets with which to carry the thinly sliced whale meat and blubber. The men were agreeable when they split the meat among themselves. As they cut the whale, the older men sang a prayer of gratitude to the whale for this truly was a gift. The dried whale meat was excellent for ceremony or a delicious luxury if someone were to visit for dinner. When the men returned to the river paths, *NrtMry* went north while *Hliul'íl* and his friends took the southern route.

It was well past dark before the older men returned to their homes, calling out their find. They were greeted first by the children, then by their smiling women with three wide tattoos marked on their chins. These strong women removed the heavy baskets from their men. Cooler weather was blowing in from the ocean. A ceremonial deer dance was planned to happen in four days' time. The whale meat would dry if the sky stayed clear and the sun remained hot. Young women were busy weaving willow redwood branches mixed with spruce twigs into the huge baskets formed on twine wrapped hazel frames. Different barks or firs were stripped from the trees, soaked, and then intertwined around the hazel basket frames. This was a learned traditional art.

The Autumn Deer Dance was to celebrate life with an appreciation to the supernatural. This was to show loyalty to ancestors and share in a huge feast. The *Yurok* did not have a potlatch. The older girls gathered wild berries to have full baskets sit on the embankments inside their redwood cabins. Grandmothers who had worked all summer to scrape fur from deerskins and sun bleaching them white were busy cutting the leather to sew moccasins, blankets, folded deerskin loin cloths, capes or thinly cut leather thongs for basket head straps, headboard wraps or cradle basket straps. Fish meat jerky soaked in herbs and seaweed was soaked for salt.

Landowners of great acreage and those who prepared the most food were considered wealthy and voted in as chiefs, administrators and leaders. Designated areas were allocated to specific families for hunting, fishing and farming. Men wore aprons of civet cat or deerskin about their waist. Necklaces of dentalium and beads were worn around their necks to bounce and jingle as they danced. *Dentalium shells* were used as currency. The more one had the wealthier one was within their class. Young men were earning their tattoos by hunting wolves, eagles, woodpeckers, civet cats and deer. The wolf's fur was worn as forehead bands for the wolf fur fell over their eyes for shade. The headbands had a stick poking straight up from their head with tied eagle feathers to resemble an enormous sacred feather, the stick covered with woodpecker scalps that showed wealth.

Hliul'íl washed the sand off his naked body after handing the cut whale meat to his elderly mother and sister who were tending to the whale meat with the other village women. This group of women rattled off stories of their men and whale hunts, laughing and joking as they cut and cleaned meat with professional ease. Outdoor pit fires were burning with kindling, while large blubber pots filled with water boiled. Whale blubber was boiled down into oil, used in cooking and for human needs. Children raced through the village with hoops and sticks, calling to one another, dogs barked at their heels. Babies slept in cradle baskets hanging on the backs of their mothers with the holding leather straps were placed around their mother's foreheads. One mother leaned forward to shift the baby's weight onto her back rather than on her forehead and neck. Mothers were explaining to daughters how to grind acorn nuts into a fine white powder for baking bread and large chunks were put into stews. *Pa'ah Chi'ish* squatted with his family's other fishermen in the middle of the village, discussing the salmon run for the next day.

Hliul'tl entered his family cabin, squat crawling through the small door. His wife *Ta'anep* was stirring their dinner in the huge cooking pot hanging from the planked ceiling. Her woven apron and skull cap were her only clothing. The rich aroma of fish mingled with the tart smell of wild plant tubers. *Hliul'tl* called to *Ta'anep*, "We need to talk about our son and his relationship with *Ch'uch'ish Ko'm.*

Chuckling under her breath, she answered, "There is nothing to speak about for they are going to have a marriage at the Deer Dance in four days."

Hliul'tl stood upright, banging his head on the low ceiling beam, he screeched, "Ow! What? Why wasn't I told of this marriage?"

"My man, didn't you learn from the Shaman? Instead of speaking with your son, you went out with the older men to find whale. I'm glad you found the whale for we can use the meat at the ceremony, but you could have spoken to *Pa'ah Chi'ish* first."

Clicking his tongue, *Hliul'tl* shook his head, "I was with *NrtMry*, *Ch'uch'ish Ko'm's* father. We spoke of their relationship, but he said nothing of marriage! He wanted us to have his family here for a dinner! Can you imagine such a thing? We are interested in his daughter and he wants us to invite them here!"

Tromping down the dirt steps into the home's center cellar to *Ta'anep*, he barked out, "Do you know *NrtMry* has only one stripe on his shoulder? Obviously, he has no land, probably doesn't have much wealth either. I'm not sure if this is such a good match, *Ta'anep*, for we have worked hard to acquire land and to raise all of our children."

Hliul'tl raised his hand to point at the interior of the cabin, asking, "*Ta'anep*, where will we put the married couple? Your family is in here and my family is here, I don't think there is enough room for them." He abruptly sat on a woven mat to lean against the dirt wall of the cellar.

Ta'anep placed the dripping wooden spoon on a basket lid. Her large brown eyes sparkled as she spoke, "Husband, most of the land we own came from my father as did our fishing areas. Your mother lives with us for this is tradition and you are responsible for your sisters now their husbands were taken by the ocean. Your son will sleep with you in the *sweat lodge* and *Ch'uch'ish Ko'm* has plenty of room in here, until then, we'll manage until something else happens."

Hliul'tl shook his long hair free as he removed his headband. The whale oil on his naked body glistened by the cooking fire, "This is all sudden! There is no time to prepare! The Deer Dance is in a couple of days and *Pa'ah Chi'ish* didn't fish even this morning. We won't be ready, this isn't a good time." He added a cocky smile as he studed her expression, "We should wait until I'm ready."

Ta'anep sat next to him on the mat, "*Hliul'tl*, you have not been listening or understanding this event. *Ch'uch'ish Ko'm* and her mother asked me about this wedding in the early spring. I gave my permission." She patted his knee to add, "You were consulted and your answer was 'go ahead.' You weren't listening were you?"

Hliul'tl jumped up, "What? I was asked? I don't remember! When were you going to tell me the marriage ceremony is this Deer Dance? You women plan everything and *NrtMry*, who is the bride's father, didn't even know about this!"

Laughing, *Ta'anep* returned to stir the fish stew in the large cooking pot, "Oh, ah-hah, or maybe he didn't want to mention the wedding? After all, you probably acted as if you had no idea who he is!"

Pacing while shaking his head, "How can I get everything in order? The family council needs to be informed and...."

She raised her hand, "You can stay busy with your whale finding and not worry about this. We have it all planned." She fixed him a bowl of stew and brought it to him.

Slurping the delicious meal, *Hliul'tl* smiled at his wife, "You are the best cook in the village. We have a good life, but *Ch'uch'ish Ko'm* is not you!"

Ta'anep frowned, "Compliments aren't going to win this argument. The council was informed in the spring after your gave your consent. You must agree this will be a good marriage. She's a fine young woman who is excellent at basket weaving and she's a good cook."

Hliul'tl returned to sit on the mat, "I don't even know what she looks like!"

His mother-in-law came down the mud stairs to the cellar, she smiled, "Who are we talking about in here?"

The oldest son followed behind her, "I believe they're referring to *Ch'uch'ish Ko'm*. Don't worry father. She's a beauty. Also, don't worry about living space, *Pa'ah Chi'ish* is building her a cabin to live in with her parents. They're getting older and her mother can help with their children as your mother helped with the raising of all of us."

Hliul'tl's face turned red as he murmured, "As a parent in this family, it is up to your mother and myself as the ones who should give the permission. We both agreed for you to marry your woman." He slurped his hot fish stew, picking up the salmon meat with his bone spoon. His family stood around the cooking pot, watching him. "Well, sit and eat. Evidently, my opinion is not important. Eat!"

After serving everyone a large wooden bowl of fish stew, *Ta'anep* spoke softly to him, "Yes, you are important in this family. You, who are always busy with important matters. So, you give your permission, right?" Her hands were on her hips as she studied him.

Wiping his mouth on the back of his hand, he nodded to her, "Of course, who am I to go against your word? After all, you women hold all the magic." He put out his hand to hers.

Intertwining her fingers with his calloused ones, she said, "Remember when you asked me for marriage at the Deer Dance? You could hardly speak. I had to nudge you to open your mouth and look at us now? We're happy, we have four children who are excellent at their work and will someday take care of us. We did well to marry and we're still doing well, right?"

Proudly lifting his strong chin, *Hliul'tl* laughed, "Yes, we're a good family. We take care of our parents and our children listen to us. I will do a better job of listening to them."

He went outside to find *Pa'ah Chi'ish* kneeling in a circle with the other men. They were drawing diagrams of the river and where they might place the nets for the early morning salmon run. *Hliul'tl* pulled his son aside, "We need to take a walk. Come with me." *Pa'ah Chi'ish* nodded to the other men and obeyed his father.

They walked to the tall trees outside of the village. *Hliul'tl* spoke first, "Son, your mother informed me that you wish to marry *Ch'uch'ish*

Ko'm. Is this what you want or what your mother wants?"

Pa'ah Chi'ish studied his father's expression. "Father, it is what *Ch'uch'ish Ko'm* and I both wish. She is not of our clan and she is not married. I am not of her clan and I am not married. We want to become a couple. This would make both of us and our families strong and we believed you would agree." Staring at the ground, he asked, "Would you agree?"

Hliul'tl said, "Yes, Son, it is important to marry a woman you want to share your life with, as your mother and I have. If this is what you both want, then I wish this as well."

Pa'ah Chi'ish bent down to pick up an acorn, tossing it away, he added, "Father, I am building a cabin at the east side of our village for *Ch'uch'ish Ko'm* and her family. When I tried to speak to you about this before, you told me not to bother. Did you understand what I was saying or do you want us to all live with you and mother?"

"Ah, yes, I remember part of that conversation." *Hliul'tl* frowned, "Evidently, I didn't understand why you wanted to live in a different cabin. Now I know. Your mother and the mother of *Ch'uch'ish Ko'm* are planning this wedding. I spoke with *NrtMry* this morning and he appeared to not know about this wedding either."

Pa'ah Chi'ish put his hand up, "What the women do is their business, but I did ask *NrtMry* for his permission to marry his daughter and he consented."

Shaking his head, *Hliul'tl* frowned, "Well, I must have appeared to be a fool in front of the soon to be father-in-law." He explained his first meeting with *NrtMry*. They both smiled. Father and son strolled into the village. Both of the men were tall, muscular, their skin dark, their brown hair fell to the waist of their naked bodies. *Hliul'tl* turned to his son, "Come on. Let's tell the others, unless they already know?"

Pa'ah Chi'ish shook his head, "No. No one knows but you and mother, well, and of course, her family. We haven't told anyone."

Hliul'tl abruptly stopped, "The Deer Dance is only four days away! Has your mother made your leather loin cloth? Has *Ch'uch'ish Ko'm* and her family put together what they will need for this special ceremony?"

Staring at the ground, *Pa'ah Chi'ish* nodded, "Yes, we have been preparing for a while now. I didn't know how to tell you."

Solemnly, *Hliul'tl* waved his hand to the men deep in conversation, "Come, let us inform the village and have a ceremony like no other!"

Immediately, the village people shifted their energy into decorating for the marriage. The wealthy chief arrived to congratulate father and son, telling them he would gladly deed over a piece land for their wedding gift. *Pa'ah Chi'ish* was deeply honored for now he would have wealth of his own. The fishermen joked with him about his wedding night and his need to improve on his salmon catch. Village women giggled, telling him *Ch'uch'ish Ko'm* was beautiful and kind and she was always eager to help the other mothers and their children.

Vines were gathered with their bright red leaves and berries to decorate the poles around the village cabins. Young boys gathered kindling for the outdoor bonfires used to cook all the necessary food for the feast. Non edible berries were mashed to soak as dyes for colorful geometric designs to be drawn on the deerskin aprons, skirts, kilts and moccasins. Seaweed pods were gathered by the girls to use the raw salt to set dyes, young women worked pounding acorns into flour for fancy shaped breads. Older women wove magnificent skull caps with intricate designs, adding carved wood sculptures on top.

Old men disappeared from the village to teach dance steps to the young. Only males were allowed to dance and the oldest man became the single chanter for the dancers. The oldest man in the village was bathed, washed with oils and given time to rest for he would be the one to call the all night chant for ten days. After a hard day of work, the men stayed in the sweat lodge, preparing for this spiritual event.

The women's work was to cook, handle the children and the elderly and control the bartering and sharing of goods. Hazel willow baskets appeared full in front of each of the homes. Dried fish and dried whale meat were guarded and kept clean, away from the fall winds and the hungry wild critters of the forest. Each day fish were brought in, from the sea and the rivers, to be gutted, boned and skinned. Some fish were dried, others cooked with herbs and seeds. Conical baskets were heavy with ocean muscles and mollusks. Four, thirty-foot long canoes came in at nightfall, loaded with three grown sea lions, speared and cleaned. This feast would be one to remember. Women who had been excluded to the menstruation house were brought food and told the latest news.

Finally, the day arrived. At sunrise, there was the cleansing of the dancing men. Each of the men was washed in ocean water. Their bodies were rubbed with fish oil. Drums beating, brought the oiled, painted men into a circle. Dye sticks had drawn elaborate designs on their naked bodies. The men's bleached white leather kilts of civet cat skin and deerskin illustrated with geometric designs contrasted with their dark skin. Fringed leather at the base of the kilts was knotted with beads and shells to jingle while they danced. Feathers floated around the wolf fur headbands and skull caps placed on their newly brushed hair.

Proud grandfathers handed the dancers carefully decorated poles. Each pole held a deerskin head stuffed and attached to the pole. The white, light gray, black or mottled deerskin had ears, mouth and throats with a false tongue decorated with woodpecker scalps, leaving the body of the deerskin and legs to hang loose. Wives arrived with colorful deerskin kilts and beaded moccasins. Layered necklaces of beads and shells hung around the women's necks covering their naked upper bodies.

Pa'ah Chi'ish, Hliul'ĭl and *NrtMry* danced with the other men. Whistles trilled in the cool morning air to hasten supernatural and ancestral blessings. The men and boys were given water while they danced for ten days and nights. Dried fish was shoved between their teeth once in the morning and then at midday to help them retain their strength. Some of the older men were given a chance to sit and rest. While others would laugh and point at them in fun. The women stayed close to the dancers to watch and comment on the performance. There was great pride in the dancers' stamina and strength to last all of the ten days and nights.

During the last morning of the dance, an ocean whirlwind grew in strength to bring a pelting of hard rain down on the dancers. Then a blast of hurricane wind flung ignited kindling across the open dance ground. Dancers leapt over the hot coals and burning sticks. Small children screamed as hot char burned their skin. Dogs barked wildly, chasing flying baskets and a flurry of feathers. Hurriedly, women covered the cooking pots, grabbing food baskets in an effort to protect the prepared feast. The village turned into chaos as people ran for shelter, grabbing children and pulling the elderly out of harms way.

Pa'ah Chi'ish's older sister *Wohpe'kumew* cried out in dispair, "This isn't good. This is a bad omen! What are we to do?"

Ta'anep said nothing as she continued to stomp on the hot coals. Then, suddenly the sun pushed through the thick clouds. The air became still. Fires calmed. Families returned to the village center. Clouds moved off to the west as the tall redwood trees became still. Many of the wind ripped branches were removed by the younger women as the dance area was swept clean and the dancing men resumed their dances until sunset. When the whistles stopped and the drums settled, the old man stopped chanting. Now it was time for each of the village chieftains to come forward to announce their individual village news.

More than one chieftain spoke on and on, proud of what his

village had achieved during the summer months, while other chiefs were thoughtfully short in their speeches. The last village chief to speak was the leader of *Hliul'tl*'s village for this village was hosting the dance. The chief lifted his hands to quiet the crowd, "Today, we are proud to have the longest canoes and the greatest number of fishermen. This is certainly an honor. Yet, we pray the other villages will soon pass us and we can visit their village for the food." People laughed and clapped.

The chief raised his hands as he continued, "There were many times the *smelt fish* were not hungry enough to come inland for us to net, but with the help of the monsoon winds we were able to bring in at least twelve harvests. The summer months proved to be warmer than we expected and only four mothers were able to birth infants. The redwood trees have allotted us enough wood to build ten new cabins."

Hliul'tl subtly wove his way through the male dancers to arrive at the chief's elbow. The chief did not waver, "If the whales are eager for us to find them, they are found. Although, we are needing the whale spirit to be kinder to our men out on the ocean in their canoes. Speaking of canoes and fishing, it is a great honor for me to introduce our greatest fisherman's father *Hliul'tl* who is poking me in the arm!"

People laughed, clapped and smiled as he stood forward to address the crowd. *Hliul'tl* wore his leather belt, holding his handcarved knives with handles of whalebone and deer bone. His body was completely covered with tattoo stains, detailing his wealth. Speaking loudly, he said, "This is the time for my son *Pa'ah Chi'ish* to marry the daughter of *NrtMry*. *Ch'uch'ish Ko'm* is to marry *Pa'ah Chi'ish*! It is time to add to our Deer Dance celebrating the union of these two young people."

Pa'ah Chi'ish held his breath. *Ch'uch'ish Ko'm* peered over her mother's shoulder to smile at *Pa'ah Chi'ish* in the group of dancers. Slowly, *Ch'uch'ish Ko'm* and her family moved to stand in front of the main bonfire. People gathered closely, eager to participate in the ceremony. Woman held leather wrapped gifts and baskets.

Pa'ah Chi'ish quietly separated from the male dancers to stand beside his father. *Hliul'tl* placed upon the ground a finely worked blanket of bleached deerskin for the two young people to stand upon in union ceremony. Joining the hands of *Pa'ah Chi'ish* and *Ch'uch'ish Ko'm* in front of him, he nodded to the drummer. A soft beat echoed through the village, silencing the people as *Hliul'tl* whispered to the couple. Then with a roar, he lifted their clasped hands into the air. Villagers shouted and laughed. Fast as lightning, *NrtMry* grabbed his daughter, pushing her behind him. The men whistled as the women clapped their hands.

Ta'anep quickly handed her son a leather pouch. *NrtMry* kept his eager daughter *Ch'uch'ish Ko'm* behind him. *Ch'uch'ish Ko'm* tried to push her father's hands away, but *NrtMry* scolded her profusely, "He is not your husband until he pays for you! Until then, you remain my daughter. Stay there!" Grandmothers clicked their tongues as others agreed with him.

Pa'ah Chi'ish nodded his head to *NrtMry*, "Rightly so, I do not wish to take your daughter illegally. Here in this pouch are Dentalgia shells. These I have collected over five years. These are enough for you to buy the land your cabin stands upon and once you have agreed to come and live in *Yurok*, you are welcome to live in our cabin." The leather pouch was given to *NrtMry*. Bowing his head, *Pa'ah Chi'ish* added, "You are now able to pay for the blood money owed and be a free man."

Whirling around to face his daughter, *NrtMry* opened the pouch, "Daughter, let us find out how much your love is worth. Stay!" He peered into the deep pouch to laugh, "My daughter, you are worth more than I thought! Go! Go and be with your fine man!"

Ch'uch'ish Ko'm raced around her father to *Pa'ah Chi'ish*. She took his hand, placing it on her cheek, loudly stating, "Now, you are to take your orders from me!"

Catcalls and jovial laughter swirled around them as conical baskets filled with carved fish fetishes were given to the newly married couple's fathers. The mothers *Ta'anep* and *Who'pek* gathered wedding presents, wrapping them in woven palettes, to carry into *Ta'anep*'s cabin. The two mothers laughed and planned as they spoke of their adult children's new lives.

Villagers shouted as more presents arrived. *NrtMry* handed *Pa'ah Chi'ish* a quiver made from raccoon's skin turned wrong side out. It was sewn tightly with leather. At the inside base of the quiver was a marten's skull filled with moss. Wrapped around the quiver were whittled arrows tied with sharp arrowheads. The feathers were for *Pa'ah Chi'ish* to find and tie.

Hliul'tl returned from his cabin to hold out to *NrtMry* a newly woven salmon net woven of fine roots, grasses and a leather handle twisted with tree resin. Along with this net, were cut sticks wrapped and lashed to long poles. This would be used as a fishing booth to put across streams and tributaries. *NrtMry* looked into *Hliul'tl*'s deep brown eyes, "This is not necessary."

Hliul'tl nodded, "Yes, if we are to fish together you will need this. I don't share my fishing booth with anyone!"

Fresh bread and fish stew ladled into deep wooden bowls were handed to hungry dancers. The drum picked a beat while children playfully danced and fishermen sang traditional songs as the feast continued until after midnight. *Pa'ah Chi'ish* took his bride to a makeshift cabin on the east side of the village. They stayed for four days. Their parents brought them food, placing it at the closed cylindrical doorway.

Then, as if nothing had changed, *Pa'ah Chi'ish* was fishing salmon with the others by the river. *Ch'uch'ish Ko'm* was sitting with the other women, weaving baskets and mashing berries in her husband's village. Life continued on as it should. *Smelt fish* were sighted in the Klamath River. *Pa'ah Chi'ish* pulled out his cylindrically woven nets with the small openings at one end. As the waves rolled from the ocean into the river, he dove down underwater, holding his net firmly. The net was brought up filled with *smelt fish*. The trout sized fish had tender meat, the oils used for healing and heating in the cold winters. The taste and odor were learned and appreciated over time. Life was good in this village.

Although, weeks went by with no news of *Ch'uch'ish Ko'm* being with child. The winter was cold and long. Food was monitored for the ocean winds were steady and strong. Rain fell and at times sleet hit hard on cabin roofs. Firewood was kept under the cabin roofs' overhang and slowly it dwindled as fires were needed to keep every cabin warm. *Pa'ah Chi'ish* finished a tiny room for their new cabin and the two of them lived it in for several weeks until they ran out of firewood. *Pa'ah Chi'ish* kept his sweat baths with the other men. *Ch'uch'ish Ko'm* stayed in the menstrual house with the other women when it was her time. The winter was colder and firewoord became scarce.

Pa'ah Chi'ish and *Ch'uch'ish Ko'm* moved back in with her family for her elderly grandmother was ill. The firewood lasted longer when the families doubled. The men continued to go out fishing if weather permitted. Women wove and shared stories and songs as they raised the little ones in the redwood homes of each perspective family group. Although, during daylight work hours. Discretely *Pa'ah Chi'ish* visited *Ch'uch'ish Ko'm* alone in their one room cabin.

Finally, spring arrived with the singing of birds, the ocean warmth and the leaping salmon. New buds appeared on the trees. Many had died during the winter and it became time for the transmigration of souls. Elders went through a ceremonial cleansing, prayers were said in each of the deceased homes and rafts with the dead were sent across the river to the Land of Death. It was believed those who died returned as birds, squirrels, rabbits and other small animals. Those deceased who had been greedy or wicked transmigrated as animals who were quickly hunted and eaten either by other animals or by humans.

The April Ceremony was a ten day dance. Families gathered hopeful for news of *Ch'uch'ish Ko'm* being with child. There was no such news. Summer was busy with fishing, dead whales were found washed ashore, deer were hunted in the northern mountains and the river ran strong. Dams were built and *Pa'ah Chi'ish* netted many fat fish to take home. During the evenings, he continued to build onto the strong plank home for his wife.

The plank log house was finally completed with high stacks of firewood lining the interior walls. Before the fall dance, *Ch'uch'ish Ko'm* went to her sister-in-law *Wohpe'kumew* for advice. She knelt beside her as they wove baskets, "What am I to do? I cannot become with child? *Pa'ah Chi'ish* says it is because of the cold wind at our marriage ceremony, but I believe there is something wrong with me." Tears fell from her eyes, "What am I to do? I will disgrace my family, my husband and myself." Sobbing, she covered her face with her hands.

Wohpe'kumew put her arms around her, "There is someone you need to ask for help. She is old and lives upstream by the old forest hut. Put down your weaving, let's go and speak with her right now. We will be back before the sun sets, come."

Telling *Ta'anep* where they were going, the two women followed along the riverbank. Avoiding the fishermen, they arrived at the top of the river's waterfall. There inside a thick hedge of willow was an old hut. They called out for *Pom'Pui*. There was a rustling of leaves hanging from the doorway. A cane appeared first, then a withered calloused foot, finally with great diligence came a bent dark-skinned woman. Her head was mostly bald with long wisps of hair floating around her forehead and ears. Her arms were bare, wrinkled with bulging blue veins. Piercing dark-brown eyes were sunken into her withered wrinkled face. The hand holding the cane had only two fingers and a thumb. The other hand had no fingers at all, only a stump of a thumb.

Fringe hung from a filthy deerskin skirt, revealing boney ribs and shoulders. The three wide tattoos on her chin had faded into one gray stubble of hair. "What! What do you want? Why do you interrupt my life? What do you two want from an old woman?" Her scratchy voice was a harsh whisper.

Ch'uch'ish Ko'm withdrew from her sister-in-law's tight hold. *Wohpe'kumew* stood tall, "*Pom'Pui*, we have been taught that you know the ways of spirits and curses. Would you be kind enough to help us? We have come to you for help that is all."

Pom'Pui snarled, sucking on her lower lip, "Yes, I know the ways of spirits and curses, but they have left me alone because I have left them alone. What is your problem?" The old woman did not move toward them.

Wohpe'kumew carefully hung an intricately woven pouch on a tree branch near the old woman, "This is for you. It is filled with seeds and fresh berries."

Pom'Pui glared at her, "I'm not starving, but I thank you for your gift." Instantly, she jerked the pouch from the tree branch to examine the contents.

Gently shoving *Ch'uch'ish Ko'm* forward, she continued, "This is my sister through marriage. She is not able to become with child. We think she may have been cursed by the winter wind, can you remove such a curse?"

Pom'Pui stared at the pouch in her withered hand, to croak out, "Stay here. Let me think."

Scurrying into her hut, the old woman disappeared. The two women waited as the sun moved slowly across the sky. When they were about to give up and leave, the leaf doorway moved. *Pom Pui* appeared, smoking a pipe filled with foul smelling tobacco. She blew the smoke in front of herself as she hobbled toward them.

"Here, have your sister drink this tea. She is to stay away from her man for ten days after she drinks this tea. If this does not work, she is not cursed. She is not blessed. Take this and go away!" They took the handful of dirty tea leaves from the old woman to race back to the village.

Ch'uch'ish Ko'm made tea from the leaves and drank until there was no more. She remained alone in her newly planked home for ten days and did not come outside. *Pa'ah Chi'ish* was worried about her, but did as he was told. They waited for another month, no news. *Wohpe'kumew* took *Ch'uch'ish Ko'm* to two other healers at nearby villages who both said she was healthy and there was no reason for her not to conceive.

The salmon run was soon to come and the men were busy with their nets. *Ch'uch'ish Ko'm* was becoming more and more depressed. *Ta'anep* brought fresh acorn nut bread to her daughter-in-law, "There is a young Shaman woman who lives between our village and your family's. She is said to have knowledge of the Blessings of Water. Perhaps it would be wise if you visited her with my daughter?" All the women knew something needed to be done soon or the families would be disgraced.

Ch'uch'ish Ko'm told Wohpe'kumew she was tired and perhaps it was time to accept her fate. She would accept being ostracized from the villages to live a life alone in the forest. The spirits had deemed for her to help raise other people's children and she was not to have children herself. This would allow her husband to find another wife who would be fertile and give him lots of children. Ch'uch'ish Ko'm was firm, she was not going to visit anymore healers. .

Wohpe'Kumew arrived at her door the next morning, "We are going with or without your choice. You are not going to stay here and give up on yourself or my brother. We are going and we are leaving right now!"

The two women left that morning while their men were readying to go fishing. These wives said nothing to their men, but moved through the village with firm conviction. This was a two day journey. The northern winds were stronger as they marched forth, chewing jerky and only stopping to drink from streams. They did well to arrive the evening of the second day.

A woman met them outside of a small village, "The winds told me of your coming. Please, enter my home and rest. The other women are already here to help you with your healing."

Hot tea was brought to the sisters. Ch'uch'ish Ko'm was given a special strong tea, which made her sleep. Before dawn, eight women arrived with woven mats and plant soaps. They took Ch'uch'ish Ko'm to the river's edge where upon disrobing her, they wrapped her in thickly woven mats. After she was firmly wrapped, she was placed, lying face upward onto their arms. The women carried her to the bank of the river where they slid her into the water. Slowly, as she floated in her wrap of mats, her body was pulled free and placed on top of the mats to float. Soaps lathered and washed her from the top of her head to the soles of her feet. Women sang songs of life, joy and freedom as they scrubbed her. Ch'uch'ish Ko'm let her mind relax and her

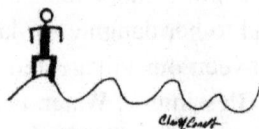

Water Blessing Yurok Tribe Story Number 10

spirit rise as the women's voices surrounded her consciousness.

An older woman arrived as mid-day approached. Sliding *Ch'uch'ish Ko'm* off of the floating mats into the river water, the women held her body afloat as the older woman rubbed *Ch'uch'ish Ko'm* with salve. Keeping her head above water, the older woman continued to rub salve deep into each part of *Ch'uch'ish Ko'm*'s body. The women sang. Salve was rubbed. This lasted until dusk. Slowly, the women wrapped the mats around *Ch'uch'ish Ko'm*, carrying her face up through the water onto the shoreline. There they left her alone to sleep.

Before the ceremony, the women had placed baskets filled with berries, wild plants and herbs and small animal furs, along the river's edge. As they had sung their songs, one by one a basket had been offered to the river spirits and allowed to float downstream. When darkness arrived, they awakened *Ch'uch'ish Ko'm*, guiding her into the women's longhouse. There she slept for four days.

On the fifth day, *Ch'uch'ish K'om* and *Wohpe'kumew* returned home to their village. The village was busy as usual. No one had taken notice of their return except for *Ta'anep* who was anxious for news. *Pa'ah Chi'ish* returned from the sweat house in the morning to find his wife was too weak to talk. Lying in her bed palette, she nodded to him and went back to sleep.

The following morning, *Ch'uch'ich K'om* raced outside to heave up her breakfast. *Pa'ah Chi'ish* sent for his mother *Ta'anep* who arrived with a basket of herbs and a huge smile. After caring for her daughter-in-law, *Ta'anep* hurried to *Wohpe'kumew* with the news.

The two mothers took *Pa'ah Chi'ish* outside for a conference, "My Son, you are soon to become a father. The ceremony for your beautiful wife was successful!"

Pa'ah Chi'ish stared at them, "What ceremony? What are you talking about?"

Ta'anep and *Wohpe'kumew* burst out laughing, "Didn't you miss your wife over these last few days?"

He shrugged, "I thought she was busy."

Hliul'tl pulled his son aside, "This is an important time in your life, please, show more emotion. This is excellent!"

Pa'ah Chi'ish smiled, "I am excited, although it has been exhausting. Seriously, these last few days were a time of resting." Glowing he added, "Finally, we're to have a family!"

Hliul'tl clapped his son on the back, "Now, you must be brave for pregnant women are not easy to live with as they require care, love and much patience. Somehow they believe we don't feel their pain, but we do.

Be prepared to know how your stomach will ache, your feet will swell and your mind will race as to how this child will grow strong with your guidance."

During the fall Deer Dance, news spread quickly as Ch'uch'ish K'om waddled to sit with the other expectant mothers watching the dancers. *Pa'ah Chi'ish* danced with pride. His family had begun and would continue. Great are the gifts of the water spirits when you are wise in knowing who to ask for assistance. It was true for *Ch'uch'ish K'om* and *Pa'ah Chi'ish* had four children, as was the tradition, and each of them grew to be healthy, helpful and to care for their parents.

Notes:

Blessings come from internal strength and belief in one's self. This story is of the Yurok people who live in Northwest California between the Klamath River and the Pacific Ocean. Every culture is filled with individuals and each individual comes with their own complications. No matter what continent, each must find their own way. These two stories are very similar and filled with trials. Women come together to help one another through difficult times and in their strength, they succeed. This story was shared at a Great Goddess conference in Utah, 1997.

Glossary:

Aiyu quo – Greeting, 'you are here too.'
Ch'uch'ish Ko'm – Bird Who Hears.
Dentalium Shells – Used as currency and in ceremonial decorations.
Harpoon – A long spear or javelin used to hunt large fish, seals or whales with a sharp arrow head at the front.
Hliul'tl – Slang for 'Father.'
Karok or Karuk – Up River People.
May-poot – Salmon Fish.
NrtMry – Wise Man.
Olekwo'l – People.
Oyuukwi – Friendly greeting.
Pa'ah Chi'ish – Water Dog.
Pom'Pui – Wise Woman.
Pohar'mts – Healer.
Pulikla – Down River people.

Smelt Fish – Small fish, resemble tiny trout, caught in tight nets.

Sweat Lodge – Men's sleeping quarters, also used for cleansing or purification as a steam bath. Natural material hut, dome shaped lodge.

Ta'anep – Chirping Mother Bird.

Unuh mrh – Village or closed family community.

Wohpe'kumew – Widower across the ocean.

Yurok – Down River people who live ner Clamath River and Pacific Ocean.

Map Related to Asian Indian Stories

Area in Map	Area Name	Story
1 and 2	Gujarat State and Madhya Pradesh State	The River Goddess Appears
3	Maharashtra State	Rain Stopped for Prasad Bhojan The Saviour Sea God – Bordeo Borivas Well and The New Bride Dangya Lake and Whooping Cough An Angry River Calm Down The Legend of the Ghost in Kirtan Wadi Lake The Story of the New Mother Well – Red Water Well Blessings of Bhivai Devi
4	Karnataka State	Eternal Holy Nanak Zara

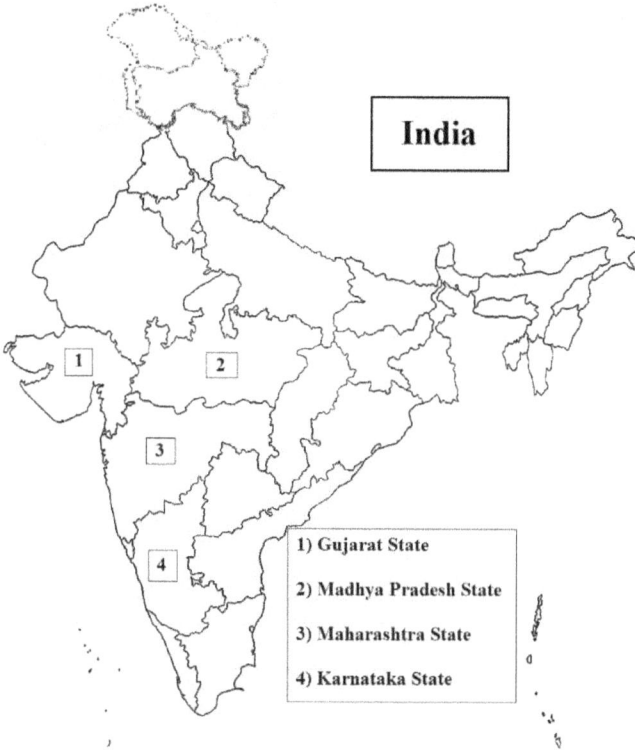

India

1) Gujarat State

2) Madhya Pradesh State

3) Maharashtra State

4) Karnataka State

Map Related to Asian Indian Stories

Maps Related to Native American Stories
North America and South America

Symbol	Area Name	Story
	South America	
A	Guiana or Guianas People, Venezuela	*Stopping the Rain* / Guiana
	North America	
B	Iroquois and Onondaga Tribes: Great Lakes Region Southern Canada into New York state.	Deganawida, the Peace Maker
C	Southern Arizona, New Mexico, Nevada, West Texas, Northern Mexico.	Water Flows / Chiricahua and Lipan Apache Stolen Wife / Cochiti Pueblo, New Mexico (Northwest of Albuquerque, New Mexico) Story of the Rain Na'wai, Tsia / Pueblo (West of Albuquerque, New Mexico)
D	Brule Sioux Tribe: West bank of Missouri River and in South Dakota.	Stone Boy Saves Uncles – Brule Sioux
E	Tsimshian People: Their communities are mostly in coastal British Columbia and far southern Alaska, around Terrace and Prince Rupert in British Columbia, and Alaska's Annette Islands.	The Lake of the Beginning – Tsimshian Mythology
F	Paiute Tribe: Their story takes place when Paiute roamed Nevada and Utah states.	Spirit Woman Ghost – Paiute
G	Chickasaw Tribe: Their story is related to Tennessee and Ohio river valleys.	Chief's Burial – Chickasaw
H	Yurok Tribe: 44 mile stretch of Klamath River in Del Norte and Humboldt, California.	Water Blessing – Yurok Tribe story

Venezuela

A

Created with mapchart.net ⓒ

Map related to Native American stories

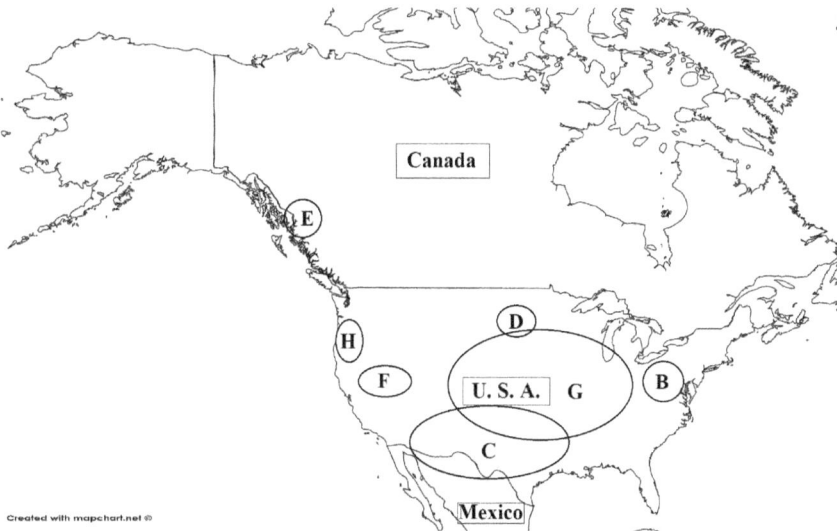

Canada

E

H

D

F

U. S. A.   G   B

C

Mexico

Created with mapchart.net ⓒ

Maps Related to Native American Stories

Asian Indian Bibliography

Anwekar, Nitin. *Bhuyikot of Solapur (Marathi language)*. Solapur: Self-published, 2016.

Bal, Sarjit S. *Life of Guru Nanak*. 1969. Reprint, Chandigarh: Publication Bureau - Punjab University, 1984.

Boas, Franz. *The Mind of Primitive Man*. New York: The Macmillan Company, 1938.

British Government. *Gazetteer of the Bombay Presidency Sholapur Vol-xvi*. Bombay: James M. Campbell, 1884.

Dasganu. *Shri Gajanan Vijay (Marathi language)*. Shegaon: Gajanan Maharaj Sansthan, 1973.

Deogaonkar, S. G. and Deogaonkar, S. S. *Native Americans and Native Indians*. New Delhi: Concept Publishing Company, 2002.

Deshmukh, Vasudeo V. *Charitra Chintan Vasudevanand Saraswati Tembe Swami Maharaj (Marathi language)*. Vasai: Shashwat Prakashan, 2005.

Ekholm, Gordon F. "A Possible Focus of Asiatic Influence in the Late Classic Cultures of Mesoamerica." *Memoirs of the Society for American Archaeology* 9 (1953): 72–97.

Lal, Chaman. *Hindu America*. Bombay: New Book Company, 1940.

Matlock, Gene. *India Once Ruled the Americas!* San Jose: Writer's Showcase - iUniverse, 2000.

Ryan, Charles J. "Early American and Hindu Culture." *The Theosophical Forum* 22, no. 3, (1944).

Singh, Jogendra and Singh, Raja D. *The Great Humanist Guru Nanak*. New Delhi: The Unity Publishers, 1958.

Virajananda. *Shri Vasudev Yati (Marathi language)*. Mumbai: Popular Prakashan, 2014.

Vokes, Emily H. "A Possible Hindu Influence at Teotihuacan." *American Antiquity* 29, no. 1 (1963): 94–95.

Native American Bibliography

Boas, Franz. *Tsimshian Mythology, BAE Annual Report, no.31,* Washington, DC, 1916.

Curtis, Edward S. *The North American Indian. Vol.13.* Cambridge, Massachusetts. University Press, 1924.

Erdoes, Richard and Alfonso Ortiz. *American Indian Myths and Legends.* Pantheon Books, New York, 1984.

Forde, C. Daryll. *Folk-lore.* William Glaisher for the Folk-lore Society. London, 1930.

Gifford, Edward W. *California Indian Nights Entertainments.* Glen*dale,* California, Arthur H. Clark, 1930.

Goodwin, Grenville, *Myths and Tales of the White Mountain Apache.* American Folklore Society, vol. 33, New York, 1939.

Marriott, Alice and Carol K. Rachlin. *American Indian Mythology.* New York, T.Y. Crowell, 1968.

Nicolar, Joseph. *The Life and Traditions of the Red Man.* Bangor, Maine, C.H. Glass, 1893.

Pijoan, Teresa. *Pueblo Indian Wisdom, Native American Legends and Mythology.* Sunstone Press, Santa Fe, New Mexico, 2000.

———. *American Indian Creation Myths.* Sunstone Press, Santa Fe, New Mexico, 2005.

———. *White Wolf Woman and Other Native American Transformation Myths.* August House Press, Little Rock, Arkansas, 1992.

———. *Healers on the Mountain and Other Myths of Native American Medicine.* Sunstone Press, Santa Fe, New Mexico, 2010.

Swanton, John R. *The Indian Tribes of North America.* Bulletin of BAE, Washington, DC, 1952.

Van Etten, Teresa. *Ways of Indian Magic.* Sunstone Press, Santa Fe, New Mexico, 1985.

White, Leslie. *The Pueblo of Sia, New Mexico.* Bureau of American Ethnology, Bulletin 184. Washington, DC, 1962.

www.ingramcontent.com/pod-product-compliance
Lightning Source LLC
Chambersburg PA
CBHW020526270326
41927CB00006B/458